Cults and Nonconventional Religious Groups

A Collection of Outstanding Dissertations and Monographs

Edited by
J. GORDON MELTON
Institute for the Study of American Religion

A GARLAND SERIES

SILVA MIND CONTROL
An Anthropological Inquiry

ANALINE M. POWERS

GARLAND PUBLISHING, INC.
New York & London
1992

Library of Congress Cataloging-in-Publication Data

Powers, Analine Marie, 1948-
   Silva mind control : an anthropological inquiry / Analine M. Powers.
       p. cm. — (Cults and nonconventional religious groups)
   Includes bibliographical references.
   ISBN 0-8153-0770-5
   1. Silva Mind Control. I. Title. II. Series.
BF1156.S55P68 1992
158'.9—dc20   91-39376
                                                                CIP

#24846295

Printed on acid-free, 250-year-life paper

MANUFACTURED IN THE UNITED STATES OF AMERICA

To My Parents

and

Dr. Leonard W. Moss

My advisor,
whose absence during the writing phase
of this work was keenly felt.

PREFACE

Silva Mind Control International is a parapsychological, self-help organization which claims to use meditation, self-hypnosis and guided fantasy in order to achieve relaxation, personal growth, altered states of consciousness, and psychic functioning. This international organization has developed as the result of twenty-two years of research by its founder, José Silva. The stated purpose of Silva Mind Control International (SMCI) is to serve humanity by teaching individuals a method that they can use to improve their own lives. The Silva Method is taught through a series of lectures and mental training exercises presented in a forty to forty-eight hour course known as the Basic Lecture Series (BLS). Currently, the BLS is being taught in sixty-one countries and fourteen languages.

In January 1974, I became interested in Silva Mind Control and took the Basic Lecture Series. Six months later, I took what was then, the four day graduate course taught by José Silva. For the next two years, I attended workshops and courses, taking notes on what I heard and saw. For multiple reasons, my contact with the Silva organization ceased until my formal fieldwork began in 1982. During this time, however, I did continue to use the Method and some of the techniques I learned during the BLS. I also began writing graduate course papers on SMCI during this time.

Because of my previous experience with and knowledge of SMCI, it seemed the logical choice for my dissertation research. The potential problem of bias (because I had used the Method) was overcome by doing an ethnography. Since I focused on description, the validity and/or proof of the Method were inconsequential. I do not deal with proof or disproof of SMC in this dissertation; nor do I include much discussion of my personal experiences with the Method. Those experiences may have influenced my choices and, perhaps, my perception. Hopefully, my awareness of the possible problems and biases has kept them in check--as has the vigilance of my dissertation committee. In any case, I assume full responsibility for the contents of this study. Any errors are mine alone.

The primary purpose of this study was to produce an ethnography of SMCI. Fieldwork was conducted between November, 1982 and October, 1984. Data was gathered through participant-observation at the local Silva Mind Control Center in Southfield, Michigan and at the International Headquarters in Laredo, Texas. Chapter Two is a description of the methodological approach used for data collection. An historical overview of SMCI is presented in Chapter Three, beginning with José Silva's early influential childhood experiences and culminating with the international expansion of the organization. Chapter Four is an examination of the Silva Method of self-mind control as presented in the BLS. Some students choose to learn advanced healing techniques and more about the history of SMCI. These topics are taught in Graduate Courses, which are also described in Chapter Four. The first BLS was taught in Texas in 1966. Expansion out of the state occurred in 1969. Since that time the organization has grown to a multi-million dollar enterprise. Chapter Five explores the bureaucratic structure of SMCI.

A secondary purpose of this study was to determine to what degree the individuals attracted to SMCI became involved with the Method and the organization; in other words, to ascertain if Silva Mind Control became a way of life for its members. To gain as much information as possible and to reach as large a population as the study would permit, questionnaires were used to supplement the primary technique of participant-observation. The questionnaires were designed to gain information in four categories: (1) demographic data; (2) opinions about the BLS and the Method; (3) ideological orientations of the respondents; and (4) degree of involvement. The results are described in Chapter Six. The final Chapter of this study presents conclusions and some speculations about the phenomena this organization represents.

As with most endeavors in life, this project could not have been successfully completed without the assistance and cooperation of many others.

Dr. Leonard W. Moss advised me throughout my graduate career. His assistance and counsel during the data gathering phase was invaluable. Without his support, this study would have been impossible. In January 1984, his sudden death left a major void--not only in my committee but also in the Anthropology Department, the University and the community.

Dr. Helen Hause graciously assumed the role of committee chair upon the death of Dr. Moss. Her assistance during the final writing phase of this dissertation was extremely helpful. My other committee members, Dr. Sue Taylor, Dr. Elaine Beane and Dr. Joseph Albini also made valuable contributions and suggestions for this final product.

This study would not have been possible without the cooperation and assistance of Mr. Louis Barbone, the Silva Mind Control Director for the state of Michigan. From my first telephone conversations to the final writing, Mr. Barbone assisted in whatever way he could. Not only did he spend many hours in conversation but he allowed me access to information and situations which resulted in a broader understanding of this organization. Likewise, the assistance of his wife, Therese, and the FTI staff was also appreciated. The two SMCI lecturers working with Mr. Barbone, Mr. Stanford Math and Ms. Barbara Goushaw, also helped me gain a better understanding of SMC. Mr. Math was especially helpful during my Laredo fieldwork.

Fieldwork in Laredo, Texas was possible only because of the partial funding provided by the local Silva

International Graduates Association. Without the data from Laredo, this study would not have been as thorough.

While in Laredo at the International Headquarters I received help and cooperation from all of the officials of SMCI. Mr. Alejandro Gonzalez, Jr., assisted me numerous times despite the busy schedule of the Convention. Mr. Harry McKnight, director of the SMC lecturer training program, allowed me to attend that ten day course. And of course, I must thank José Silva for the interview he allowed while in Detroit for the Ultra Seminar. I would also like to thank Mr. E. Bernd and Mr. Saul Gonzalez for their assistance while I was in Laredo.

The editorial assistance of Ms. Dana Leasendale was invaluable and is greatly appreciated--as was her continual encouragement and support. This task was simplified by the assistance of the Anthropology Department in the text processing of this manuscript. Access to the Departmental computer terminal permitted the timely completion of the work.

My family has been very supportive throughout my graduate career and without them I would not have finished. The unaltering emotional support and continual urging of Dr. John Katharopoulos was important in the completion of this task.

And finally, I wish to thank the lecturers and students of the Silva Method who kindly assisted me. Without them, there would have been no study.

TABLE OF CONTENTS

LIST OF TABLES

LIST OF CHARTS

CHAPTER ONE

INTRODUCTION

I. STATEMENT OF THE PROBLEM

Anthropology is a holistic discipline. It studies all aspects of social life, all expressions of culturally patterned behavior. As Alfred Kroeber once said, the subject matter of anthropology is limited only by the imagination of man.

This study is a expression of the range of interest within anthropology. The focus, Silva Mind Control, is an international organization and is studied as such. The ideology of the organization (which must necessarily be addressed) and the growth of that organization, however, set it apart from topics traditionally studied in anthropology.

The basic anthropological interest of this study is that the Silva Method may represent a Western cultural manifestation of phenomena expressed in non-Western societies through the magician, the shaman, or the traditional healer. Of additional significance is the possible relationship between the relaxation technique SMC claims to teach and stress management. Recent research has shown that unmanaged stress leads to numerous diseases and illnesses. The Silva Method may become a supplement or an alternative to conventional stress management therapies. Finally, not only is SMCI part of a larger, growing self-help movement, but its success demonstrates a growing interest in the West--among the general public and the scientific community--in parapsychological phenomena. Perhaps by understanding why SMCI has grown, we can gain insight into the popularity of parapsychology.

II LITERATURE REVIEW

A. Healing

1. Shamanic

In cultural anthropology healing has been studied primarily in terms of shamen and traditional healers. The shaman is a religious specialist able to enter into direct contact with the supernatural, usually in a controlled trance state. S/he, as Eliade states, is "at once magician and medicine man, healer and miracle doer, psychopomp, priest, mystic, and poet"(1964). Many of the feats claimed by shamen seem similar to those claimed by advocates of Silva Mind Control.

Shamanism has been studied from numerous perspectives. In a social/structural-functional analysis, Landy(1974) examined the shaman's social role as cultural broker in acculturation situations. From a psychological perspective, shamanism has been linked to almost every psychopathology;

for example, schizophrenia (Wallace 1966; Silverman 1967) and mental derangement (Devereux 1965,1961). Conversely, it has also been examined for its therapeutic aspect (Ackerknecht 1943; Eliade 1964). Schweder (1979) has focused on the unique cognitive capacities of the shaman, showing how he is able to give meaning to ambiguous situations, "avoid bafflement and impose form on unstructured stimuli"(p.331). Others have examined the psychological meaning of the shaman's vision quest. Despite views of shamanism as pathological, others have stated that there is no reason to consider shamans as pathological or abnormal (Sasaki 1969; Gillin 1948; Lantis 1960; Fabrega and Silver 1970; Torrey 1974).

Of the many roles the shaman plays, that of healer is most relevant to this study. Eliade (1964), in his extensive work on shamanism points out that throughout Asia, North and South America, and Indonesia the shaman performs the primary role of doctor and healer. In Central and North Asia, for example, the shaman's principal function is magical healing. Disease results primarily from soul loss. The shaman must retrieve the soul to achieve a cure(p.215). Among the Eskimo, where illness is believed due to violation of taboos (leading to soul loss), the shaman is expected to heal the individual by counteracting the effects of taboo violation in the spirit world (p.289). In South America, the shaman relies on magical healing which is supplemented by the use of medicinal plants and animals and massage to bring about a cure (p.327).

In each of these examples, as in most cultures with shamanic beliefs, the principal cause of illness is spiritual, according to Eliade. It includes either "the flight of the soul or a magical object introduced into the body by spirits or sorcerers" (p.327). In these cases a shamanistic healing is the only option--even in those societies which have secondary religious practitioners such as diviners or healers.

In Western society, the correlate to spiritually induced illness is psychosomatic illness and disease, both physical and emotional. In these cases, however, the 'agent' or cause of the illness is the individual self rather than a deity, unhappy spirit, sorcerer, or ancestor. The Western "shaman"--psychotherapist, medical doctor, priest--must help the individual realize the relationship between mind set and physical condition. If they can, then occasionally a "cure" is achieved. The actual percentage of disease and illness induced by the individual self has not been firmly established. Some estimates are as high as ninety percent. Regardless of the actual percentage, it is generally agreed that the mind is a powerful agent in health maintenance.

According to Silva Mind Control, the individual is responsible for her/his own state of health and well-being. The individual causes the illness or maintains the state of well-being. As noted above, anthropologists working in non-Western societies have demonstrated the external (to the individual) spiritual causes of illness. In Western society the cause is frequently also "spiritual" (i.e. non-physical/mental). It is the locus which differs. Here that locus is the individual self. This idea of individual responsibility for one's state of health meshes well with the strong individualistic orientation of American culture and the emphasis on personal responsibility for success or failure in life. As such, Silva Mind Control may be a reflection of basic American values and it may be useful to study its development as a barometer of change for those values. However, it is antiposed to the ideology of allopathic medicine (the dominant U.S. form), which sees disease and illness as caused by external, intrusive agents.

2. Spiritualist

A second type of healing which has been of anthropological interest and which is relevant to the discussion of SMC, is spiritualist healing (see Macklin 1974; Aguirre 1978; Kearny 1978, 1961; Trotter and Chaviro 1978). Spiritualism shares with shamanism, beliefs in soul voyaging, spirit-familiars, contact with spirit beings and possession by them (Kearny 1978; Foster and Anderson 1978). Foster and Anderson (1978:259) view spiritualism as "civilization's attempt to structure and pattern and to validate the near-universal belief in spirits that harm human beings, who can be dealt with by means of human intermediaries". In spiritualist therapies, healing is achieved by the curer (trance medium) contacting spiritual beings (often of dead doctors), channeling mental energy from the healer's mind to the patient's affected body area, and then cleansing the body of all negative "vibrations" (Trotter and Chaviro 1978).

Although found throughout the world, spiritualist practices have increased dramatically, particularly in Latin America and especially along the Mexican-American border (Ibid). As Foster and Anderson point out, spiritualism (along with faith healing and other religious cures) has become the alternative health care system in the area at the expense of curanderos, root doctors, herbal and home remedies, and other traditional curers (Ibid, p.259-60). The Silva Method was developed in this area (Laredo, Texas) by a Mexican-American (José Silva). The success SMCI claims in this area (and throughout Mexico and Latin America) may be due, in part, to the apparent similarities between the Silva Method and spiritualist healing.

The essential features of spiritualist therapy, according to Kearny, are its

> ability to evoke powerful imagery, especially of body parts and aspects of the spiritual cosmology, and to loosen blocked emotions. Powerful suggestions, experienced as visualization of body ailments and their magical treatment, serve to remove many symptoms, especially those of a hysterical nature, and also are no doubt quite effective in generally mobilizing natural healing(1978:37).

Imagery, clear visualization of the body, its ailments and their psychic treatment are also claimed to be the bases of healing in Silva Mind Control. There is, however, a major difference: in spiritualism, the patient must go to individual healers for a cure, with Silva Mind Control, each person is believed capable of self-healing.

B. Cults

Anthropology has long concerned itself with social movements in non-Western societies. In the literature, these movements are termed cargo cults, millenarian, messianic, nativistic or revivalistic movements by various authors (e.g. Linton 1943; Cochran 1979; Worsley 1970; Belshaw 1972). Anthony Wallace (1956,1966), who has done extensive work in the area, classifies all of the above as revitalization movements. These "conscious organized efforts to construct a more satisfying culture" have two major aims: (1) to provide immediate personal salvation to those currently afflicted; and (2) to reorganize the culture so that a better life replaces the old. As Wallace points out, they most frequently occur in societies, or groups within a society, who are in an identity crisis.

In non-Western societies, this identity crisis usually was precipitated by contact with Europeans. In the decade of the sixties, however, a large proportion of the population of the United States underwent an identity crisis. The result was that a tremendous number of cult groups arose throughout the U.S. Many were prime examples of a revitalization movement (e.g. neo-paganism). Some authors view this cult phenomenon in the United States as a modern resurgence of shamanism.

A major portion of the literature on American cults is explanatory. It deals with psychological or socio-cultural/ functional explanations for the existence and popularity of these cults, including the personality characteristics of the individuals attracted to them. For example, Armond Nicholi (1974) relates religious preoccupation and cult participation with changes in the American family. Michael Barkun (1972,1976) demonstrates how some of these cults (specifically millenarian movements) are functional for modern society. Some of the most extensive sociological work has been done by Roy Wallis. Although his primary concern has been Scientology, his observations are applicable to many modern U.S. cults (1973,1974a,1974b, 1975,1976,1977,1979). Joseph Washington (1972) has explored the relationship between black religious cults and social conditions. (See also Balswick 1974; Nelson 1969; Rossell 1974; Beckford 1977; Zaretsky and Leone 1974). Psychologically oriented explanations for the rise and popularity of cults are provided by numerous authors. Most focus on need fulfillment, anxiety reduction, feelings of alienation, or the therapeutic aspect of cult membership (see Adler and Hammet 1973; Evans 1973; Penner 1972; Tiryakian 1972).

A second major area of cult literature focuses on descriptions of various cults, usually accompanied by explanations for their existence. Jacob Needleman (1970) has focused on Eastern Philosophy oriented groups. Glock and Bellah (1976) provide us with information about and explanations for groups from many different traditions. Likewise, Robert Ellwood (1973) examines numerous cults in his book, Religious and Spiritual Groups in Modern America. Wallis (1977) gives us his view of the Children of God movement while Berkely Rice (1976) enlightens us on the Reverend Sun Myung Moon and his Unification Church. (See also Carroll 1973; Lofland 1973; Marty 1970; Balch and Taylor 1976; Woodward 1976; Newsweek 1974).

Different types of cults or new religions that arose during the sixties and seventies attracted different types of people. By far the vast majority, the most popular and well known groups were part of a specific age stratum, those under thirty (e.g. Balswick 1974; Scott 1980; Ellwood 1973; Wallis 1977). A few examples of these are the Unification Church, the Children of God, Meher Baba Movement, and Hare Krishna. Virtually none of the cult groups from the last two decades had general population appeal, spanning from child to senior citizen, lower class to upper class, Christian, Moslem, or Jew. Consequently, there has been little extensive work done with broad spectrum appeal cult groups. One prominent exception to this is the topic of the present study, Silva Mind Control International. SMCI is a group which, according to Ellwood's criteria (1973) can be classified as a cult yet its members seem to come from all age groups, from blue collar workers, clerical, professionals (educational, medical, athletic), clergy, and homemakers. These people are not from the traditionally dispossessed, alienated, counterculture, or marginal individuals. Rather, they seem to be members of groups which are central to the character of industrial society. That is, they come from the middle and upper class "establishment". Empirical data is needed on these types of groups.

One of the characteristics of American cults is an interest in healing (see Ellwood 1973). The degree and importance of healing does, of course, vary according to the particular cult. The Rosicrucians, for example, place a special emphasis on healing. Members are taught, in great detail, how bodily systems work. When healings are performed, members (the healers) are encouraged to be in the presence of the person being healed and actually touch the individual to facilitate that healing; although healings with the patient not present do take place. The Aetherius Society[1], a cult which believes all major religions are the result of contact with extra-terrestial beings, also places a great deal of importance on healing. In addition to weekly prayer circles (for healing), healing services accompany most of the other organized activities at the meeting center. In the case of the Aetherians there is generally no physical contact between the members and the individual "being healed". Healing energy is "sent" to the person by the group (see also Wallis 1974a, 1974b).

A well known group that places perhaps the greatest emphasis on healing is Christian Science. Although beginning as a cult, it has now gained the status of a religion (e.g. Podmore 1973; Fradkin 1975). Nonetheless, mental healing is the base of its ideological system. Although each individual is believed responsible for her/his own state of health or illness, there is a select group of members who are trained as "practitioners" or healers. Members are expected to utilize the services of a practitioner whenever a health problem arises--the only exception being broken bones for which an MD may be used. The practitioners charge for their services and are also reimbursed by Blue Cross. Since incorrect thinking, improper thoughts, are the cause of illness, it is the task of the practitioner to correct the ill person's thoughts through an argumentative form of prayer. Illness is infants and children is believed to be the result of improper thinking by the parents. It is their thoughts that must be corrected to cure the infant.

Silva Mind Control appears similar to Christian Science in the importance it places on healing and self-responsibility for one's state of well being. However, whereas Christian Science and medicine are polemic systems, Silva Mind Control accepts interface with traditional medicine: they are not mutually exclusive. One of the investigative questions of this study concerns the degree to which the Silva Method becomes an alternative or supplement to conventional medicine for some of the members.

C. Way of Life Movements

Christian Science is a way of life for its believers (Fradkin 1975). The ideology permeates into every aspect of their daily living. Likewise, certain cults, either with a full communal life style or those less inclusive, also are way of life groups (e.g. Hare Krishna, Unification Church). Silva Mind Control appears to be a broad spectrum appeal group. Its members seem to have heterogeneous backgrounds (economic, social, occupational). In this study the degree to which SMC succeeds in becoming a way of life for those members is considered to be significant. The literature addressing itself specifically to way of life movements is scarce. Consequently, this study provides a needed contribution to that literature.

The literature on Silva Mind Control has appeared primarily in the popular press(an exception being Brier, et al. 1973). For a selection of these works see the Selected Bibliography on SMC at the end of this work.

ENDNOTES

[1] Unless otherwise indicated, all information on the Aetherius Society is based on data collected during fieldwork in 1973.

CHAPTER TWO

METHODOLOGY

I, FIELDWORK

A. Problems of Fieldwork

The anthropological process of fieldwork--whether in non-Western or Western societies--is inherently fraught with problems; but the nature of the problems differs between the settings. Among non-Western cultures, the anthropologist must face such basic problems as language differences, housing, food, and acceptance into the community. Much of the data the anthropologist in these settings obtains is learned by simply "being there".

In Western society, the anthropologist working among her/his own culture faces problems which are different, but of equal magnitude. Westerners do not feel comfortable with strangers or "semi-strangers" just "hanging-around". They want clear identifications and specific questions so they know exactly what is taking place. In non-Western settings the anthropologist frequently has trouble maintaining her/ his own privacy. In Western society, on the other hand, it is the people being studied who guard their privacy so closely. They are sophisticated yet at the same time

14

suspicious of those asking questions. Likewise, the note taking necessary for fieldwork can cause concern. In my situation it was necessary to explain to a number of people what I was writing.

Omnipresent for the Western researcher is the difficulty of perceiving the patterns of behavior and gestaults with which the anthropologist has been raised. Biases are likely to be in favor of the people or behavior observed. When the anthropologist goes abroad to the field, s/he leaves behind family and friends and is able to devote full-time to the data collection. The anthropologist who stays near home for fieldwork is continually faced with family obligations, interactions with friends and (most probably) the requirements of the job necessary to support the fieldwork. The result is that the fieldwork itself sometimes becomes secondary to other considerations.

For this study, there were additional potential problems. Because of my association with SMCI during the 1974-1976 period, I had some preconceived ideas and expectations. Also, because of my previous training in the 1974 BLS, I had used the Method. I began this fieldwork knowing that the Method had worked for me many times in numerous ways. Although I was constantly aware of these biases and my function with the organization, my observations, my choices, and my conclusions may have been influenced by these factors. In addition to my own awareness, I relied upon my committee to help ensure the objectivity of this study. It was also because of these same factors that I chose to do a descriptive study. By focusing on a description of SMCI, Inc. it was not necessary to deal with the validity or proof of the Method.

While these factors posed potential problems they also were assets. My pre-exposure to the organization and the Method not only gave me a time depth for comparison purposes but it gave me access, acceptance, credibility and trust from the very beginning. All of this would not have been there had I not been a Silva graduate. Without doubt, it would have taken much longer to obtain the data and achieve understanding, had I started without this background.

B. Location

Fieldwork for this study was carried out primarily in the Metropolitan Detroit area at the Silva Mind Control Center in Southfield, Michigan. Known as the Forward Thinking Institute (FTI), it is Regional Center for the state of Michigan and was chosen because of its convenience and accessibility. In addition to numerous "drop-in" visits at the Center, I attended Introductory Lectures, Basic Lecture Series (BLS) courses, and workshops at the Center and the Ultra Seminar held at the Southfield Civic Center. This part of the fieldwork began in December 1982 and lasted approximately one year. Follow-up visits continued into 1984.

Secondary fieldwork took place in Laredo, Texas. Although the length of time was short, the amount of data collected was enormous. Without this segment of fieldwork the study would have been superficial. For approximately two weeks in August 1983, I attended the activities surrounding the annual SMCI International Convention. This included the BLS taught by Jose Silva, the convention activities, the graduate course and the Lecturers Development Seminar by Harry McKnight, and interviews with key personnel at the International Headquarters. Tapes of most of these activities were either made by me or purchased from SMCI.

II. THE SAMPLE

The largest portion of the sample for this study was drawn from the Metro-Detroit area. It consisted of 114 persons who, at some point, attended activities sponsored by the Forward Thinking Institute. From these 114 individuals, I chose 32 for a follow-up group. The criteria for selection included age, sex, race, income, marital status, and year the BLS was taken. I attempted to get as broad a representation as possible in each of the categories. Each of the follow-up respondents was mailed an open-ended questionnaire (labeled #2 in Appendix Eight) accompanied by an explanatory cover letter. Of the 32, 19 returned the completed questionnaire.

The second largest portion of the sample consisted of 62 individuals who attended activities in Laredo, Texas during the 1983 convention. This portion of the sample is divided into two subsets:

1) Laredo Functionairies; 30 lecturers who were in Laredo for the August 1983 convention and the Lecturers Development Seminar.

2) Laredo Graduates; 32 SMCI graduates who attended the same convention. Both groups are from the United States and numerous other countries.

As a direct result of the Laredo fieldwork, data was obtained on a small group from Indianapolis, Indiana. While in Laredo, some of the lecturers requested copies of that questionnaire to use with their graduates. Twelve individuals from the Indianapolis SMC Center returned the completed questionnaire.

The total number of people who responded to the questionnaires is 188. This is a convenience sample; that is, it consists only of those individuals who were willing to take the time and make the effort to answer the questionnaires. Consequently, the descriptions and conclusions based on this data do not necessarily represent all persons who have taken the Silva Mind Control Basic Lecture Series. In addition to the 188 respondents to the questionnaires, I also talked with approximately 150 other individuals on various topics. Nonetheless, the sample is biased. In the Metro-Detroit area, I have only persons who attended activities at the FTI or the Ultra Seminar at the Southfield Civic Center. There is low representation of students and graduates from the other lecturers in this area. For the Laredo groups, the fact that they were in Laredo attending the convention or Lecturers Development Seminar makes them different from other SMC graduates. To incur the expenses (both monetary and temporal) of going to Laredo for three days to two weeks would seem to indicate that these people are committed (to some degree) to the organization and/or the Method. The study in general, has low representation of those who took the Silva training and then stopped associating with the organization and/or stopped using the Method.

III. DATA COLLECTION TECHNIQUES

A. Participant-Observation

The primary means of data collection was participant-observation. I attended workshops, Introductory lectures, and BLS and graduate courses. For some of the sessions, I participated in the mental training exercises. For others I simply observed. While in Laredo, I attended the SMC courses and convention activities. I was also allowed by SMCI, to participate in and tape record the ten day Lecturers Development Seminar. As a researcher, I was not charged the fees for the LDS or the convention (nor, likewise, for workshops at the FTI). I was required, however, to sign a contract ensuring that I would not teach the Silva Method, on my own, for one year after the Lecturers Development Seminar.

At the beginning of all activities I attended at the FTI, I would give about a five minute introduction of myself to ensure that everyone knew who I was and why I was present. I included my background with SMC, my present status as a graduate student doing research, the purpose of my study, and the fact that I was completely independent of SMCI and the Forward Thinking Institute. I also mentioned participation in the study was completely voluntary and all information obtained would be strictly confidential. A similar procedure was followed while in Laredo.

B. Formal Interviews

In addition to the face to face informal conversation, that are a natural part of anthropological fieldwork, I also conducted formal interviews with certain officials of SMCI. In Metro-Detroit, Mr. Barbone, the Director of the Forward Thinking Institute, repeatedly set aside time for interviews. Mr. Barbone also arranged for me to have an interview and dinner with Jose Silva while he was in Michigan to teach the Ultra Seminar. Although not necessarily formally arranged, a good deal of information was also obtained from telephone conversation with Mr. Barbone and other key informants in this area.

While in Laredo, interviews were held with Juan Silva, the Director of Foreign Countries; Alejandro Gonzalez; Saul Gonzalez, Director of Silva Sensor Systems; and Ed Bernd, BLS lecturer for Laredo and responsible for various duties at SMCI Headquarters.

C. The Questionnaires

There are over four million individuals who have taken the Silva training. Because of the constraints of the study, it was not possible to reach even one-half percent of that number. In the Metro-Detroit and Laredo populations there were well over seven hundred people. It was physically impossible to talk with each of them, even superficially, due to time constraints. Consequently, in order to reach as large a population as the study would permit and to gain as much information as possible, a traditionally non-anthropological data collection technique (questionnaires) supplemented the primary technique of participant-observation. The questionnaires were of three types:

1) General Background; designed to gain demographic information.

2) Extensive Laredo; in addition to demographic data, also designed to gain information on the respondents opinions about the BLS and the Method, their ideological orientation, and their degree of involvement.

3) <u>Follow-up</u>; used to supplement the general background questionnaire for a portion of the Detroit population.

For the first two questionnaires, during my introduction, I explained the questionnaires and their purpose. Not only during the introduction but also on the face of each questionnaire were statements indicating my independence from SMCI and the FTI. Also indicated was the fact that participation was completely voluntary and all information obtained would be confidential. Piles of these numbered questionnaires were placed in conspicuous places and/or gathering areas for the length of the courses. Respondents had the choice of handing the completed questionnaire to me personally, mailing it to me, or--for the Metro-Detroit people--returning it through the FTI. Also for the Metro-Detroit group, for those who did not wish to have their name on the questionnaire, a detachable slip of paper with the corresponding questionnaire number and identifying information could be handed in separately. Less than five people chose to detach their name from the questionnaire itself. The respondents to the Laredo questionnaire did not have that option. Their identifying information was incorporated into the last page of the instrument.

The follow-up questionnaire was sent through the mail. It had an explanatory cover letter reminding the person of the study and describing the purpose of the questionnaire.

A deadline was included for their return. For those not returned by that date, a reminder post card was sent indicating I was still interested in hearing from them. The end result was that nineteen of the thirty-two were returned.

IV. THE QUESTIONNAIRES

A. Introduction

There were three questionnaires created for this study. Each was specifically designed for a particular population (see above). In each case, the respondents represent a convenience sample--i.e. those who took the time to answer the questionnaires are represented. As mentioned above, it is not random nor can it be said to be representative of all persons who have taken the SMC BLS. The response rates for each of the questionnaires was exceptionally high (see Chapter Six).

B. Types

1. General Background

The General Background questionnaire was designed for the Metro-Detroit sub-group. It consisted of forty-five forced choice questions with the primary purpose of gathering general demographic data. The topics included sex, age, income, education, religion, marital status, number of children, race, employment status, SMC history, involvement with other organizations, belief in parapsychology, and use of a psychic. This questionnaire was pre-tested on thirty-five individuals. With the exception of question numbering, virtually no changes were necessary. As such, the data from the pre-test was included in the total Metro-Detroit group responses. In Appendix Eight, this questionnaire is labeled #1

2. Extensive Laredo

The extensive Laredo questionnaire was designed for those attending the 1983 SMCI International Convention in Laredo, Texas and the participants in the lecturers training which immediately followed that convention (see Chapter Four). In addition to all the questions contained in the General Background questionnaire, the Laredo questionnaire also included twenty-six open-ended questions. These questions were designed to generate information concerning the respondents' (1) opinion about the BLS and the Method, (2) ideological orientation, and (3) degree of involvement with SMCI and the Method. This questionnaire is labeled #3 in Appendix Eight.

3. Follow-up

Because of the success of the Laredo questionnaire and the amount of data obtained from it, I developed a similar instrument for a portion of the Metro-Detroit group. In addition to the twenty-six open-ended questions from that instrument, this questionnaire had eight additional open-ended questions aimed at degree of involvement. This questionnaire is labeled #2 in Appendix Eight.

CHAPTER THREE

A BRIEF HISTORICAL OVERVIEW OF

SILVA MIND CONTROL INTERNATIONAL

I. INTRODUCTION

Silva Mind Control is an international organization which developed as a result of twenty-two years of research by its founder, José Silva The stated purpose of Silva Mind Control International (SMCI) is to serve humanity by teaching individuals a method which they can use to improve their own life. The Silva Method is taught through a series of lectures and mental training exercises contained in a forty to forty-eight hour course. What began as research in Laredo, Texas in the mid-1940s, has expanded to classes[1] taught in sixty-one different countries.

This chapter will briefly trace the historical development of Silva Mind Control International. It will begin with a look at the personal history of José Silva. The circumstances which lead to the development of the Silva Method will be discussed next. Once the Method was developed, Silva attempted to get others interested in his findings. In 1963, Silva started teaching the Method to select groups. The first classes, from 1966-1969, were held within Texas. In 1969, Silva expanded out of the state.

Shortly after that, Silva Mind Control became an international organization.

The information contained within this chapter has come from one or a combination of the following sources: (1) the available literature on Silva Mind Control; (2) Silva Mind Control lectures presented during the courses; (3) personal communications from lecturers and students of the Silva Method.

II. PERSONAL HISTORY OF JOSE SILVA

A. Early Life

Born in 1914 in Laredo, Texas, Jose Silva, the second of four children, began his life in extreme poverty. In order that her child would be born a United States citizen, Jose's mother Isabel Silva, left the family home in Monterrey, Mexico and temporarily went to her mother's home in Laredo, Texas. At this time, Mexico was in the throes of a revolution, with severe economic conditions. In 1918, Jose Silva's father died as a indirect result of the violence which occurred during that revolution (Silva,1983:17-25).

Widowed and pregnant with her fourth child, Isabel Silva brought her family to live with her mother in Laredo, Texas. Support for the family fell to Jose Silva's matrilateral uncle, Manual. Eventually, Isabel Silva remarried. She and her new husband moved away, taking

Jose's younger brother Juan with them. Jose's youngest brother, Albert, went to live with an aunt, while Jose and his older sister, Josephine, remained with their grandmother who served as mother. Jose's uncle Manual became, in effect, his father and assumed the social responsibility for his upbringing.

At the age of six, it became necessary for Jose Silva to supplement the family income. He began by shining shoes and selling newspapers. Within a short time, his daily earnings reportedly equalled the average weekly adult wage ($1). By the time he was seven, it is claimed he was earning as much daily as his uncle Manual weekly. Consequently, the decision was made that he would continue to help support the family and not attend school. His business ventures rapidly expanded to include distributing weekly circulars and nightly janitorial service for local offices. When Jose Silva was seventeen, he had accumulated enough capital to go into business, wholesaling locally unavailable merchandise from San Antonio and selling it door to door in Laredo (Ibid:27-37).

As Jose was busy working to help support the family, his brother and sister were going to school. In the evenings, they would give their daily school lessons to Jose. He became quite interested in language and reading, practicing daily by using Spanish and English comic books. The neighborhood barbershop always had a large supple of comic books so he would spend most of his free time there.

Eventually, he began reading other material, including a correspondence course in electronics. The barber agreed he could borrow the weekly lessons for a one dollar fee per lesson, if he agreed to sign the barber's name to those lessons. José agreed to the terms and completed the course. The barber received the diploma which he displayed on his barbershop wall as he continued to cut hair. Silva learned electronics and at the age of fourteen began his own electronics business (Ibid:39-45; Silva and Miele,1977:22).

His first business venture in electronics was radio antenna installation. This lead to radio repair and the eventual establishment of his own radio repair shop. In turn, this expanded to include the sale of used radios for homes and automobiles (Silva,1983). His electronics business grew rapidly and eventually became "the most successful in Southeast Texas". It was the success of this electronics business which provided the one half-million dollar financial base for the research which lead to the development of the Silva Method (Silva and Miele,1977:22).

B. Adult Events

In 1940, at the age of twenty-six, José Silva married Paula, who was and continues to be a driving force in his life. By 1983, they had 10 children and 21 grandchildren (see Appendix One). His children were his first subjects in his research. Today, most of his children and many of their spouses are actively involved in the running of Silva Mind Control International (see Chapter Five).

In 1944, José Silva, then the father of three children, was drafted into the United States army. Because of his fourteen years of electronics experience, Silva scored highly in the electronics areas of the army entry testing. He was eventually assigned to the Central Signal Corps School and served in the Signal Corps until the end of the War (Silva,1983:89-113).

It was during his service in the Army that José Silva began to study psychology. During his induction procedure, it was necessary for him to speak with the Army psychiatrist. The psychiatrist's probing questions and subsequent discussions aroused Silva's curiosity in psychology. He bought and read as many psychology books as he could find. This interest in psychology continued and was influential in shaping the Silva Method (Ibid; Silva and Miele,1977:23).

After World War II ended, Silva returned to Laredo. While rebuilding his electronics business, he taught at Laredo Junior College where he created and supervised its electronics lab. With the advent of television, his electronics business became very successful and it was necessary for him to spend all of his time working at it. Accordingly, he resigned his teaching position (Silva,1983:116-117;Silva and Miele,1977:23-24).

III. DEVELOPMENT OF THE SILVA METHOD

During the late 1940s, José Silva expanded his interests from psychology to hypnosis. Initially, this began as an attempt to help his children with their school work. Later, it expanded and became a major influence in the development of the Silva Method.

A. Interest in I. Q.

Three of Silva's children were having a great deal of difficulty with their school work. Upon talking with their teachers, he was told their I. Q.s were low. This aroused his interest and lead him to I. Q. research. He concluded that I. Q. primarily measures experiences, that it is not fixed, and that with training I. Q. could be improved. He felt the real problem with his children was their lack of concentration on the lessons being presented. Drawing on his background in psychology and his new interest in hypnosis, he developed a training routine to improve their performance.[2]

B. Hypnosis

His initial goal was to relax the children so they would be able to learn. From his electrical background, Silva knew that the ideal circuit has minimum impedance and maximum electrical energy use. Based on this, he reasoned that the brain--a complex electrical circuit--could function more efficiently if its impedance could be lowered. To achieve this he began using hypnosis (Silva and Miele,1977:24). In hypnosis, the hypnotist takes the subject into a deep state of relaxation where the subject is extremely susceptible to suggestion and is under the complete control of the hypnotist. Silva would hypnotize each of his three children, read them a lesson and then bring them out of their hypnotic state (Silva,1983:126-127). As a result of his observations, he concluded that the brain does receive and temporarily store more information at lower frequencies. But, it is also completely passive. He concluded that there is no reasoning or questioning which are crucial for understanding the material (Silva,1983:202;Silva and Miele,1977:24). After five years, he became dissatisfied and abandoned hypnosis as a technique.

While Silva was doing this early research and using his children as subjects, other family members were also using hypnosis. Isabel, Silva's oldest child and first subject, learned hypnosis by reading one of her father's books. She would regularly hypnotize her younger brothers and sisters. It became a game for her, as she left harmless and amusing suggestions with them (Silva,1983:181-184). Paula Silva, initially hesitant about the use of hypnosis with the children saw how effectively preconditioning worked and learned to do it herself (Ibid:175). Jose Silva had worked with all his children and preconditioned them to enter an hypnotic state on cue. One day, Antonio had a medical emergency. Jose Silva activated the cue (thumb on forehead) and Antonio entered an hypnotic state during which his wound was treated and he felt no pain. After seeing this, Paula Silva realized the usefulness of the technique and learned the procedure. They both reportedly used the cue on their children a number of times as they were growing up (Ibid:167-175).

C. Controlled Relaxation

Silva next began experimenting with techniques that would lower the brain wave frequency yet keep the mind alert. Through these early years of research, he decided that ten cycles per second is the frequency at which the brain is most energetic and synchronized and it is the optimal frequency for information impression and recall (Silva and Miele,1977:24). He investigated zen, yoga, and other meditation systems but was dissatisfied with them because they induce a five cycle/second frequency in the meditator (Silva,1979:22-23). All or part of various mental training exercises were tried until Silva was satisfied that he was achieving the desired results (Ibid:23-25). He then felt he had a method which could achieve a ten cycle per second brain wave frequency with complete alertness and self-control--controlled relaxation.

As a result of the training and the focussed attention associated with it, the Silva children reportedly improved their school performances. By the early 1950s, the original goals of the research had been achieved. The children had learned to relax and reduce their stress. Their concentration and attention span had increased and their grades in school had improved (Silva,1983:129). News of the success of the Silva children gradually spread throughout the neighborhood. By 1953, thirty-nine children had been brought by their parents to Silva for his help[3] (Silva,1983:211;Silva and Miele,1977:25-26). For the next ten years, Silva worked individually with each of these first thirty-nine non-family subjects.

D. First Expression of Psychic Ability

In 1952, after working with his children a number of years, José Silva witnessed a completely unexpected event. While working with Isabel on a poetry lesson, Silva observed that Isabel would recite the next poem before he had presented it to her. He tried several more times and she continued to respond to the questions or recite the poem just before he presented them. Since he continually changed the order of presentation, she could not have known before-hand which poem or question would come next. Silva concluded that she was receiving the information in some other way, possibly "reading his mind" to telepathically get the information before he had asked. Silva had read about clairvoyance, clairvoyant diagnosis, and Edgar Cayce when he was studying hypnosis (Silva,1983:127-129). Intrigued by this new development he abandoned any further research on ways to improve I. Q. and devoted his efforts to developing ways to enhance the "guessing factor"--the psychic ability that Isabel had displayed. He designed numerous experiments to test Isabel's apparent psychic ability (Ibid:129-130;Silva and Miele,1977:25).

IV. ATTEMPTS TO MAKE OTHERS AWARE OF HIS WORK

A. Dr. J. B. Rhine

In 1953, the leading researcher in extrasensory perception or psychic phenomena was Dr. James B. Rhine of Duke University. Convinced he had trained Isabel to be a psychic, Silva wrote to Rhine explaining what had happened. Rhine's response, which came from an associate, was guarded. Rhine, like most researchers in parapsychology at that time, believed that the psi factor, or psychic ability, was unchangeable.[4] They believed some people were just natural psychics, while others never would be. They concluded Isabel must have been a natural psychic. Without any proper pre- and post-testing there would be no way to be certain (Silva,1983:131-132;Silva and Miele,1977:25-26).

Disappointed but still convinced he had discovered something, Silva continued to work with other subjects. It took ten years to individually train the first thirty-nine subjects. During this time, Silva repeatedly invited Rhine to come to Laredo and investigate his research. Rhine never accepted (Silva,1983:133). By 1963, after the training of the first subjects was complete and they all were reportedly functioning psychically, Silva was certain of his technique (Ibid;Silva and Miele,1977:26). He was convinced that he had developed a method which could train a person to be a psychic while at the same time teach them how to relax, concentrate and recall information more effectively.

For the next three years (1963-1966) Silva worked on perfecting the Method. He began by training groups of twenty, one group at a time. Silva experimented with the age and sex composition in these first groups (all male, all female, coed, same age) to see if that would have any effect on learning the Method (Silva,1983:212,229). No differences were found. Silva continued to modify the techniques and decrease the training time until, by 1965, he was satisfied with the basic method of training (Ibid:229).

B. National Aeronautics and Space Administration

In early 1965, Silva became aware that Dr. Everett F. Dagle, a National Aeronautics and Space Administration scientist, was interested in extrasensory perception (ESP). They corresponded and designed experiments to test clairvoyants' ability to mentally influence an astronaut while in orbit. Three of Silva's most experienced and accurate clairvoyants were chosen as senders. The orbital flight of Grissom and Younge was chosen as the target. The objective of the first experiment was to get the astronauts to hallucinate/receive smells, tastes, sounds, sights and touches. The second was designed to increase the astronauts' blood pressure and heart beat. The exact time of every projection was recorded and both experiments were witnessed by a representative from the Mind Science Foundation[5] (Silva,1983:237-242).

After the experiments were finished, a notarized copy of the schedule was sent to Dr. Dagle for comparison with NASA data. Despite numerous attempts over the next two years, Dr. Dagle reportedly was not able to obtain the NASA data. All the data had been classified and thus not available. Because of the difficulty in getting feedback, Silva abandoned these types of experiments (Ibid).

C. President Lyndon Johnson

Convinced he had developed a mental training method that could benefit everyone, in August 1965 José Silva wrote to President Lyndon Johnson. Silva offered to turn over all his research findings, including the Method itself. All the material could be used at the President's discretion with "no strings attached". Two weeks later, Silva received a response. President Johnson turned the offer over to the National Science Foundation. Randal Robertson, Associate Director of Research, expressed gratitude but indicated that there was no need for Silva's work at that time (see Appendix Twc) (Silva,1983:229-232). According to later accounts of this incident, Silva's primary purpose in writing to President Johnson was to give the Method to the government so that it could be taught in every school throughout the country.

V. GROWTH OF THE ORGANIZATION

A. Within Texas

Undaunted by Johnson's rejection, Silva decided it would be up to him to get his Method to the people. In September, 1966, José Silva started teaching what is now referred to as the Basic Lecture Series. The first class was conducted Amarillo, in the panhandle of Texas.

Nelda Sheets, who later became the first female lecturer for Silva Mind Control, was a member of a group interested in hypnosis and extrasensory perception. She invited José Silva to come to Amarillo to speak to her group. After his lecture they were so interested they wanted him to teach the Method to them. He was not yet teaching his course in a class format but after some persuasion he agreed to do so (Sheets,1983, personal communication). The composition of this first class was approximately ninety percent female, and many of the class went on to be part of the first lecturer training course in 1968.

The first course was very different from the way it is today. At that time, Silva drove up from Laredo once a week and taught the forty to forty-eight hour course in four-hour weekly components and it took almost three months to complete the course. Today, the course is usually taught on two consecutive weekends. For the next three years, Silva taught the Basic Lecture Series throughout the state of Texas.

B. Outside of the State

In March, 1968, José Silva conducted the first training course for those interested in teaching the Silva Method. Now staffed with others who could teach the course in Texas, Silva planned for expansion outside of the state. In July, 1969, the first Basic Lecture Series was taught outside Texas in Chicago, Illinois. In August, it was taught in Detroit and in September it was offered in New York. Harry McKnight taught these first BLS courses and was responsible for opening up subsequent new territories. York. Today, the Basic Lecture Series is taught in virtually every state, several times a year. Most states have at least one lecturer with some of the more populated states having several lecturers. José Silva now teaches the Basic Lecture Series only once a year during the week preceeding the annual International Convention in Laredo, Texas.

C. International Expansion

As Silva Mind Control continued to grow, expansion outside the United States was possible. The Organization gradually spread into Mexico, Canada, Central and South America, Europe, and Africa, with the fastest growth presently occurring in Mexico, Central and South America. (This point will be expanded in Chapter Five.) Today, the Silva Method is taught in sixty-one countries and fourteen different languages (see Appendix Three) with a worldwide membership in the millions.

ENDNOTES

[1] Although the terms "teach" and "classes" are used throughout this dissertation, they are technically incorrect. According to SMCI, since they do not have credentials for "teaching" they do not "teach" but rather "lecture". Likewise, they do not have "classes"; they have "lectures".

[2] This sequence of events is the one generally presented in the Basic Lecture Series. A slightly different version is presented in the autobiography. According to this version, Silva first read the literature on hypnosis and took hypnosis courses throughout the United States for five years. He then wanted to practice the theory so in 1949 he started helping his children with their school lessons (Silva,1983:180).

[3] In all but one of the references to these first 39 subjects they are referred to as school children. The notable exception is Silva's autobiography. In this he states the first 39 subjects were "men, women, and children" (Silva,1983:133). I suspect the majority were school children with perhaps a few family members or close friends also trained.

[4] In 1966, ten years after the Silva research, J. B. Rhine reportedly changed his mind and said the psi factor could be changed or enhanced with training.

[5] The Mind Science Foundation is an organization interested in studying paranormal phenomena.

CHAPTER FOUR

THE SILVA METHOD OF SELF MIND CONTROL

I. INTRODUCTION

The Silva Method of self-mind control[1], developed
after years of research by José Silva, is based on the
assumption that the brain functions most effectively, for
certain tasks, when it is at a brain wave frequency of ten
cycles per second. At this frequency, new information is
imprinted strongly, information learned in the past is
recalled more easily, and psychic functioning is enhanced.
It is also at this frequency, according to Silva Mind
Control (SMC), that the body's immune system is activated
and health is improved (see Chapter Six). Based on this,
the Silva Method is designed to train an individual to enter
ten cycles per second at will. The training takes place in
a forty to forty-eight hour course referred to as the Basic
Lecture Series (BLS). This basic course is all that is
necessary to learn the Silva Method. If, however, an
individual is interested in learning more about the history
of the organization or is interested in learning additional
healing techniques, graduate courses are occasionally
offered. Additionally, there is an annual instructors

training course given for persons interested in teaching the BLS (see Chart 1).

CHART 1

Courses of Instruction

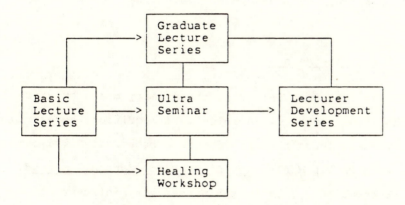

This chapter will describe the Silva Method and it will examine all of the instructional courses through which the Method is taught.

II. THE SILVA METHOD

A. Defined

The Silva Method is a mental exercise in which the individual consciously and with control, enters a state of physical relaxation and altered consciousness²--an alpha level of mind (10 cps). By entering this "level of mind", the individual is believed able to have conscious control over bodily systems (both autonomic and and sympathetic), to have access to a wide range of unconventional problem solving techniques, and to improve physical and mental health. It is also maintained by SMC that regular functioning at alpha increases creativity, promotes healing and recuperation, and sharpens intuition or psychic functioning.

B. How to Learn the Method

The Basic Lecture Series is the primary means by which the Method is taught (see below). In addition, however, many individuals learn the Method from a book Jose Silva co-authored with Philip Miele, The Silva Mind Control Method. From my observations, this book has been very influential in getting people to come and take the course itself. The other means through which individuals learn of the Method (or parts of it) is through graduates of the BLS. These graduates often teach their family and friends the Method and some or all of the techniques. These family members and friends often will then take the Basic Lecture Series themselves

C. Relevant Research

There are two areas of research relevant to the Silva Method. The first concerns electrical brain wave activity—electroencephology. The second is biofeedback research.

In the late 1920s, Hans Berger a German psychiatrist, conducted the first experiments measuring the electrical activity of the brain (Lawrence,1972:74-75). In these pioneer studies, Berger actually discovered the alpha and beta brain wave frequencies. He also speculated about the relationship between these brain wave frequencies and levels of consciousness. Berger's research was abruptly and permanently interrupted in 1938 with the rise of the Nazis (Ibid). Other researchers, however, were able to continue brain wave frequency investigation in other countries.

In the last decade, there has been a tremendous amount of work done on brain wave activity. The result is a much greater, but far from complete, understanding of the electrical activity of the brain. Researchers have found, for example, that there are four brain wave frequencies; beta, alpha, theta and delta. All four frequencies are always present, but at any particular moment, one of the frequencies generally dominates (see Brown,1974). Each of the four brain wave frequencies also has been found to be associated with specific physical and emotional states. Beta, which ranges between fourteen and approximately twenty-eight cycles per second', is generally associated with physical activity, rational thought, tension and anxiety. Alpha, ranging between seven and fourteen cycles per second, is associated with relaxation, tranquility, creative thought, intuition, meditation, psychic functioning, and recall. Theta, four to seven cycles per second, is related to deeper levels of meditation, concentration, accelerated healing, greater learning and recall capabilities. Finally delta, at zero to four cycles per second, is usually found in association with deep sleep and unconsciousness (Lawrence,1972; Brown,1974). During sleep, people continually cycle through all four of these levels. Most people, however, spend their waking hours functioning primarily at beta. Silva maintains that with training, a person can learn to function with conscious awareness at any of these levels, even delta.

It was the work of Berger and subsequent researchers which eventually led to the development of todays ideas about biofeedback. Biofeedback (also known as biofeedback training, BFT) is a technique by which the individual learns, through cues presented by electronic measuring devices, to regulate and control physiologic functioning and brain wave activity (Brown,1974). The initial discovery and definitive research in biofeedback is credited to Barbara Brown. Since those first years of research in the late 1960s, thousands of experiments and investigations of biofeedback have taken place (see Brown,1975).

José Silva, primed by his electronics background, was quite interested in brain wave frequency and biofeedback research. By the late 1960s, the Silva Method had already been developed and classes were being taught throughout Texas (see Chapter Three). Silva had already recognized the benefits of functioning at "alpha" frequency levels and had been teaching people to do so since the early 1960s. He maintains, however, that sophisticated instruments (e.g. EEG machines, galvanic skin response devices) are not necessary to achieve control over alpha production. From Silva's perspective, the biofeedback research simply reinforced the claims he had been making since the early 1950s. Conscious regulation and control of psysiologic functions and controlled alpha production are possible. But, Silva asserts, this can be achieved through the use of the Silva Method and without the aid of external cues. In fact, students are discouraged from using any mechanical devices until they have learned the Method and finished the Basic Lecture Series'.

The impact of this research on Silva Mind Control can be seen in three ways. First, this research, combined with his own investigations, reinforced Silva's belief in the importance of functioning at alpha frequencies. Secondly, the electroencepholographic instrumentation conformation of controlled alpha functioning of Silva graduates lend credence to the Method. Finally, it was partially from these two areas of research that Silva developed his brain wave frequency chart (see Appendix Four) which is utilized throughout the Basic Lecture Series.

III. INSTRUCTIONAL COURSES

A. The Basic Lecture Series

The Basic Lecture Series (BLS) is approximately forty hours long. It is divided into four segments of about ten hours each. Known respectively as MC101CR, MC202GSI, MC303ESP, and MC404AESP each of the segments builds upon the previous one. It all culminates in the final session, MC404AESP. The first two segments deal primarily with relaxation and problem solving techniques. It is in the final two segments that the parapsychological or psychic aspects of the course are expressed.

The typical BLS is presented over two consecutive weekends. The four ten hour days are divided into morning and afternoon sessions. Each session is composed of a series of triadic components which are (1) lecture, (2) pre-conditioning, and (3) conditioning or mental training exercise (see Chart Two). Locally, a forth segment, the break, is added to this cycle.

CHART 2

BLS Triadic Components

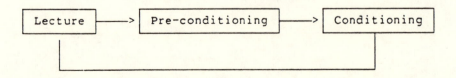

The lecture component is intended to prepare the student for the mental training exercise. During this component the lecturer' introduces ideas relevant to the upcoming technique. Research on the subject is presented and relevant literature discussed. During the pre-conditioning, the lecturer reads through the up-coming mental training exercise just as it will be presented while the students are "at level". This enables the students to know precisely what will be said to them and dispels any possible fears that may exist about the lecturer introjecting something harmful. The primary purpose of the lecture and pre-conditioning is to set the stage and establish the proper mind set for the mental training exercise. The examples used, the orientation and the literature discussed, however, are all determined by the lecturer. Technically, every lecturer is required to do a pre-conditioning for each of the conditioning cycles. Actually, some skip this segment, going directly from their lecture to the conditioning.

It is in the mental training exercise that the techniques are introduced. The exercise is composed of a series of steps. The entry procedure changes as the student progress but the remaining portion stays essentially the same. After the morning of the first day, the students use the "3 to 1" method to enter their "basic plane level" (see below). Once at level, the same sequence is always followed. The following are the steps followed in a typical mental training exercise or conditioning cycle, during the BLS.

1) <u>Enter level with the 3 to 1 method</u>: (discussed below).

2) <u>Deepening</u>: countdown from 10 to 1 to enter a "deeper level of mind"--become more relaxed.

3) <u>Eye-lid relaxation</u>: a forty-five second substitute for the long relax (see below) in which the student consciously releases tension in all parts of the body.

4) <u>Ideal place of relaxation</u>: early in 101, the student mentally creates a place to which he can "project" himself. It can be any place or situation that the student perceives as relaxing, e.g. sitting alongside a gently flowing stream in the middle of a forest. The lecturer pauses about thirty seconds to let the students enjoy their ideal place of relaxation. Although the pause is half a minute, most students report, after the exercise, that they perceived the time spent there as three or four times longer.

5) <u>Rapport</u>: at this point the lecturer reads four statements intended to establish/maintain rapport with the students. The first directs the student to continue to listen to the lecturer's voice and follow the directions which are given. The second associates the word "relax" (which is occasionally

repeated throughout the exercise) with being physically and mentally relaxed. The third statement reaffirms that the lecturer can bring the student out of any level of mind by counting from 1 to 5. At the count of 5 the person will be in perfect health and feeling fine. The last statement is directed at the rare individuals who might not open their eyes at the count of 5. Instructions are given that when the lecturer touches the student's left shoulder three times he will be wide awake and feeling fine.

6) Genius statements: two statements affirming the individual is special and that she is able to use more of her mind are read. From this point on the student mentally repeats the statements as the lecturer reads them.

7) Beneficial statements: this is a series of positive statements designed to increase the individual's confidence in their own control and in the benefits of positive thinking. Also, the ideological position that the students' "increasing mental faculties" are to "serve humanity" is stated.

8) Protective statements: these are the only statements that do not appear in any of the manuals. The reason given is that after the BLS there is no need for the statements. The statements themselves are important, however, in

that they reflect a basic underlying belief of SMC. The statements, which are presented throughout the 101 and 202 sessions, are:

This is Mind Control. Your own self mind control. You are always in control. You may accept or reject anything I say, any time, at any level of the mind. You are always in control.

9) Preventive statements: these statements are directed toward better mental health. They include a series of phrases in which the person states he will "never learn to develop physical or mentally" physical ailments such as heart disease, leukemia, diabetes, arthritis, glaucoma, cancer, circulatory ailments, mental disorders, or any psychosomatic disease. The students also affirm that they will always have a perfectly healthy mind and body and that negative thoughts will not influence them.

10) Effective sensory projection statements: in the pre-conditioning for the introduction of these statements, the students are told that they are not expected to believe the statements. The only request is that they suspend disbelief, allow for the possibility that ESP might exist. The students are told they are able to project their intelligence (awareness) to any point on this planet or any planet in our universe; that they can project into any of the three matter kingdoms (inanimate, plant and animal, and human); and that they can detect and correct any abnormalities

found there. These activities are possible, it is said, only if it "is necessary and beneficial for humanity". The students also reaffirm, again, that negative thoughts have no influence over them.

11) Programing: this is the point in the cycle when the lecturer reads the techniques discussed below.

12) Post-effects: these are positive statements concerning how the individual may use the levels of mind achieved. The students are told they benefit physically and mentally from using these levels of mind, that they can help themselves or any one else who needs help at these levels of mind, but that the levels should only be used in "a constructive, creative manner, for all that is good, honest, pure, clean and positive". If they try to use the levels of mind achieved to hurt others, they "will not be able to function within these levels of mind". There is also a statement included here which is another expression of the underlying ideology:

You will continue to strive to take part in constructive and creative activities to make this a better world to live in, so that when we move on, we will have left behind a better world for those who follow. You will consider the whole of humanity, depending on their ages, as fathers or mothers, brothers or sisters, sons or daughters. You are a superior human being, you have greater understanding, compassion, and patience with your fellow man (Graduate Course: MC1001 GC manual,1973:15).

It is also at this point that the lecturer would introduce any preparation for the next conditioning cycle.

13) <u>Bring-out</u>: in this last phase of the cycle the lecturer counts slowly from 1 to 5, affirming that at the count of 5 the person will be "wide awake feeling fine and in perfect health, feeling better than before". At the count of 5, the lecturer snaps his/her fingers and the students open their eyes.

1. The Introductory Lecture

The first segment of the Basic Lecture Series, MC101CR, begins with a lecture in which a general overview of the course is presented. This overview is approximately three hours long and is referred to as the "Introductory Lecture". Generally the Introductory Lecture is presented two or more times in the week(s) prior to the BLS itself. These "Intros", as they are called, are extremely important. It is here that the instructor "sells" the course and gets the students to register for the BLS.

The cost of the "Intro" is determined by the individual lecturer. Most often the lecture is free of charge. Some, however, combine it with a particular technique usually learned later in 101 and charge a slight fee for the lecture. The number of times the "Intro" is offered before the BLS is also determined by the lecturer.

Most will offer the Introductory Lecture at least twice before each class.

It is in the content of the "Intro" where one sees the greatest variation among lecturers. All Introductory Lectures should include a short history of SMC, a basic overview of the course, the meeting schedule, and the cost. Beyond that, the individual lecturer may add whatever he or she chooses. Often, this is a demonstration of the "memory pegs", a technique learned later in the course. One very successful lecturer, Marcelino Alcala, uses the "mental house cleaning" session--usually covered later in the BLS -- as the basis for his Introductory Lecture. Most lecturers, however, will use some memory trick during the "Intros" to get the audience attention. Frequently, this will be learning the names of all present as they arrive and register. Later, the lecturer is then able to address each individual by name.

The approach in the "Intro" varies almost as much as the content. Some lecturers will take a strict business orientation. Others will be more "spiritual" or "self-help" oriented. Both the content and the approach taken depend on the background of the lecturer. (A more detailed discussion on the importance of the Intro is included in Chapter Five).

2. Controlled Relaxation--MC101CR

The first segment of the Basic Lecture Series itself is entitled, "Controlled Relaxation", MC101CR. The primary function of this session is to teach the individual how to relax. This is done through the use of a series of progressive relaxation exercises. Then, the first of the "techniques" are introduced. These include: (1) sleep control; (2) to awake control; (3) awake control; (4) dream control; and (5) headache control (see Table 1).

TABLE 1

MC101CR

Content/Techniques	
1. controlled relaxation	4. awake control
2. sleep control	5. dream control
3. to awake control	6. headache control

In the first portion of 101, the student learns how to achieve the state of relaxation which will be needed whenever the Method is used. This state of relaxation, known as "controlled relaxation", is learned through a series of progressive relaxation exercises. In these exercises the students are asked to close their eyes, focus on a particular part of the body, mentally feel the skin, the nerves, the blood, and then consciously try to relax that area by letting go of all tensions there. Known as the "long relax", this exercise begins at the top of the head and progressively works its way down to the soles of the feet.

It is during this "long relax" that the student learns
to identify different levels of relaxation; physical
relaxation, mental relaxation, and the "basic plane level".
Physical relaxation is defined by SMC as a state in which
all physical tension and stress is released. Mental
relaxation is identified as regular alpha rhythm which is
sometimes felt as deep calm. Brain wave frequency research
has shown a correlation between deep physical relaxation and
alpha brain wave frequency production (see Brown and
Klug,1974). The "basic plane level" is a particular brain
wave frequency ("level of mind", altered state of
consciousness) which becomes the "working level" for the
individual. It can vary from person to person and
fluctuates depending on the particular task upon which the
individual is working--i.e. the purpose for entering the
level. Ideally, according to Silva, the basic plane level
should be at ten cycles per second. This is especially true
when the practitioner is working on health cases. Actually,
as presented in the BLS lectures, the level is said to
fluctuate throughout the alpha brain wave frequency range.
It is believed, however, that with practice the basic plane
level will center at ten cycles per second since this is,
according to Silva, the most effective brain wave frequency
for problem solving and case working.

Learning to identify these different levels is
correlated with associating a particular number with each of
the three basic levels. each of the three basic levels.

Central to the relaxation technique is a series of count down exercises designed to relax the nervous system. An association is established between counting down and becoming more relaxed with each decreasing number. The final result is the student learns to associate the number "3" with physical relaxation, the number "2" with mental relaxation, and the number "1" with the basic plane level. Known as the "3 to 1" method, it involves closing one's eyes, taking a deep breath and while exhaling, mentally visualizing and repeating the number "3", three times and then repeating the procedure for the numbers "2" and "1". By the end of the 101 session, the student uses only this "3 to 1" method to enter her/his level'.

After a series of trial exercises and a few relaxation exercises the first of the techniques, "sleep control" is introduced. Sleep control is designed to help those individuals who have difficulty falling asleep at night. Since the cause for the restlessness is frequently stress or stress inducing thoughts, this technique provides a means to eliminate those thoughts and relax the body. Using the technique the individual imagines a chalk board or which he draws a circle and writes the word "deeper" outside the circle. Starting with the number "100", the person writes the number within the circle, erases the number, and traces over the word "deeper". The same procedure is followed with each decreasing number until the person falls asleep. Since it is difficult to hold two opposing thoughts simultaneously, concentrating on the procedure and counting down seems to effectively eliminate the stress inducing thoughts and restlessness. Also, the technique, if practiced as directed, is boring. The effect is similar to that achieved by repeating a sound or word, by counting backward from 100, or just counting sheep. In any case, attention is focused on non-threatening thoughts.

The second technique introduced, "to awake control", is intended to provide the individual with a method to awaken at a desired time without the use of an alarm clock. Each person has within them an internal time keeping mechanism, a circadian clock, which allows the estimation of time passage. Transcontinental travelers frequently suffer jet lag and disorientation until this internal time piece resets itself. Many individuals are consciously or unconsciously using their circadian clocks everyday. The Silva technique of "to awake control" brings conscious awareness to the mechanism. Because it is dependable and easy to use, practicing this technique provides the student with early successes which build the confidence necessary for later techniques.

This technique is practiced just before going to sleep. The person enters "his level" and visualizes a clock. The current time is seen first then the hands of the clock are moved forward to the desired wake-up time. The person suggests to himself that "this is the time I will awaken". For many, to awaken by the use of this technique (or a variant of it) is a more natural and pleasant experience than the harsh awakening of an alarm.

"Awake control", the third technique introduced in 101, is used when a person is drowsy yet needs to stay awake. The technique involves entering "your level", then mentally telling yourself that you want to feel wide awake and alert. You then count out of level from 1 to 5 and at the count of 5 you should be wide awake and able to continue your task in an alert state.

"Dream control", the next technique, is based on the assumption that it is possible to use one's dreams to achieve answers to questions and to solve problems. Interest in the interpretation and use of dreams spans decades.' Silva believes that the time spent sleeping should be used for more than just physical relaxation. Since the mind is never unconscious, mental activity during sleep--dreaming--should be directed toward specific purposes. To do this, Silva developed a three step dream control technique. In each step, before going to sleep the person enters "level 1". In step one, the person programs-- suggests to himself--that he' will remember a dream. When he is able to remember a dream on command, he moves to the next stage. He programs himself in step two to remember his dreams for a specific night. When he can do this satisfactorily he moves to the final phase where he programs to have and understand a dream which will solve a particular problem. The use of dreams in this manner is considered important because it is believed to help in the mastery of self mind control.

The final technique is the first of many directed toward personal health maintenance. "Headache control" is based on the belief that the brain can control certain stimulations, including pain. As such, the person should be able to rid himself of pain/discomfort through suggestions he gives himself while "at level". In this technique, as in the previous ones, the individual enters level with the "3 to 1" method. At level, the person acknowledges that he has a headache but that he does not want the headache. He then suggests to himself that at the count of five, when he opens his eyes, all pain/discomfort will be gone; he will be in perfect health and feeling fine. This technique can be applied to both tension and migraine headaches. For tension headaches one application is suggested. According to SMC, migraine headaches usually require three applications, five minutes apart.

3. General Self Improvement--MC202GSI

The second segment of the Basic Lecture Series is entitled, "General Self Improvement, MC202GSI". As the name implies, the primary goal is to teach the individual techniques that can be used to improve their mental and physical well-being. This is done through memory, problem solving and habit controlling techniques. These include: (1) the mental screen, (2) memory pegs, (3) three fingers technique, (4) mirror of the mind, (5) hand levitation, (6) glove anesthesia, (7) glass of water technique, and (8) habit control (see Table 2).

TABLE 2.

MC202GSI

Content/Techniques	
1. mental screen	5. hand levitation
2. memory pegs	6. glove anesthesia
3. three fingers	7. glass of water
4. mirror of the mind	8. habit control

The creation of the "mental screen", an area that the individual can focus attention on, is the first task in 202. It is used for a variety of purposes--including use as the area on which the individual will project (imagine) objects and people. According to the BLS manual, the mental screen is a means of providing order and continuity of experiences and of separating empty or meaningless imagery from purposeful creative problem solving (p.49). To create the mental screen, the individuals enter level and with their eyes still closed, are directed by the lecturer, to raise their eyes to an angle of about 20° above the horizontal plane. The area that they imagine is their mental screen. The students are encouraged to enhance the screen by projecting brightly colored images on it--including memory pegs, which is the next technique learned.

The "memory pegs" is a technique adapted from a system developed by Bruno Furst (1944). It is used primarily to memorize and recall lists of sequential numbers and items by associating a key word, a number and a vivid image. First students memorize a standard list of letters and peg words for each number (1-100). While at level, the instructor reads a letter and peg word and the students visualize an image of the peg word on their mental screen. For example, the letter for "2" is "N" and the peg word is "NOAH". The students are instructed to project an image of an old man with a long white beard on their mental screen. Another example would be the letter for the number "7" as being "K" and the peg word is "KEY". The image to project is a large gold key. After learning the above, the students are then asked to associate items with the numbers and peg words. For example, if the second item in the list is the Rocky Mountains, the person would associate Noah (the number "2" peg word) with the second item (Rocky Mountains). This is done on the mental screen by having the students visualize an image of Noah standing on a mountain, in front of a mountain, etc. Another example might be if the seventh item on the list is "fish", the mental screen image might be a fish with a large gold key in its mouth. The more imaginative the association, the stronger the impression.

Before the mental training exercise in which this technique is presented, the lecturer demonstrates the technique to the class. The lecturer elicits a list of thirty items from the class. After the list is generated, the lecturer (with his/her back to the list on the board) recites that list in any order requested by the class--1 to 30, 30 to 1, even numbers, every third number, etc. A demonstration of this technique is frequently used during the "Intro" because of its attention getting value.

The three fingers technique is a fast and easy way to "enter level". It originally developed out of research with the Silva children as an aid in learning their lessons. Today, it has grown to become a symbol of SMC graduates worldwide. The technique, which involves bringing together the tips of the first three fingers of either hand, is a triggering mechanism to "instantly" enter an alpha brain wave frequency. It is believed that superior memory, concentration, and recall are available at this level. According to Silva, the technique can be used when reading something to be remembered, when hearing a lecture, and when taking an examination. Graduates, however, report using the technique unofficially for various things including remembering phone numbers or names, finding lost items, getting someone to phone, and even finding a parking space close to the door of their destination.

To learn the technique, the students enter their level and the lecturer reads the program. The students are told that whenever they bring the "tips of the first three fingers of either hand" together, they will enter a level of mind at which information is impressed and recalled more

effectively. They may use this level to read a lesson, hear
a lecture or take a test. The proper way to use the
technique is given for each of the suggested applications.

The "mirror of the mind" is the power technique
underlying the Silva Method. An aspect of the mental
screen, the mirror of the mind is a problem solving
technique used when the desired solution to the problem is
known. In this case, the individual creates a blue framed
mirror on his mental screen. Within the blue framed mirror,
he visualizes his problem or project as clearly as possible,
looking at all aspects. After he has satisfactorily
examined the problem, he creates a white framed mirror. In
this mirror, the person imagines, in as much detail as
possible, the desired solution to the problem. Thereafter,
whenever the person thinks of the problem/project, he only
sees the desired solution in the white framed mirror. The
negative aspects of the problem are not thought of again.
The assumptions upon which this technique are based are
central to the whole Silva Method.

The mirror of the mind is based on the belief that
thoughts influence behavior and events in life. A person's
beliefs and attitude toward a situation will influence the
way he performs. As such, the person is directed to focus
only on the desired results. Silva suggests the individual
create the desired result in his mind (thoughts); think
positively about it (energize the scene); and he will
achieve the desired result. This is tied to another pivotal

belief, "whatever the mind can conceive, it can achieve", a phrase frequently repeated throughout the BLS.'

The next two techniques learned, hand levitation and glove anesthesia, are quite closely related. Hand levitation functions primarily as a deepening mechanism. That is, it enables the student to enter deeper levels of mind than can be achieved by the 3 to 1 method alone. Hand levitation is based on a method developed by Milton Erikson, who had polio and developed it to control the pain. SMCI uses the Method with his permission. The mental training exercise, or conditioning cycle, in which these techniques are presented is one of the longest. It begins not in the usual 3 to 1 fashion but with the eyes open and the hands resting on the knees. The lecturer instructs the students to concentrate their attention on the back of their dominant hand. Slowly, the lecturer counts down from 10 to 1, making suggestions that the hand is becoming lighter and lighter as he counts. At some point in the countdown, the hand should rise, although the students are instructed not to raise their hand consciously. When/if their hand does rise, the students are to touch the face (cheek) with the back of the hand and close their eyes. If anyone's hand has not risen by the count of three, they are consciously to bring it up to their face (cheek) and close their eyes for the final 3 to 1 count. It is maintained that it is not concentrating on the hand which causes it to rise but rather the instructions given to the "inner conscious level" by the lecturer. This was one area where the explanation given during the lecture and pre-conditioning was rather ambiguous. It is believed that concentrating on the hand in this manner, and thus eliminating other stimuli, will take the person to a theta brain wave frequency (similar to that achieved through mantra use). Theta, which requires extreme relaxation to achieve, is the brain wave frequency necessary to short circuit pain (according to Silva), which the next technique is designed to control.

Once the students have entered this deeper level of mind achieved by hand levitation, there is a countdown deepening and then glove anesthesia is presented. While they are still at level, the students are instructed to put their dominant hand down at their side in an imaginary pail of ice water. They are to imagine it becoming colder and numb with each passing moment. Their other hand is put in an imaginary pail of hot water. To fill the time necessary for these feelings to develop, the lecturer reviews the memory pegs presented earlier. After the review is finished and a few minutes have passed, the students are told that the sensation they presently feel in their hand is glove anesthesia. Next, the students are instructed to raise that hand above their head without touching anything. As they hold it up, the hand is to become even colder as it "dries" in that position. Holding the hand down for that length of time and then raising it up to head level creates physiological changes (e.g. blood flow) which produce physical sensations (e.g. tingling, vibration, heat) all of which are to be associated with glove anesthesia. Finally, the students rest their hand on their leg, test for sensitivity, and rub it to return normal feeling. The anesthesia achieved can be transferred to any part of the body to eliminate surface pain and to control bleeding. It can also be transferred, according to the lecturer, to other people to eliminate their pain.

The next technique introduced, the glass of water technique, is designed to solve problems for which the solution is not known. It can be applied to any type of problem and will work even for those who have not had the Silva training. Students are, in fact, encouraged to share this non-exclusive technique with non-grads. This technique, which requires the use of a clear glass filled with about six ounces of water, is used at bedtime. The student thinks about the problem and while drinking half of the water, mentally says "this is all I have to do to find the solution to the problem I have in mind". In the morning, upon awakening, the student drinks the remaining water, following the same procedure. At some time within the next seventy-two hours the solution will appear. According to the lecturer, this technique acts as a triggering mechanism to turn the problem over to the inner conscious level. If, after seventy-two hours, a solution is not found, the procedure is repeated or another technique is tried.

The final technique learned in 202 deals with habit control. Although the technique can be applied to any undesirable habit, those specifically dealt with are weight and smoking control. The purpose of this technique is to eliminate any repetitive behavior pattern which is no longer desired.

Since habits are multifunctional, to successfully eliminate a habit the individual must fully analyse that habit to determine the cause, the needs being met by the behavior, and the circumstances under which it is expressed. Once this is done, the person can apply the technique to control the habit. Using the technique, the person utilizes the mirror of the mind to analyse the present condition and to visualize how they would prefer it to be. In weight control, for example, the person sees himself in his mirror of the mind, looking the way he desires. For added effect, he also sees his desired suit size and the weight he wishes to achieve. Whenever he thinks of his weight, he sees himself as he wants to be.

4. Effective Sensory Projection

It is in the third segment of the BLS, MC303ESP, that the parapsychological components of the course are first expressed. The letters "ESP", in popular usage mean "extrasensory perception". According to Silva Mind Control this ability is innate in everyone and not "extra". They also claim that we not only perceive but also send information. In SMC, it is maintained that the person "projects" his/her awareness to other people and places. During the process, the individual is supposedly able to receive and transmit information. Hence, in SMC terminology, "ESP" means "effective sensory projection". In this segment the students begin their exploration of "ESP" by projecting into (i.e. imagining what it would be like to be within) different types of metals, plants, and animals. They also create a mental laboratory to work in and two mental assistants to help them (see Table 3).

TABLE 3.

MC303ESP

Content/Techniques	
1. metals	4. creation of laboratory
2. plants	5. creation of counselors
3. animals	

Beyond the continuing attempt to get the students imagination[10] working, this segment tries to break down the enculturated inhibitions against using one's imagination. This is accomplished in a variety of ways. In this segment the students go through a series of exercises designed to activate their "inner conscious level", their "inner senses". The primary purpose is to add to their arsenal of tools to come up with relevant information to solve problems. In so doing, they establish "subject points of reference"; identifiable, fixed experiences which can be used, according to SMC, whenever they are at the inner conscious level. Similar to geographical markers at the physical level, these subjective points of reference, however, are unique to the individual. A fracture, for example, may appear as a white line on the bone to some while to others it may be a gap in the bone. In either case, that is how each will identify fractures at the subjective level.

The exercises in this segment begin with the familiar and move to the increasingly unfamiliar. In the first exercise, the students project themselves to (imagine they are at) their own house. They begin on the outside then go into the living room. Once inside, they are directed to face the south wall and minutely examine it, seeing as much detail as possible. Next they imagine they are within the wall and "mentally test" the temperature, odors, etc. Finally, again facing the south wall, they do a series of color changes and object (e.g. chair, fruit, etc.) projections against the wall.

During the break following this mental exercise the students examine the cylinders/cubes of stainless steel, copper, brass, and lead which have been set out in the room. In the next exercise the students "project themselves" into each of the metals, imagining/experiencing in as such detail as possible, the differences and similarities among the metals. To help the students experience this, the lecturer leads them through a series of "tests" for each metal and and then a comparison of results for all four metals.

The next exercise involves projection into plant leaves. Two different species of plant leaves are provided for the students to examine. During the exercise, the students are again lead through with a series of "experiments" to carry out for each leaf and a comparison of the two at the end.

In the final exercise of this series, the students are directed to choose a furry pet which will be the object of examination. During the exercise the students project the animal against their south wall, turn it around and examine it from different angles. Next, the students are directed to project themselves into their pet. They begin with the bone structure, work their way through the circulatory system and then into various organs. All the while they are led through and suggestions are given about what they might see. The purpose is to familiarize them with a living system and prepare them for the next day's projections. If, while examining their pets, they detect what they feel is an abnormality, they are instructed to do whatever they feel is right to correct it. The major functions of all three of these exercises are to get the imagination working, familiarize the students with functioning at an altered state of consciousness, and establish points of reference which can be used from this point on.

There are only two more things accomplished in 303 --
the creation of the laboratory and the introduction of the
counselors. The laboratory is a mental work place and a
"level of mind". As a level of mind, it is considered
"deeper" than that achieved by the 3 to 1 method. After a
series of steps, the laboratory level is reached by a final
10 to 1 deepening countdown. In this exercise the students
mentally create their labs. They decorate and fully furnish
their labs with a chair, a desk, water, a clock, a perpetual
calendar, an informational system (computer or file
cabinets), chemicals, medicines, and tools for any project.

In the final exercise of the day, the lab creations
are completed with the addition of a mental screen on the
south wall and the introduction of the two counselors. The
counselors are lab technicians, assistants to help in what
ever way they are needed. According to SMC, the counselors
are geniuses in all fields and have access to what ever
information the person may need. They are there to serve
and will do what ever is requested of them, according to the
lecturer.

Who are the counselors? There is no set response to
that question. To José Silva they represent a level on the
continuum of intelligence (discussed below). To lecturers
and students metaphysically inclined, they are guides,
teachers, spirits. To some in the Christian tradition, they
are guardian angels. While to others, they are one's alter
ego, or the source of universal information. In any case,

after they are "created" they can be used or not used at the individual's option.

The idea of counselors evolved out of Jose Silva's work with his children. While Isabel was working the health case of a mental patient, she became quite frightened by what she was experiencing. Silva suggested Isabel create a protector, an advisor to be with her in her lab. This counselor could answer questions about things she was not sure of and at the same time protect her if she became frightened again. It is reported that because of her Spanish cultural background, Isabel felt uncomfortable talking about certain subjects with a male advisor. So she also created a female advisor. In 303, two counselors are still created during the exercise. It is left up to the individual how he or she utilizes either or both counselors.

When using the laboratory level there is a standard entry and exit procedure to be followed by the students. Once at the lab level, the procedure begins with a greeting to the counselors, a welcoming prayer as Jose Silva refers to it. The purpose of this greeting/prayer is to acknowledge the presence of the counselors and attune to them. The greeting can be an extensive prayer such as the "Lords Prayer", or it can be something very simple like "hello, glad to see you". After the greeting, the person reviews the most recent successful case they have worked on at that "level of mind". Case working is done next and when it is finished a farewell prayer is recited. Again, it can

be elaborate or simply "thanks for your help". The purpose
is to demarcate the end of the laboratory session. The
final step is the count out from 1 to 5. In the last
session of 303 and thereafter, the lecturer no longer guides
the students in or out of level, nor is the alpha sound
used. The students enter and leave their level completely
on their own.

5. Applied Effective Sensory Projection

The final segment of the Basic Lecture Series, Applied
Effective Sensory Projection, MC404AESP, pulls together all
the previous exercises and the students apply what they have
learned. There are no new techniques introduced, just an
expansion to the human level of what was begun in 303. The
two short exercises in this segment are merely
informational. Both deal with the human anatomy. The first
covers the brain, the skeletal structure, the heart, the
blood, and the lungs. The second begins in the stomach,
moves to the intestines, the pancreas, the liver, the gall
bladder, and the kidneys. The subject of the investigation
is someone the student knows who they believe to be healthy.
A healthy individual is chosen because the purpose of this
exercise is to establish "points of reference" for healthy
organs, systems, and structures. As the students are guided
through the human anatomy in these exercises, the lecturer
suggests how healthy organs or structures should appear and
how possible defects may be manifested. For example,

arthritis may appear as a white powdery substance in the joints, a fracture may appear as a white line in the bone, or a missing organ may appear as an opaque spot in the body. As the students are mentally examining their subjects' body, they are directed to correct with "healing energy", any condition they feel is abnormal. The correction of abnormalities--health case working--is the concern of the remaining part of this segment.

In the last part of 404, after a discussion of the importance of health and of working health cases, the lecturer calls upon one of the new students to demonstrate health case working for the class. The volunteer/draftee is always a new student, not a repeating graduate. He or she goes to the front of the room, enters lab level and is given the name and location of an individual who is severely ill. The student then proceeds to tell all that he feels is wrong with the person. His responses are compared with a previously written health card on which a description of the person and the problems are listed. After the demonstration and subsequent discussion, the class divides into pairs to work health cases on their own.

In health case working, two individuals pair off. One acts as the psychic--the person working the health case. The other serves as the director--giving the psychic the name of the subject, leading him through the body if necessary, and recording the responses for later comparison with the health card. After the psychic has worked two or three cases, the pair switches statuses.

The names and descriptions of people used as subjects during these case working sessions are provided, for the most part, by the members of the class. Toward the end of 303, health case working cards are distributed to the class. Each student is asked to fill out two or three cards on individuals they know who are ill. The more severe and extensive the ailments, the better. According to SMC, severely ill individuals are preferred because in the early stages of health case working, it is easier to detect serious illness. If not enough cards are available, the students can draw from a general file from past classes. In either case, the student who is acting as psychic and working the case has supposedly had no previous contact with the card or the individual described thereon.

After each student has had time to work six or eight cases, the class reassembles for the closing remarks and the distribution of the graduation certificates. In the closing remarks, the lecturer informs the students of the graduate courses available, the Mind Control Newsletter, and the graduate magazine Alpha Amigos. They are also informed of their eligibility to become members of the relatively new graduates association known as, Silva International Graduates Association or SIGA (discussed in chapter 5). Graduate activities offered by the lecturer, such as workshops, are also discussed and the students are reminded of their repeat privileges and money back guarantee.

One of the unique aspects of Silva Mind Control International is the repeat privilege it offers. Once the student has completed the Basic Lecture Series, s/he may repeat the course, free of charge, as often as desired and with any lecturer in any country the BLS is offered. The same policy applies to the graduate courses.

Another unique aspect is the money back guarantee offered by SMC. During the Introductory lecture, before the students register for the course, they are informed of the money back guarantee (see appendix 5). After having completed the BLS, (which includes participating in all the exercises), if the student is for any reason dissatisfied, he may request and be given a complete tuition refund. It is reported that less than one percent of the graduates have requested a refund.[11]

The certificates of graduation are awarded by the lecturer. As each new student's name is called, he or she walks to the front, is congratulated by the lecturer, and is given a certificate with his/her name, date and the lecturer's name (see Appendix 6). Along with the graduation certificate, the students also receive a wallet sized card containing the same information. This card--or the certificate--is needed if the student repeats the BLS. Some lecturers also will give the students a memento such as a lapel pin with the Mind Control logo. Generally, after the awarding of the certificates, the class disperses.

6. Major Themes Presented in the BLS

In addition to the techniques taught during the Basic Lecture Series, some major themes also are presented throughout the course. The pivotal triad upon which the whole Silva Method rests is "desire, belief, and expectance". These are, according to some, the "pillars" of Silva Mind Control. Nonetheless, some lecturers spend very little time discussing them while others devote a whole lecture to their importance. "Desire", according to Silva, is the key. As explained in the lectures, it is desire which is the motivating force, or the triggering mechanism for the mind control process to happen. Desire creates the ability to perform. Without desire, the student can correctly follow the steps of the Method but its effectiveness is questionable. According to Silva, not only does the person have to want to perform but he must also "believe" that he can perform. Belief is created by the presentation of "facts" throughout the BLS. The "facts" include relevant research and anecdotal accounts of using the Method. Eventually, the person uses their own experiences as the basis of their belief.

"Expectancy" is based on experiences, according to the lecturer. Beginning with the apparent small successes achieved with the early techniques (e.g. to awake control), the students gradually build their repertoire of reportedly successful experiences. By the time they have reached the final sessions of the BLS, they expect to get results when they use the Method. Any lingering doubt appears to vanish after working their first health case. The students then appear completely convinced. According to the lecturer, each success after that should reinforce their "desire, belief, and expectancy".

"Better and better" is a phrase used throughout the mental training exercises and the lectures. The etiology of the phrase can be traced back to Emile Coue' and his psychotherapy based on autosuggestion in the early 1900s. It was Coue's contention that, (1) we can "think of only one thing at a time", and (2) concentrating on a thought causes that thought to become true because our "bodies transform it into action"(Silva and Miele, 1977:61). To trigger the body's healing mechanism, Coue's famous phrase "Day by day, in every way, I am getting better and better", is repeated twenty times twice a day in the Coue' method(Ibid). The heart of The Coue' Method, according to Silva, is in Mind Control. Jose Silva, however, has changed the phrase to "Everyday, in every way, I am getting better, better, and better". It is said only once while at level. Silva also includes the phrase "negative thoughts, negative suggestions, have no influence over me at any level of mind" because of Coue's influence (Ibid:61-62).

The function of the phrase is to continue to create the positive mental attitude necessary for successful programming/functioning. The phrase also becomes a symbol for Silva graduates. In response to the question "how are you?", a Silva grad (at least at Silva functions) usually responds with "better and better". During the BLS, as the course progresses and the socialization process occurs, the new students gradually begin to use this response. By the 303 session if they respond to a query about their state of being in any other way, someone present will "correct" them with the proper response. The symbolic nature of the phrase is also evident in its use on bumper stickers advertising Silva Mind Control.

The importance of a positive mental attitude is also reflected in the "mental housecleaning" lecture. Since it is believed a person's words reflect their attitudes and influence their behavior, Silva maintains that those words should always be positive and constructive. In this lecture, the students are told that phrases and words used routinely and usually without much thought, can have a major influence on them and their lives. The purpose of the lecture is to tighten up one's vocabulary by eliminating the use of negative words, phrases and attitudes. The use of the words "can't, kill, sick, died or pain", for example, are discouraged. "Can't" and "try", it is argued, are simply acceptable ways of deferring responsibility for something you have no desire to do. "Pain" or "sick" used in phrases such as "that's a pain in the neck", or "he makes me sick" are completely unacceptable. It is maintained that each time the phrases are said or thought, it reinforces the belief that the person or thing has a negative effect on the individual saying the phrase. Allegedly, by constantly programming that belief, the speaker eventually does develop a pain in the neck or become sick (i.e. what others refer to as autosuggestion).

An area of research which receives major discussion throughout the whole course is brain hemisphere functioning. In addition to the research of Hans Berger with brain wave frequencies (EEG) and Barbara Brown's biofeedback work, much mention is made of right and left brain hemisphere functioning.[12]

The benefits of functioning at high alpha production (alpha brain wave production, hereafter, referred to as "functioning at alpha" or "at level") are presented during the "Intro" and the first session of the BLS. According to Silva, activating the right hemisphere, (functioning at alpha), can: improve physical, mental, and emotional health; speed recuperation; increase creativity; heighten intuition or psychic abilities; and facilitate self-reprogramming or habit change.

The last major item introduced in 101 is the "Silva Mind Control Sound". About midway through the afternoon of the first day, the lecturer dims the lights and introduces a background sound for the programming sessions. The sound is an alpha rhythm click combined with the drone of a metronome. It is believed that the sound helps the individual "center" at ten cycles per second. From this point until the individuals attempt health case working, the sound accompanies the mental training exercises.

As the course progresses, additional terms are defined and new ideas are presented. Visualization and imagination, for example, are thoroughly distinguished. Visualization, according to the lecturer, is a process of retrieving from memory something that was actually seen before. Imagination is projection on one's mental screen of things that have never been seen. It also involves recombining or editing images in totally new ways. Imagination, because it is central to the Method, is discussed a great deal. It is pointed out by the lecturer that many people are enculturated to feel guilty about using their imagination. In SMC, however, imagination is the key to attaining one's goals: it is an essential ingredient in the successful use of the Method. As noted above, many of the exercises are designed to get this faculty operating more effectively.

Along the same line and also touching upon the underlying ideological system, is the premise that "whatever the mind can conceive, it can achieve".[13] Based on the assumption that our thoughts influence matter and behavior (and by extension our life circumstances), it is maintained that whatever the mind is able to conceive at the alpha level can be created or brought about in the physical realm, the beta level. It is believed that physical events can be traced back to the alpha "dimension".

In MC303, the basic ideology of SMC is expressed overtly. As presented in this segment, the universe is composed of matter kingdoms: inanimate, vegetable, animal and human. Using the Silva Method, it is maintained one can enter these kingdoms to establish points of reference, detect and correct abnormalities, solve problems and generally enhance psychic ability.

Closely akin to the ideology of the matter kingdoms is that concerning the hierarchy of intelligence in the universe. According to Silva, each of the matter kingdoms has intelligence, or the ability to solve problems. The inanimate, the vegetable and the animal kingdoms, however, are quite limited in their problem solving capacity and therefore, in their intelligence. At the human level there also is variation in intelligence. Those individuals who have a greater capacity for problem solving are, according to Silva, more intelligent. Also, individuals may be quite effective problem solvers in some areas and less effective in others. Intelligence--i.e. problem solving--is relative.

One of the purposes of SMC, according to José Silva, is to make people more effective problem solvers by teaching them how to gain access to information and techniques not generally available. Beyond the human kingdom, the hierarchy of intelligence continues. This point, however, is not discussed in length until the graduate courses. It

is in the graduate courses that the Silva concept of "god"
is explained.

The other major idea presented in the 303 session is
"programming at a distance". Similar to the mirror of the
mind and health case working, programming at a distance is
used to commmunicate with another person. In this
technique, before going to sleep the Silva grad suggests to
himself that he will awaken when the target is at a level of
mind which is most receptive to communication. When/if he
then awakens during the night, the grad enters level and
communicates his message to the target. It is believed that
communication between individuals at an alpha level of mind
is more effective because it is done without the defenses
necessary at beta.

The technique was designed for parents to use on
their children, the purpose being to get the children to
change their behavior or see the consequences of an
activity. According to Silva, this is permitted ethically
since it is part of parental responsibility to influence
their children's behavior. The technique, however, is
reported by graduates to work on adults as well. Although
not officially endorsed, it is pointed out by the lecturer
that using the technique on adults will work only if it is
something that will benefit the individual (i.e. the
target). Again, the basic philosophy is that a person can
do no harm to themselves or to others at the alpha level.

In the 404 session there remains only two major ideas to be presented, the soul mold and psychorientology. The focus of the last session is health case working and both concepts stem from this. The "soul mold", a term which comes from Silva's strong religious orientation, is the ideally healthy human. It is the abstract blueprint for perfection, the correct genetic code for the structure. Each species has its own specific soul mold to which all members of that species compare. It is maintained that when working health cases, the only modifications which can be made are in the direction of health and perfection. That is, one cannot create harmful or abnormal conditions or remove essential structures. It is asserted that the Method will not work to do harm to anyone or anything. This idea is presented in the programming sessions throughout the course.

When Silva began his research, he maintains there were no terms which adequately described the work he was doing. He says he found it necessary to create his own term, "psychorientology". As explained in the lecture, psychorientology is the "science of orienting the mind" (psyche)--psych/orient/ology. It is applied specifically to health case working with the psychic being the case worker and the orientologist directing at the beta level. In the Basic Lecture Series Manual, however, a more detailed explanation is given.

Psychorientology means (1) to help to reinstate the mind to its own inner world; that is, its own native dimension; (2) to continue to guide, direct, and educate its functioning within this dimension; (3) to develop, increase, and control its psychic perceptions which comprise those sensations proper to the mind; (4) and to continue this education for further growth and development in psychic applications; by making these applications the mind learns to use its own field of sensation with at least the same facility with which it presently uses the field of biological sensation. Learning to do this is known as Subjective Education and this is what Mind Control is all about. (1977:7)

B. Graduate Courses

Silva Mind Control's Basic Lecture Series is concerned primarily with instruction in the Silva Method. The orientation is toward teaching the techniques with little attention given to the history of the organization and the underlying ideology. Graduates of the BLS who desire to know more about these topics and to learn additional techniques take graduate courses. These include the Graduate Lecture Series, the Graduate Seminar, the Ultra Seminar, and the Holistic Healing Workshop.

1. Graduate Lecture Series

The most extensive graduate training occurs in the "3-Day Graduate Lecture Series"(GLS). In this course, the students learn additional problem-solving techniques, ways to teach others to function at ten cycles per second, and age regression methods. A comparison of the Silva Method with other systems, and the underlying ideology of the Method and the ideological orientation of the lecturer are also presented. The course has been taught by José Silva, Harry McKnight, J. Hahn, and George DeSau.

The GLS begins with a review of the techniques and major ideas presented in the BLS, followed by a more detailed discussion of the history of SMCI. This includes its present subsidiaries (see Chapter Five), and outside research which has shaped the Method. The Method is then compared with zen, yoga, transcendental meditation, hypnosis and biofeedback. New techniques are also introduced.

In the GLS, two new problem-solving techniques are presented. The first is the "special glass of water technique". This differs from the glass of water technique learned in the BLS. In this version, which is used primarily for health problems, three drops of lemon juice are added to the water. The second technique is a method to "send problems to the center of the galaxy" for answers. It is believed by SMC, that the center of the galaxy is a very spiritually advanced and knowledgeable "location". In the GLS, students are taught to imagine the center of the galaxy above and behind them. When they have a problem no other technique has solved, they are instructed to bow their head and "send it off to the center of the galaxy" for the solution. The students are also advised to "align themselves with the center of the galaxy" when they are working health cases.

Another major technique students learn in the GLS is how to teach non-graduates the Method and techniques. This is done primarily through the "special cycle". This is a long deepening exercise in which the technician (Silva grad) physically interacts with the trainee to help him achieve a deep level of relaxation. The interaction includes a series of arm lifts and drops and countdowns until a "deep level of mind" has been achieved. At that point, the technician reads the rapport statements, programming statements (techniques), and finally,the standard "bring out". The graduate can also use the "standard cycle" to teach others. In this case, the graduate reads the "long relax" from the BLS and inserts the programming just before the post effects and bring out. In either case, it is suggested that the subject go through ten hours of training before the graduate can be sure the subject is at ten cycles per second and are able to enter level on his own by the 3 to 1 method.

For members of the graduates families, Silva offers a quick way to teach them to enter level. Known as the "thumb on the forehead technique", the program is read to the subject during the standard or the special cycle. While reading through the program, the graduate actually places her thumb on the subject's forehead, while telling him that whenever she does so he will enter a deep healthy level of mind. Thereafter, whenever the graduate puts her thumb on the subject's forehead, he should enter a state in which he produces predominantly alpha brain waves.

Another major area covered in the GLS is age regression. After extensive discussion of reincarnation research (by Silva and others), the students are taught techniques for self-age regression and age regression for others. Regression, according to Harry McKnight, is walking back upon your experiences of life. In regressing others, the Silva grad helps the subject enter a physically and mentally relaxed state through a series of deepening exercises. Then the subject is gradually led back through life experiences to childhood. At each step back in time, the subject is directed to "recall" the circumstances surrounding that time. For self-age regression, the graduate directs him or herself back through their own life.

The final activity of the GLS is case working. The class pairs off and each student works a few health cases. After this, the class reconvenes and the lecturer awards the graduation certificates. The same procedure as in the BLS is usually followed for the awarding of these certificates.

2. 2-Day Graduate Seminar

A condensed version of the GLS is offered in the "2-Day Graduate Seminar". This course presents the "special cycle", age regression, case working and the underlying ideology of the Method and the lecturer. The course, which is currently taught by Harry McKnight, George Desau, James Needham, and J. Hahn, is offered, on the average, four times per month throughout the United States and certain other countries. Harry McKnight, for example spends the equivalent of nine months per year on the road teaching the

2-Day Graduate Seminar (personal communication,1983).[14] The 3-Day Graduate Lecture Series, although still "on the books", is offered very infrequently, if at all.

3. 2-Day Ultra Seminar

Another condensed version of the GLS is the "2-Day Ultra Seminar" which is taught almost exclusively by José Silva; occasionally, Laura Silva Gomez, his daughter will also teach it[15]. Like the 2-Day Graduate Seminar, this course is offered throughout the U. S. and certain other countries. The primary emphasis is on health. In this course, Silva teaches the students how to create four states of mind which are conducive to thought transference for healing. These are: (1) a state of confusion, (2) a state of expectancy, (3) triggering the survival mechanism, and (4) slowing down brain wave frequency. After creating one of these states, the graduate transfers "healing thoughts/ energy" to the individual.

José Silva is familiar with magnetic fields because of his electronics background. Based on this, Silva teaches a healing technique which use a tape recorder and the alpha sound. Silva maintains that the immune system is activated at 10 cps and that healing is assisted if the injured areas are placed in a field vibrating at 10 cps. To achieve this, a tape recorder with a recording of the alpha sound is placed close to the afflicted area for 15 minutes, twice a day. It is believed this will speed up the healing process.

If the person is generally healthy, it is suggested the sound can by applied to the area of the solar plexis to stimulate the immune system. The technique is based on the belief that 10 cps (brain wave frequency or vibration) is optimum for health.

Silva claims to have investigated and worked with healers from all parts of the world. As a result of this, he has developed two holistic healing techniques. Both are intended for use on others and involve a number of different physical actions by the healer. The first method, known as the "Silva Special Healing Technique", is intended primarily for localized problems. The technique involves placing the hands in different positions while physically vibrating them at "10 cycles per second". The healer first places her hands on the patient's head, next the afflicted area (e.g. knee), and finally once again on the head. With each position the hands are vibrating, the breath is held, the eyes are closed, and the healer is thinking "this is all I have to do to correct the problem" while "sending" blue/ white energy[1] to the patient. After demonstrating this technique to the audience, Silva asks for volunteers--both healers and those with persistent pain. He chooses three for each category and pairs them off with each other. Each healer performs the procedure on their patient. After they finish, the patients claim from 30% to 80% reduction in pain. Silva maintains that those who report only 30% reductions should receive another application to get an

additional 30% reduction.   Then a different healer should be
used   to   achieve   a   complete   healing.   After   the
demonstration,   the   class   pairs   off   to   practice   the
technique.

The   "Standard   Silva   Healing   Technique"   is   more
complex.   In   this method, the healer must make a series of
hand "passes" and movements over the body to prepare it   for
healing.   Then the healing is supposedly done by placing the
hands   on   either   side   of   specific   areas and visualizing
energy flowing and the problem corrected.   As in the Special
Technique, Silva demonstrates the technique with a volunteer
and the class pairs off to practice.

Since it is José Silva who teaches the Ultra   Seminar,
it   is during this course that his ideology and the ideology
underlying the Method is most extensively expressed.[17]   José
Silva   has   always   been   a   devote Roman Catholic and that
belief predominates.   Silva claims, in fact, that one of the
most influential events during his early   research   was   his
exposure   to   a   particular   picture of Christ with the poem
"One Solitary Life" on the back.   In   the   lectures,   Silva
continually   makes   reference   to Jesus (whom he calls Rabbi
Jesus) and to God.   Silva quotes Jesus repeatedly;   many   of
these   Biblical   quotations   are reinterpreted, with psychic
explanations. For   example,   the   "Kingdom"   talked   of   so
frequently   by   Jesus   is   viewed   by   Silva as being at the
"alpha dimension". The "keys to the Kingdom"   are   seen   as
being the Silva techniques to function at 10 cps.

Silva asserts that intelligence is hierarchically arranged. The levels of intelligence--from the "inanimate" kingdom" to the human level--were discussed above. According to Silva, there continues to be a hierarchy of "higher intelligence" beyond the human level. Some of these higher intelligences are "assigned" to watch over our solar system. Another group watches over our galaxy. Still others watch over groups of galaxies. Each ascending level has access to more information and greater problem--solving ability. Over it all is "God", the "Almighty". "God", according to Silva does not deal with each person individually. We communicate with God through these higher intelligences. Even at the center of the galaxy we have not yet reached "God", but just a more advanced stage of the hierarchy.

"God" created us and we are "supposed to help God shape up this planet". "We were sent to correct the problems of the planet Earth, to make it better." "We were created in God's image to do this"(Silva). The more knowledge/intelligence, the greater one's ability to solve problems and the more god-like one is. If you create problems, Silva declares, you go in the other direction-- i.e. there are influences and ignorance which keep you from doing the right thing toward God. "It is called the devil."

God, Silva states, created us to be healthy. He gave us everything we need to maintain that health; "it is all within each of us". Illness and disease are the result of improper thinking. Those who think at ten cycles per second (go to level at least twice a day) are "centered". These people, Silva asserts, are healthier--since they reinforce their immune system each time--and are more spiritual. Ignorance of this creates "90% of our health problems". "You make yourself sick." "We are all healers. We suffer only because of ignorance."

There are some individuals who are "natural right brain users", who are always centered, according to Silva. These are the people who are natural psychics, healers, (prophets and wisemen from the past). Silva refers to these as "10%ers" since, according to his findings, only 10% of the population naturally function at 10 cps. Moses, Buddha, Krishna, and Jesus were all 10%ers, Silva purports, because they helped humanity and knew "how to act properly".

These are just a few of the ideological points touched upon in the Ultra Seminar. Beyond them, Silva also discusses auras, magnetic fields, certain diseases (e.g. cancer, AIDS), the counselors, extra-terrestial life, and any other topic which comes up during the numerous question and answer periods throughout the course. [1]

Until the late 1970s, the only graduate course offered was the Graduate Lecture Series which was being taught by Jose Silva, Harry McKnight, J. Hahn, and Jim Needham. Silva's GLS classes were always huge, however, numbering in the hundreds. The other graduate lecturers, conversely, had relatively few new students, but large numbers of repeating students. The students were opting to take the course for the first time with Jose' Silva and then exercise their repeat privileges with the other graduate lecturers. This presented a major problem. Since the lecturers are supported by the revenue generated from the GLS and only new students were required to pay, these other lecturers were earning much less than Silva for teaching the GLS. To solve this, Silva agreed to divide the graduate course into two segments, the 2-Day Graduate Seminar and the Ultra Seminar. The other graduate lecturers would teach the Graduate Seminar and only Silva (or one of his family) would teach the Ultra Seminar. There is a minimum number of new students which must be guaranteed before a graduate course will be taught. Based on the frequency with which these two courses are offered, this arrangement seems to be working quite well.[1,9]

The Holistic Healing Workshop is a four-hour condensed version of the Ultra Seminar. Unlike the three other graduate courses, the Workshop is open to the general public. It includes Silva's ideological orientation, the "Silva Special Holistic Healing Technique", and use of a tape recorder and the "alpha" sound for healing. The Holistic Healing Workshop (which is offered, on the average, four times a month throughout the U. S. and certain other countries), is taught exclusively by Jose' Silva. At this time, Jose' Silva spends approximately 90% of the year on the road teaching the Ultra Seminar and the Healing Workshop (personal communication,1983).

Many individuals who become involved in Silva Mind Control and the Silva Method decide they want to teach what they have learned to others. To do this on a regular basis, they must become SMCI lecturers. The process of becoming a SMCI lecturer is discussed in the next chapter, as is the organization itself.

ENDNOTES

[1] The other terms used include: The Silva Mind
Control Method, The Silva Method, Mind Control, and
Psychorientology.

[2] In an ordinary state of consciousness, the
individual adapts to the physical world--i.e. through
problem solving, physical interactions, reality testing. An
"altered state of consciousness" (ASC), is anything that
differs from this ordinary state. There are numerous ways
to typologize ASCs but most seem to link the ASC with
individual subjective reality, the mystical or the
supernatural. But, as Bourguignon points out, all ASCs are
"not necessarily religious". For an extensive discussion of
altered states of consciousness see Bourguignon, 1974,
"Culture and the Varieties of Consciousness".

[3] There is debate concerning the boundaries between
frequencies. Delta is defined by some as 1 to 3 cps and
others as 1 to 4 cps. Alpha ranges between 9 to 13, 8 to
13, 7 to 12, and 7 to 14 cps. Some measure beta at 13 to 18
cps while others use 14 to 28 cps See Brown,1974;
Lawrence,1972; Tart,1976 for a more detailed discussion.
There is also individual variation in frequency production,
detection locations and corresponding behavior and emotional
characteristics (Brown,1974:34).

[4] SMCI began developing its own biofeedback equipment
in the mid-1970s because of its increasing popularity.
Today, SMCI has a number of biofeedback instruments
available and many more in the planning state. See Chapter
Five for a detailed discussion of this topic.

[5] The term "lecturer" is preferred over instructor
because the latter has academic overtones Silva prefers to
avoid.

[6] In hypnosis, the usual procedure is to count up to
get the subject deeper and to count down to bring him out of
the hypnotic state.

[7] For example, see Current Research on Sleep and
Dreams.

[8] Rather than continually repeat s/he, herself/
himself, her/him, etc., I will be using the male version.
It is meant to refer to both males and females and is used
only as a matter of convenience in this study.
Unfortunately, English does not provide us with usable
neutral terms.

' This is based on the following phrase by Napoleon Hill, "whatever the mind of man can conceive and believe, it can achieve"(1959,Think and Grow Rich). Hill used the phrase in the general sense. He felt whatever humans, as a species could conceive and believe, they could collectively achieve. In Mind Control it is used in that sense also, but it is most frequently brought down to the individual level.

[10] In SMC terminology, imagination means creating an image in your mind of something you have never seen before. Visualization means creating an image in your mind of something you have experienced in the past. As the course progresses this distinction is made and the lecturer switches from using the term imagination to visualization.

[11] In all the BLS courses I attended in 1974-1976 and during the past 14 months I did not find one individual who was not satisfied with the course or the results achieved.

[12] Based on thousands of studies, it has been concluded that people use their brain bifunctionally. The left hemisphere is associated with rational tasks--e.g. language processing --and analytical thought, while creativity, intuition, and spatial abilities are linked to the right hemisphere. For a detailed discussion, see Ornstein, 1972, 1973, 1976.

[13] See Endnote # 9

[14] Harry McKnight was the first lecturer to join SMCI on a full-time basis over 15 years ago. As of May 1984, he transferred to Alpha International Management Development, Inc. as executive vice-president. This is a new subsidiary of SMCI (see chapter 5) and McKnight will concentrate on getting it established (Mind Control Newsletter,1984(3):5).

[15] For example,in a seven month period, Jose Silva taught 14 of the 16 sessions offered.

[16] It is believed by psychics that blue-white light is very powerful.

[17] The only other opportunity to get such an extensive exposure to Silva's orientation is his once a year presentation of the BLS. This takes place in Laredo and is offered just prior to the International Convention.

[18] For a more detailed discussion of the ideological orientation of,Jose Silva see Mystery of the Keys to the Kingdom by Jose Silva.

[19] Recently another "Silva course" was introduced. Burt Goldman was a very successful SMCI lecturer in California and the surrounding area. For two consecutive

years he won the Outstanding Lecturer Award at the International Convention. He also co-authored the book Better and Better, about the Silva Method. Approximately three years ago. Goldman decided to leave SMCI to teach his own version entitled the "Supermind Seminar". Because of the great degree of similarity between the Silva techniques and what Goldman was offering in "Supermind" and because his advertising brochures implied approval from SMCI, a number of problems developed (including legal problems with copyright infringement). After much discussion, the situation was resolved and as of May 1984, Goldman's Supermind is now advertised in the SMC Newsletter and offered as the "Silva Supermind Seminar". This was not a unique situation--although the solution was. SMCI has two full-time lawyers who handle copyright infringements. The small scale individuals are left alone but the money making business ones are sued in the courts. According to Jose Silva, SMCI has not lost a case against anyone they have taken to court.

CHAPTER FIVE

THE ORGANIZATION

I. INTRODUCTION

The International Headquarters for Silva Mind Control is located in Laredo, Texas. From here SMCI coordinates the activities of its subsidiaries, oversees all international affairs, services the Laredo area, and conducts research. It is also in Laredo where the training for new lecturers occurs and the annual International Convention is held. This chapter will examine in detail, the bureaucratic structure of SMCI. The independent lecturer is the base of SMCI. This chapter will detail the status and behavior of the independent lecturer and show how s/he fits into the regional concept. Also included here will be a discussion of the Michigan center and lecturers for SMCI. Finally, this chapter will explore the international success of Silva Mind Control.

II. THE LAREDO HEADQUARTERS

Laredo, a city of just less than 100,000 is nestled in southwest Texas. Located on the Rio Grande river its neighbor is Nuevo Laredo, Mexico. Because of its border

location, Laredo has always been an important point of entry
for people and goods. It is in fact, "one of the busiest
ports of entry in Texas, with more than 2,500,000 vehicles
and 8,000,000 persons annually crossing the International
Bridge" from Nuevo Laredo (p. 299). Consequently, there is
an abundance of unskilled and semi-skilled Mexican day
laborers and industries to accommodate them.

Established in 1755 and chartered as a Texas city in
1852 (Ibid:302), Laredo is old yet still growing. This is
reflected in the architecture and in the construction in
residential areas. Neighborhoods consist of all types of
housing: from poverty-stricken shacks in dire need of repair
to affluent new dwellings, side by side. Yet, even the
poorest looking houses have air conditioning units--some one
quarter the size of the shack they are attached to--to cope
with the incessant heat and humidity. In the area
surrounding the city, "suburbs" are developing to
accommodate the new growth with typical ranch style homes.

This is the setting for the international headquarters
of Silva Mind Control. The neighborhood is typical of any
in the city, affluence and poverty, growth and decline, co-
existing. It is in this neighborhood that José Silva has
lived most of his life.

The building, which today houses the international
headquarters, was Silva's original electronics shop. It was
here that Silva conducted research which led to the
development of the Silva Method. Over the years, his home,

which was next door, and the neighboring building were connected and remodeled to form one large complex.

This complex functions as both a center for the Laredo area and the International Headquarters for Silva Mind Control. As the SMCI Center for Laredo, it serves as the locale for classes and workshops. As International Headquarters, the complex coordinates all international affairs, arranges and coordinates the annual International Convention, teaches the annual lecturers training, and schedules all graduate courses and healing workshops. The headquarters is also the location of the family owned business, "Ltd.", of which SMCI is a subsidiary.

III BUREAUCRATIC STRUCTURE

A. Authority: The People--The Power

Silva Mind Control International began over forty years ago as a father's attempt to help his children with their school work (as noted previously). That effort has evolved into the Silva Method which today is taught in 61 countries and in 14 languages (see Appendix Three). As the teaching of the Method spread, the organization itself developed and grew into an international enterprise.

Silva Mind Control International, Inc. is a paternalistic, nepotistic organization. Jose Silva is the patriarch--founder, figure head, symbol, president, and ultimate authority. His primary activity now is to teach the Ultra Seminar and the Healing Workshop throughout the United States and certain other countries; he spends 90% of the year on the road. His longest stays in Laredo center around the International Convention and holidays. During the International Convention, Silva is kept continually busy. For the week preceeding the convention, Silva teaches the Basic Lecture Series. During the two day convention, Silva attends all the activities and is relatively accessible to the conventioneers. Following the convention, he teaches the Ultra Seminar and drops in on the 2-Day Graduate Seminar. He is also very prominent during the lecturers training which follows the graduate courses (see below). Other high ranking officials within the organization are all (with one exception) family members.

Directly under José Silva is his brother, Juan, who is Executive Vice-President and Director for Foreign Countries (see Chart 3). Juan Silva teaches the Ultra Seminar and the 2-Day Graduate Seminar in Spanish (and occasionally English) in numerous foreign countries. As Director for Foreign Countries, he is responsible for the classes, the personnel, production, and quality control in all countries outside the U. S. in which the Silva Method is taught. He is director of the Lecturer Development Seminar for Spanish-speaking countries and teaches the annual Spanish Lecturer Development Seminar.

Collateral with José and Juan Silva are two advisory groups, the Board of Directors and the Consultants. The

CHART 3

SMCI, INC.

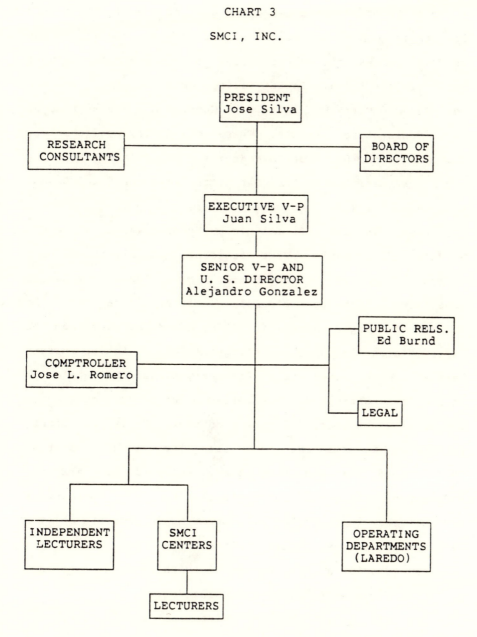

Board of Directors is a 14 member governing body responsible for major policy decisions (setting, reviewing, and revising). As of August 1983, the Board of Directors included Jose Silva, Paula Silva, Juan Silva, Alejandro Gonzalez and Harry McKnight. The Consultants are a group of five research specialists. These include Dr. George DeSau, Dr. J. W. Hahn, Dr. Richard McKenzie, Dr. Clancy McKenzie and Dr. Frederich Bremner. Two of the five (Hahn and DeSau) also teach the 2-Day Graduate Seminar.

Next in the official hierarchy of power is Alejandro Gonzalez Jr., Senior Vice-President, Administrator, and Director for the United States. Mr. Gonzalez, nephew of Jose Silva, is the son of Jose's sister (Josefina). He joined the organization in 1976 after retiring from the United States Air Force Intelligence as a Senior Master Sergeant. As United States Director, Alejandro Gonzalez is in complete control of territories, lecturers, contracts, production, and courses for this country. He is, in effect, in charge of all SMC activities for the United States. Under Mr. Gonzalez and answerable directly to him are the independent lecturers and regional directors. Gonzalez is also directly in charge of all operating departments at the Laredo Headquarters. These include:

1) Administrative: concerned with personnel records, correspondence, office personnel.

2) Operations: concerned with lecturers' contracts, travel, transportation, curriculum.

3) <u>Printing and Graphics</u>: concerned with printing and binding of manuals, books, pamphlets, and the newsletter.

4) <u>Data Processing</u>

5) <u>Marketing</u>: concerned with the purchasing, storing and distributing of materials.

At the base of the authority hierarchy are the lecturers. Independent lecturers and SMCI Center or regional Directors are equal in status. Lecturers who work for a center must answer to that Center's Director (see Chart 3). Also associated with Centers are "lecturers in training". These are individuals who believe they would like to be SMC instructors but have not yet taken the training in Laredo. They serve at the Director's discretion, attending the classes and assisting with administrative and monitoring duties.

B. The Structure--How Things Fit Together

Silva Mind Control International, Inc., along with five other corporations is a subsidiary of a larger holding company known as the Institute of Psychorientology, Ltd. (see chart 4). This parent company is owned exclusively by José Silva and his nuclear family. Comprised of twelve equal shares, they are held by José Silva, his wife Paula, and each of their ten children. The other subsidiaries of "Ltd" are (1) the Institute of

Psychorientology, Inc., (2) Silva Sensor Systems, (3) SMCI Programs, and (4) Better and Better Vitamins.

CHART 4

Institute of Psychorientology, Ltd.

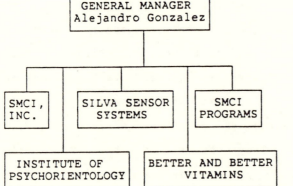

1. Institute of Psychorientology, Inc.

The Institute of Psychorientology, Inc., has two major functions; certification to teach the BLS and all printing. It is the Institute of Psychorientology which technically runs the Lecturers Development Program (see below) and grants permission to teach upon completion of the training. The corporation is also responsible for reviewing, updating and revising the SMC course manuals. The Institute holds the copyright on the Silva Method and techniques and all

materials presented in the BLS, graduate courses, and SMC
workshops.

Printing is the other major function of the Institute
of Psychorientology, Inc. This company is responsible for
all printing done for "Ltd". This includes the manuals for
the all the courses, seminars, and workshops; numerous books
written about SMCI; pamphlets, reprints and brochures
dealing with research on some aspect of SMC; lecturer's
manuals and materials; and all convention materials.

2. Silva Sensor Systems

Silva Sensor Systems (SSS) is responsible for all
electronic equipment, recordings, and related materials.
SSS began by producing review casettes of the BLS and tapes
of the alpha and "Silva" sounds. In addition to these
tapes, SSS now also produces and offers for sale casette
recordings of speakers at the International Conventions and
recordings of the Introductory Lecture by four different
lecturers (one of whom is José Silva).

Among the electronic equipment Silva Sensor Systems
produces is biofeedback instrumentation. Initially, SMCI
discouraged its students from using biofeedback equipment.
But, as biofeedback became more and more popular, SMC grads
bought the available equipment to prove to themselves they
were producing alpha waves. Seeing the inevitability of the
situation (and the potential), SMCI began producing its own
equipment through Silva Sensor Systems. The first produced
was a galvanic skin response (GSR) device. Known as

"Trainer 1", it is attached to the first two fingers and measures changes in the body's resistance to the flow of a weak electrical current. Set to begin with a pulsating beep at 18 cps, it gradually slows down as the person becomes relaxed (i.e. enters "deeper into level"). If the person starts to come "out of level", the pulsating beep speeds up. Selling for $55, this pocket sized device is the most popular available. According to SMCI, Trainer 1 is used by the public for relaxation, pain control, improved concentration, and stress relief. For SMC graduates it provides objective verification that they are at an alpha level and helps them develop more control over that level.

A more sophisticated biofeedback instrument is the Silva Educator. Like Trainer 1, the core of the Educator is a galvanic skin response meter. The oscillating frequency slows as relaxation deepens. Beyond its capability as a GSR meter, this instrument is designed to turn on a tape recorder when a specific level of relaxation has been achieved. It can be set for "light, medium, or deep levels of mind". When the desired, level is reached a tape recorder starts and continues to play only as long as that level is maintained. According to SMCI, it is a patented "Genimatic" circuit which is responsible for this capability. SMCI does, in fact, hold the U. S. patent for a mechanical device activated by brain wave frequency alone. The Educator comes with four casette programs but individuals can use any programming tape or educational program they choose. The cost of the Educator is $395.

The most advanced biofeedback instrument SSS offers is the Silva Executive. In addition to all the features of the Educator, the Executive also is a "brain wave sensor". Equipped with a head band, it measures brain wave frequency and can activate a built in tape recorder when the specified frequency is achieved. It also can require both a relaxed physical state and a specific brain wave frequency to activate the tape recorder. The Executive is priced at $495.

Silva Sensor Systems claims to have researched the area of biofeedback for three years, consulting with doctors, engineers, and "electrical psychologists" before deciding which features to include in their equipment. According to Saul Gonzalez, President of SSS and Jose' Silva's son-in-law, the Silva equipment is unique. For example, the Educator and the Executive are activated by brain wave frequency alone. Other unique aspects include the circuitry and the headband. The circuitry is discrete and the headband uses skin electrodes and input circuits which result in an immediate 1×10^6 amplification of the signal (personal communication,1983). Because SSS was not aware of the four year time period for international patents, there are currently two very similar devices being produced in France and Japan. They are each selling for $2500 (Ibid).

Future production plans for SSS include minicomputers and microprocessors in watches that could monitor brain wave frequency for one week intervals. One of the more adventuresome projects is a "Foxfire" type device. It is similar to the Executive in that it is activated by brain wave frequency alone, but with the headband incorporated into a headset. This device, however, is to be part of a video game. Rather than use "joysticks" or rolling balls, the gamester would need to achieve and maintain a specific brain wave frequency to play the game. The types of games being considered are all non-violent and non-aggressive. SSS plans to market the device initially in arcades and eventually in private homes. They plan to have a demonstration model at the 1984 International Convention in August (Saul Gonzalez,personal communication,1983).

The Institute of Psychorientology and Silva Sensor Systems are both housed in the "PSI Building". Located one block from SMCI headquarters, the building contains the printing facilities, electronic manufacturing, and research and development for electronics. Although there are a number of other printers in Laredo, the Institute of Psychorientology is the largest volume printer in the city. In fact, they have the contract to do the printing for the city of Laredo. As such, the equipment is extensive. There are five presses, two letter and three book, capable of doing two colors at once; a binder and a folder handling 70,000 pages per hour; and well-equipped plate and dark rooms. The other side of the building houses the Silva Sensor Systems equipment, assembly, and research areas.

3. SMCI Programs

SMCI Programs is the subsidiary responsible for the "Relaxation Seminar", an additional offering of SMCI. This seminar is composed of a series of mental exercises designed to enhance visualization and relaxation. Open to the public, the seminar is taught by lecturers trained by Harry McKnight. These lecturers are not usually SMCI lecturers. For those who wish to be Relaxation Seminar Lecturers but cannot go to Laredo for the training, SMCI Programs offers a Relaxation Seminar Training Kit which includes cassette recordings of the training session, an actual Relaxation Seminar, lecturer's manual and necessary supplies. This kit sells for $250. In addition, SMCI Programs also sells the Relaxation Seminar Album kit at $35 and a series of spiritual healing tapes. These healing tapes, each of which sells for $9.95, are narrated by Harry McKnight and intended to correct various health problems-- such as arthritis, diabetes, high blood pressure, glaucoma, hyperglycemia, and heart ailments.

4. Better and Better Vitamins

Better and Better Vitamins was begun in 1981 as a result of research by Dr. J. W. Hahn, a biochemist. The vitamins consist of two tablets, "super-alpha" and "super-beta". "Super-beta" is essentially a B-complex with 200mg of vitamin C, iron and calcium. It is intended to be taken in the morning to help the person get through the stresses of the day. "Super-alpha" contains vitamins A, D, E, and C combined with numerous minerals. Intended to be taken in the evening, it is designed (according to the literature), to help the body restore and rebuild itself during sleep. The vitamins are sold through an elaborate five-level distribution network. Each step up in the marketing structure nets greater returns. Discounts and incentives range from 35% to 48% or more at the upper level. A vitamin kit which costs the consumer $24.00 provides a 50% profit for the distribution coordinator, the highest position in the marketing program.

C. The Independent Lecturer

1. Territories

The independent lecturer is a private contractor who has exclusive rights over a specific territory. Territories range in size from several states to sections within one city. Although the number may vary slightly throughout the year (for reasons discussed below), as of the May 1984 directory there were 126 independent lecturers in the U. S. and other countries.

The territory is designated in a contract that every new lecturer must sign and every established lecturer annually renew. The territory (location and size) is assigned based on personal preference and on SMCI's need to service an area. The two are matched as closely as possible, according to Mr. Alejandro Gonzalez. Equally important, however, is Mr. Gonzalez's evaluation of the person's ability to handle an area requested. For example, a new lecturer may request a large, two-state area but only be given a section. Once s/he has demonstrated ability to service the area as expected, the territory may be increased. All new lecturers begin on a trial basis until they demonstrate their performance. Established lecturers must also continually demonstrate their ability to service an area. Unsatisfactory servicing of an area results in cancelling or non-renewal of the lecturer's contract.

2. Obligations

As part of the contract, the independent lecturer has certain obligations to SMCI (referred to simply as "Laredo" by the lecturers and sometimes appearing as such hereafter). First and foremost, independent lecturers are expected to produce. Each lecturer's contract specifies a minimum number of classes per year and students per class. If these numbers are not met, Laredo warns the lecturer. If no change occurs, that lecturer's contract is cancelled. The minimum numbers for classes and students are based upon the size and population of the lecturer's territory. Some areas warrant a class every month, while in others once every four months is sufficient. Usually ten or more students per class is desirable.

The independent lecturer also is required to buy the Basic Lecture Series kit for each new student. The kit consists of a BLS manual, a graduation certificate and a wallet card. These kits, which cost $70 each, must be issued to the students at the beginning of the class. If not, SMCI has the right to cancel the lecturer's contract. Because the material in the BLS is copyrighted, the lecturer is, in effect, paying a royalty fee to SMCI as part of the $70.

The price the lecturer charges for the BLS is independently determined. SMCI recommends, but cannot tell the lecturer what to charge, which would be price fixing. The price formula Laredo has found to work best is that the $70 BLS kit should be 25% of the total cost. Another 25% should be for expenses/overhead (e.g. rent, advertising). The remaining 50% should be profit. Based on this formula, the BLS should cost $280. In actuality, it ranges from $220 to $350. Most lecturers will offer discount incentives for those who sign up at the "Intro", for example charging $250 instead of $300. SMCI offers discounts for second family members who take the course within six months and who live at the same address. The suggested reduction in price is 25% (e.g. $300 to $255) with a corresponding discount on the BLS kits ($70 to $52.50). If the lecturer chooses to give only a 20% discount, then SMCI discounts the BLS kits only 20%.

Servicing an area includes more than simply offering the BLS as specified in the contract. The lecturer must also be active and fill the needs of the graduates in the area. This may be through workshops, newsletters, or other activities which keep the graduates active and provide them with an opportunity to practice the Method.

Although Laredo does not have contractual obligations to the lecturers, it does provide services for them. These include legal council, consulting, and graduate courses.

3. Lecturer Development Seminar

Some individuals, after taking the Silva course(s), decide they would like to teach the Method. To do so, they must follow a set procedure and become certified lecturers. The major part of the procedure is the Lecturer Development Seminar (LDS) held annually in Laredo. Before attending, however, the potential instructor is expected to have repeated SMC courses, done a number of suggested readings, participated in graduate follow-up groups, become a Relaxation Seminar lecturer, and fulfilled certain financial obligations.

All potential SMCI lecturers are required to have taken the Basic Lecture Series and the graduate courses (Ultra and Graduate). They then must repeat at least two complete BLS courses (Intro-404) with different lecturers (if possible) and repeat the graduate courses whenever offered in their area. All the while they are doing this, they are expected to be reading from the recommended list and developing their own outline for the course and lecture materials.

Those potential lecturers not working with a SMCI Center director, are first required to become Relaxation Seminar Lecturers. This can be done by attending the training in Laredo or by purchasing the cassette training kit. After having processed one hundred people through the Relaxation Seminar, the potential SMCI lecturers are eligible to attend the Lecturer Development Seminar.

All new lecturers are required to meet certain financial obligations before attending the LDS. As part of the new lecturers' agreement, each new lecturer must pay $700 for the LDS training and $1300 to establish an account for BLS kits and supplies.

The Lecturer Development Program, directed by Harry McKnight, oversees the Lecturer Development Seminar. The LDS is a ten day course held annually in Laredo and taught by McKnight. In the past, when demand was greater, the LDS was held twice a year. Now, it is offered once a year immediately following the International Convention. I attended the August, 1983 LDS and this information is based on those observations.

The LDS class is composed of both new and seasoned lecturers. The new lecturers are those attending for the first time. The seasoned lecturers are those repeating the LDS to complete certification and established lecturers who are speakers or are just reviewing. As part of their contract, new lecturers must return to Laredo for two years following their initial LDS. It is only after the third year that they receive full certification to teach. By requiring new lecturers to repeat the LDS for two years, Laredo is able to check on the way they present the material, ensure that they are aware of new findings and changes in perspective, and reinforce personal networks established during their initial LDS (discussed below). To ensure that established lecturers are "staying on track", Laredo is currently trying to find a way to require all lecturers to come to Laredo and review the LDS at least once every few years. At the August 1983 LDS, there were approximately 30 new lecturers and between 50 and 60 repeaters. The number of second and third year lecturers and other established lecturers decreased as the LDS progressed. Because of scheduling, many of these individuals were not able to stay the full ten days. Frequently in attendance also were members of the Silva family and some of the Laredo staff.

Each day of the LDS is divided into four-hour morning and afternoon sessions. Each session begins with a short (15 minute) mental relaxation exercise followed by lectures and demonstrations. Occasionally interspersed are question and answer periods with members of the Silva family.

The mental exercise which begins the session is the short relax. Each time, the exercise is read by a different potential lecturer. Immediately following, the reader is critiqued by McKnight and the class. This criticism is one of the mechanisms which leads to the uniformity of style (e.g. intonation, rhythm) one finds in the reading of the mental exercises.

The majority of the morning and afternoon sessions are composed of lecture and/or demonstration. Harry McKnight runs the LDS and most of the lectures are by him or his assistant, Laura Silva Gomez. In addition, there are key SMCI lecturers who discuss specific topics or give demonstrations of their approach. At the 1983 LDS, the first days were devoted to the business aspects of teaching Silva Mind Control. According to Jose Silva, in the early years, many lecturers knew nothing about running a business and consequently a good portion failed to succeed. To correct this, SMCI added lectures on Silva Mind Control as a business venture to the LDS. To conform with the schedules of some of the key speakers, the lectures on business were presented in the first few days and were of two interdependent topics: how to run a successful business and how to be a successful SMCI lecturer.

There are two prevalent attitudes among SMCI lecturers. Teaching the Silva Method is viewed as a business, or it is viewed as a service to humanity. Jose Silva, in his Ultra Seminar and in question-and-answer sessions, repeatedly speaks in terms of providing a service for humanity. In fact, the frontispiece of the SMC manuals contains the phrase, "Dedicated to the betterment of humanity" while the backcover contains "to qualify as human beings we must partake in humanitarian acts". Yet, José Silva along with the other top lecturers, is the first to admit that teaching the Method must first be approached as a business. The lecturer must be "business wise". If not, s/ he will not be successful--despite well meaning intentions.

At the 1983 LDS, to help raise the business awareness level, a number of top lecturers discussed such topics as the following:

1) Overhead-- advertising costs, rent, office expenses, salaries;

2) Advertising--how to write an ad, the type of ad to use, where to place it in the newspaper, the use of the phrase "mind control" in the ad, and press releases (free advertising);

3) Credibility--the importance of a good secretary, first impressions at the Intro (e.g. importance of appropriate dress, personal appearance and personal behavior), the lecturer's credentials, establishing a good credit rating by paying bills immediately, making one's self known to the community and the business world.

An important aspect of éclat is being a successful lecturer. To contribute to that success, useful "tips" are freely given. For example, it is suggested the new lecturers use their home as their office and always "work from behind". Of primary importance is that new lecturers have another source of income upon which they can depend. It is said that teaching SMC should be a part-time activity until the income from teaching is two thirds that of the primary income. Then, the person can be a full-time SMCI lecturer. It was suggested to me that the new lecturer needs $10,000 and three years to get well established. After that, the person should be able to do well by teaching alone.

According to the speakers, the successful lecturer is one who (first and foremost) is an example of the Method. S/he must believe in what he is doing. He must go to level (program) at least once a day, use the techniques, and _live_ Mind Control. If s/he does not, then s/he should not be teaching. There must be, according to the speakers, a congruency between what the lecturer believes and what he teaches in class. If belief, action and teaching do not interface, the students will know and will loose their confidence and belief. On the other hand, the lecturers are also warned about presenting themselves (consciously or unconsciously) as messiahs. As one of the top SMCI lecturers phrased it, "we are guides who share the Silva Method, not gurus".

Another factor which contributes to the successful lecturer is a solid graduate base. Lecturers have an obligation to serve their BLS grads by providing them with graduate courses, workshops, and opportunities to repeat the BLS. The lecturer is also expected to be available to his graduates for assistance in programming and SMC related problems. The lecturer who services his graduates well is repaid by those graduates bringing in new students. In speaking on the importance of a solid graduate base, one BLS lecturer team claims that forty percent of the students in each of their Introductory courses are present as a direct result of contact with their graduates.

Personal improvement is also an important theme in the LDS. Each new lecturer must complete self-assessment questionnaires and check sheets. Furthermore, new lecturers are required to do a video taped presentation which is later critiqued. The purpose is to help the new lecturer improve communication skills, speech, dress, and presentation of self. Some basic self-improvement psychologies are also presented. For example, many speak of "expanding your comfort zones"--a phrase directly out of "est" (Werner Ehrhardt's Sensitivity Training). Lecturers are also encouraged to use the techniques on themselves for self-improvement and for successful classes.

As mentioned above, the Introductory Lecture is crucial. Its full significance is reflected in the amount of time devoted to "Intros" during the LDS. During these sessions the new lecturer learns some effective techniques for presenting the Intro. Top lecturers discuss their method of presentation and point out crucial areas of the lecture. To provide them with the opportunity of seeing a successful lecturer at work, a leading lecturer actually presents her/his four hour introductory lecture. At the 1983 LDS, Rosa Rivas, recipient of the World Cup (see below) and "one of the hardest working and most effective people in the movement", presented her Intro.

The opening and closing segments of any lecture or presentation are critical. It is in the opening that the speaker gets the attention of the audience and establishes credibility. In the closing, the major point of the lecture is "driven home" or the "sale is made". Realizing this, successful lecturers--especially those with business or sales training--offer suggestions and demonstrations for effective presentations. They also suggest books and tapes to improve the opening and closing segments.[1]

In addition to the opening and closing, the actual structure of the Intro is also important. For example, where the price of the course is interjected into the lecture can be decisive. While presenting the Intro lecture to the LDS, the lecturer points out the crucial areas and how they have been handled. Although the potential lecturer should have attended a number of introductory lectures before going to Laredo, the demonstration during the LDS provides the new lecturers the chance to see how a successful lecturer sells Mind Control.

The primary purpose of the Lecturer Development Seminar is to teach potential lecturers how to present the Basic Lecturer Series. The process involves not only knowing the material itself but also being socialized into the Silva mode of thought and action. To ensure the material is learned and then presented correctly, each of the techniques and mental training exercises is examined in detail. As each exercise is scrutinized, suggestions are made concerning when, what type, and how much preconditioning material should be used. In the last few days of the LDS, each new lecturer is required to present a short segment of the BLS (e.g. explanation of the brain wave frequency chart) to the class. The presentation is then criticized by McKnight and those present. The end result is a uniformity of examples and ideas that cross-cut all the lecturers.

Interspersed throughout the LDS are question and answer periods with members of the Silva family. During the lectures and demonstrations, those present are free to ask questions of the lecturer whenever they desire. At numerous times during the ten days, José Silva, Juan Silva, and/or Alejandro Gonzalez stop in for varying lengths of time. Beyond this, there are semi-formal question and answer sessions, and times when one of the Silva family simply takes over the lecturn. At these times, the class is free to ask whatever they want. Questions that arise when José is not present are usually written down and handled when he arrives.

Other members of the Silva family deal with their speciality areas: Juan Silva addresses the international aspects of SMC; Alejandro Gonzalez discusses business matters. A special speaker at the 1983 LDS was Isabel Silva de las Fuentes, Jose's daughter and first subject. She spoke of her experiences during those early years of research and what it was like to grow up with Mind Control.

Lunch and dinner gatherings also present opportunities for lecturers to get to know the Silva family. During the 1983 LDS, lecturers had the opportunity to dine and spend the evening at the homes of Jose Silva and Alejandro Gonzalez; in addition, lunch was served at the homes of Juan Silva and Harry McKnight. These informal affairs provide the lecturers with occasions to talk and become acquainted with the important officials in the organization, to establish or strengthen ties, and to feel as if the Silvas are friends. This personal contact can create a strong bond between the lecturer and Laredo which, in turn, is expressed in their presentation of the BLS.

In the last two days of the LDS, while the potential lecturers are giving their presentations, Alejandro Gonzalez holds conferences. It is during these conferences that the details of the contract are finalized, any reservations are expressed, and if all agree, the contact is signed. The conference with Mr. Gonzalez is the last major step in this rite of passage. All that remains thereafter is awarding the LDS certificates and a short farewell party.

The schedule of the LDS is exceptionally tight. People spend eight hours per day in lecture, then usually lunch and dine with others from the group. For the most part, the people who attend are open, friendly, and sincere individuals who are willing to help and share experiences. Consequently, friendships and ties established during the LDS continue. The result is a bond among some lecturers that cross-cuts specific territories and strengthens the general network of Silva Mind Control lecturers worldwide.

I attended the English speaking LDS conducted by Harry McKnight. Concurrent with it was the LDS for Spanish speakers, run by Juan Silva. I was told it paralleled the English LDS in every way except for a greater emphasis on lecturer obligations to service and follow-up with their graduates. There were approximately sixty new lecturers attending the Spanish speaking LDS, thirty of those from Brazil alone. Because of the tight schedule there were few opportunities for the two groups to interact. Beyond the arranged lunch and diner gatherings, the only occasion for contact was a farewell party given by the English LDS group. Despite the language problems, most of the Spanish LDS came and seemed to enjoy themselves. It was during these informal gatherings that I had the opportunity to interact with the Spanish speaking LDS.

D. The Regional Concept/The SMCI Center

1. Development

As the Silva Mind Control organization grew, spreading across the U. S., Laredo divided the country into regions. Each region consisted of a number of states and was headed by a Regional Director. All other lecturers within the region worked under the Director who received a percentage of their BLS course fees. By 1973, just four years after the first course was taught outside of Texas, there were twenty-three regional directors. Of these, eleven had major regions directing between two and six states. Eight regions were devoted to specific cities or a part of a state (i.e. California). One consisted of areas "left-over" from other regions and three were foreign regions (i.e. Canada; Puerto Rico; and Mexico, Central and South America).

Although specific numbers are not available, class enrollment throughout most of the 70s was quite high; consequently, many of the regional directors became quite successful financially. Toward the end of the 70s, that steady growth leveled off, a number of unspecified problems arose, and numerous regional directors left the organization. Many of these started spin-off courses of their own. Hence, Laredo was forced to abandon the regional concept and return to the independent lecturer with an exclusive territory. It has been suggested that it was the inability, on the part of certain regional directors, to handle their relatively sudden financial success that eventually led to the decline of the regional concept. In May 1984, only seven of the original twenty-three regional directors were still active with SMCI. All of those now act as independent lecturers.

Today, the regional concept has been replaced by SMCI Centers. There are two types of Centers. Many independent lecturers maintain an office or suite in which class and workshops are held, books are sold, and graduates are free to stop in whenever they desire. Such a center serves as a nucleus for that lecturer's graduate base. The other type of SMCI Center, in addition to being a locale, is a concept. The territory is assigned to the director of the Center and he, in turn , has lecturers who work for him. These lecturers, known as "Center Lecturers", coordinate their classes and get their supplies through the Center. In some cases they actually teach with the Director.

There are advantages to being a Center lecturer. First, by working through a Director, the person is not required to be a Relaxation Seminar Lecturer before receiving the LDS training, nor is the individual required to establish the $1,300 supplies account. All Center lecturers' supplies are purchased through the Center without need of an independent account. The Center lecturer experiences less pressure, since he is working for an established lecturer in an established territory. He is not starting out "fresh", as must most independent lecturers. Also, the Center provides access to other lecturers, who can be relied upon in times of need. For these advantages, the Center lecturer must, of course, either pay a percentage of his BLS course fees to the Center Director or receive a salary from the Center for teaching. In February 1984, there were eight SMCI Centers of this type with fifteen associated Center lecturers.

2. Michigan and the Forward Thinking Institute

Until 1976, Michigan was the regional center of a four state area which included Ohio, Indiana and Kentucky. The Regional Director, Kenneth McCaulley, appeared quite successful. His class sizes were always large and he had a number of lecturers working for him. For personal reasons, McCaulley left SMCI and began teaching his own self-improvement course. When he left the Silva organization, he was not replaced as Regional Director. The lecturers who were teaching under him became independent lecturers. Eventually, new lecturers were assigned other territories in the four state region.

By 1979, there were only four active SMCI lecturers in the state. Sister Elizabeth Reis, assigned by the Sisters of St. Joseph to Nazareth College, was teaching in Kalamazoo and Battle Creek. Ms. Bobbie Brooks taught in northwest Detroit. Sister Blanche Cushing, assigned to St. Edmunds parish in Warren, taught at the parish. A forth lecturer, Fr. Jay Samonie, pastor of Holy Trinity Catholic Church, taught classes in his parish. Today, Sister Reis and Ms. Brooks function as they did in the past. Sister Blanche has taken a sabatical to attend the University of Detroit Law School and teaches only one or two classes a year. Father Samonie currently has two lecturers assisting him in his territory.

Fr. Samonie's territory is in Southwest Detroit. The area is low income residential and small industrial with large hispanic and black populations. This area does not have a local population or economic base sufficient to support three lecturers. They do well only because they draw their students from outside the territory. Fr. Samonie has a unique appeal. Since he is a Roman Catholic priest, there are many individuals who prefer to take the course from him. To do so they must travel to Holy Trinity since Fr. Samonie's contract does not permit him to teach outside of his territory. Also, because Fr. Samonie does not have the overhead expenses most other lecturers face, he is able to offer the BLS at a much lower rate than other area lecturers and benefit from students cultivated by local centers. The two new lecturers who currently work for Fr. Samonie did not begin training with that intention. Both planned to be independent lecturers with their own territories in this general area. Since all of the area is assigned, the only way Laredo would give them certification to teach after completion of the 1983 LDS, was to work for an established lecturer. They chose to affiliate with Fr. Samonie.

Michigan remained a state without leadership until 1979, at which time it once again became a region. This time, however, Michigan is the only state in that region. In addition to being a region, Michigan also is the site of one of the eight SMCI Centers. Located in Southfield and known as the Forward Thinking Institute (FTI), the Center's director is Louis Barbone.

The approach taken by Barbone is quite different from the other major lecturer in the region, Fr. Samonie. Being a Catholic priest, Samonie is religiously oriented; there are many individuals who prefer that approach and the perceived authority his status as priest conveys to him. Barbone, on the other hand, has a business orientation and a practical approach with few ideological overtones. Each appeals to a different type of student and meets the needs the other does not.

Louis Barbone has been interested in the potential of the mind for most of his adult life. Greatly influenced by the writing of Napoleon Hill², trained in hypnosis, and a teacher of Napoleon Hill courses, Barbone was a member of the 1969 Detroit Basic Lecture Series, the first held outside Texas. After attending only the introductory lecture to that BLS, Mr. Barbone says he recognized the "personal, business, and cultural potential of the Silva Method". He immediately attempted to gain approval for his "Personal Achievement Institute" to become the Silva Center for Michigan. His business partner was against the merger, however, and it did not materialize. In 1979, after having used the Method for ten years, he developed a renewed interest in establishing a SMC center. He then formed the "FTI" for the expressed purpose of becoming the SMC Center for Michigan. At that time he convinced José Silva to give him the opportunity to pull Michigan together as a region. When Barbone took over as state director on July 15, 1979, he brought with him a unique philosophical and business orientation.

A pivotal element in Barbone's belief system is synergy. This is most obviously expressed in the team approach that guides the Forward Thinking Institute. When Barbone became state director, he maintains he was confronted with the same serious problems that have caused SMCI to stagnate for the past seven years. Lecturers were/ are learning the Method--the techniques--but were/are not internalizing the philosophy (i.e. the unity and oneness of all). Consequently there is competition, rivalry and lack of cooperation among the independent lecturers.

The established lecturers were opposed to Barbone and they expressed their hostility in numerous ways (Barbone,personal communication,1983). Because they refused to work with him it was necessary to recruit new people who shared his philosophical orientation and long-range goals for the region. His approach was viewed as a threat by the established lecturers since they believed it necessitated giving up their independence and control. It took quite some time for most of them to begin cooperating with him. Barbone maintains that this inability of the independent lecturers to work in unison has cost Laredo millions in lost revenue throughout the U. S.

The FTI views the independent lecturers within its region as unaffiliated. These lecturers were established when Mr. Barbone became state director. According to him, none recognized or were willing to explore the benefits of becoming part of the FTI team and working with him. Although each established lecturer was given a specific territory, the change in state organization created some animosity. For the most part, the lecturers were uncooperative and antagonistic to the new Director. There was, in fact, one individual who refused to stay in the assigned territory, recruited students from outside the area, and caused numerous other problems. Today, the relationship between the FTI and this individual continues to be strained (Barbone,personal communication,1983).

In the mid-70s when Ken McCaulley resigned as regional director, there were a number lecturers teaching in Michigan; in 1979, only four were actively teaching SMC. A similar decrease was found throughout the U. S. Barbone estimates that in the last 14 years, SMCI has trained over 2000 lecturers for the U. S. Today, he says, only about 5% are still active and only a dozen make their living by teaching Mind Control (Ibid). Why do they quit? Because, according to Barbone, they have not internalized the philosophy. They have remained at what Barbone calls the "survival mode". These individuals used "dog eat dog" competitive techniques. This orientation is a complete contradiction to the approach of the FTI. Consequently,

Barbone had to look elsewhere--to new potential lecturers from his BLS courses--to make up his team.

Today, there are three certified lecturers and six lecturers-in-training working with Barbone. Two of the three, Sanford Math and Barbara Goushaw[3], have well paying, full-time jobs and teach with Barbone as a part-time weekend activity The other certified lecturer is Lou Barbone's wife, Therese. Mrs. Barbone, like the other lecturers, assists during the BLS by teaching certain segments. Additionally, she is responsible for running the FTI. In recognition of the excellent job she has done at organizing the Center, Laredo awarded her the 1983 Outstanding Organizer award at the convention. Part of this teaching team makes up a six member advisory board. During their weekly meetings, this board discusses ways to improve teaching techniques, ideas on how to make Mind Control more visible, ways to apply the Method in everyday living situations, and philosophical ideas.

A second axial component of Barbone's approach is his attempt to unit two seemingly diametrically opposed philosophical positions--subjectivism and objectivism. In response to the subjectivist philosophy developed by Descartes, expounded by Hume and Kant, expressed today as logical positivism, and basal to most religious ideologies, Ayn Rand developed her philosophy of Objectivism--a form of Aristotelianism.[4] The subjectivists, sometimes referred to as "inside-out" philosophers, take as their starting point the data of the consciousness--ideas, impressions, insights. Objectivism, an "outside-in" philosophy, begins with existence and the real world. From these basic assumptions both then proceed to major philosophical issues.

The Silva Method is individually oriented subjectivism. The students are continually advised to follow the impressions they receive while "at level". Barbone is attempting to temper this classic subjectivism with objectivism. He maintains the alpha experience needs to be objectified by testing and verification at the beta level. Both are necessary for completeness, he claims, and the Silva Method is the means to integrate the two.

A third factor influencing Barbone is his extensive business background. In addition to owning his own business, Barbone was a market consultant on the regional staff of Century 21 of Michigan. Three years ago, he acquired the Elsa Cooper School of Court Reporting and is currently training 200 students a year. He applies this business experience to teaching the Silva Method and running the Forward Thinking Institute. The FTI, for example, shares office space with the Elsa Cooper business. The classrooms in which the Silva Method is taught on the weekends, serve as the locale for court reporter training during the week. Barbone's business orientation is also expressed in the way he would like to expand the Method into the local business community. Currently, Barbone is negotiating to teach SMC to employees at Ford and GM through their "Quality of Life" programs. He also has had discussions with Detroit Tiger officials about putting the team through the training. All the instructors at the Elsa Cooper School have taken the Silva training and the students are encouraged to do so with a 50% scholarship. Barbone's attempts to get SMC into the business world predate and are independent of Laredo's renewed business orientation.

Not only do the above elements combine to make the Forward Thinking Institute a unique SMCI Center but Barbone's scenario of the future also sets it apart. Barbone sees a renewal of the regional concept--which Laredo is attempting. This time, however, the Regional Director would have power and responsibility over the other lecturers in her/his territory. All the lecturers would work as a team, cooperating and helping each other. The Director would not only oversee and coordinate, but also guide the other lecturers, making useful suggestions on ways to improve teaching techniques, for example. Barbone envisions himself with three roles. Primarily he would train other instructors to teach the Silva Method.

In Laredo, according to Barbone, they certify the person but there is not enough time to teach her/him how to be an instructor. Barbone believes techniques on the most effective way to present the ideas of the BLS should be given to new instructors. For example, slides and other visual aids can be used to integrate the subjective and the objective (such as having a slide of a large gold key during the memory peg session). Barbone would also like to devote time to presenting SMC to the corporate world and demonstrate ways to apply the Method. Similarly, he would like to make the Method more visible by developing information dissemination avenues such as a syndicated newspaper column.

The other members of the team would be responsible for teaching and administration. In the synergetic approach, Barbone states, the results are due to the work of all involved--the teacher, the administrator and the salesperson. All would be working as an interacting team, as allies not competitors guided by hostility and adversity. The end result (because of the multiplier effect) would be group success--in spreading the Silva Method, and personal success--far greater than that possible independently. The Forward Thinking Institute is a prototype of what must come for SMCI if it is to achieve its potential (Ibid).

The approach taken in class by Lou Barbone is a reflection of his philosophical orientation and background. Raised a Roman Catholic and trained by Jesuits, he no longer limits his identification to that religion alone. An independent thinker and seeker of knowledge, he is constantly adding new material and examples to his preconditioning segments. Although he sometimes oversimplifies a concept, he draws from many fields for his material. This eclectic approach makes for interesting and informative lectures. Because he is in command of the

material--both lecture and techniques--he has an air of
authority to which the students respond. Unlike some past
and present lecturers, Barbone realizes that ESP,
parapsychology, or psychic phenomena is a subject of which
many people are leery. Accordingly, the parapsychological
aspects of SMC are de-emphasized at the FTI, until the end
of 303. The focus in the Intro and through the beginning of
the course is on the relaxation and problem solving
techniques. Likewise, parapsychological examples and
psychic phenomena are not generally included in the
lectures. Personally, Barbone is open and approachable and
encourages students to question and understand the ideas
presented. Because he is able to "read the class", he can
modify his approach to meet the needs of those present.
His business background comes through in the way he has
organized his Intro, his summary newspaper handout of that
Intro, his advertisements, and the Center's Newsletter.
Although quieter and usually in the background, Mrs. Barbone
shares her husband's mastery of material and open, helpful
attitude.

Sanford Math and Barbara Goushaw attended their
initial LDS in October, 1982. They both had been lecturers
in training under Barbone before that LDS so they had a few
months of pre-exposure to teaching. During my fieldwork, I
watched a transformation of these two individuals take
place. In the beginning the insecurity of both was
reflected in their robotic "canned" presentation.

Gradually, as they mastered the material and themselves, their presentations became relaxed, free, and appeared almost spontaneous. The change in their presentation of themselves and the material was, in turn, reflected by the way the students responded to them. It is also reflected in the fact that they both received Certificates of Merit at the 1983 Convention. Together, all of these people create an atmosphere at the FTI that I did not experience at the previous Center or with other lecturers. It is one of openness, friendliness, and a genuine desire to reach out and help who ever asks for it.

The other BLS lecturers I have observed were quite different from those at the FTI; they too reflected their backgrounds and interests. The lecturer with whom I took the initial BLS was very psychically oriented which was reflected throughout the presentation of the course. Thus, my initial impression of SMC was very different than it is today, this initial impression is shared by other graduates of that lecturer with whom I have spoken. Repeating the BLS, I found other lecturers to range from a self-center guru with a god complex (who nonetheless, had interesting lectures and a large following) to the almost overly humble and very religious José Silva himself.

I have been told by a number of sources that the religious who teach the BLS orient their lectures and pre-conditioning segments around the teachings of the Roman Catholic Church. For example, one of these individuals used the whole pre-conditioning for dream control to talk about the dreams of a particular saint. Unless Laredo were to "can" the pre-conditionings as it has the techniques, there is no present way to overcome this diversity--nor should they want to. The heterogeneity of instructors is one of the mechanisms that attracts students with such a wide range of backgrounds to the BLS. Enforced homogeneity of lecturers would decrease appeal and thus enrollment.

E. The International Aspects

1. SMC in Foreign Countries

There are approximately 150 lecturers teaching the Silva Method of self-mind control worldwide. Currently, the Method is presented on a regular basis in sixty-one countries and fourteen languages (see Appendix Three). Of these countries, one of the most successful has been Brazil. SMC has been in Brazil since 1972. For the first few years everything went quite well. Then for a period of two and a half years, the director of SMC in Brazil disassociated himself from Laredo. He continued to teach the Silva Method but refused to send royalties to Laredo or allow José or Juan Silva to teach the graduate courses. Quite recently this problem was resolved and a new director appointed. None the less, according to Juan Silva, the enrollment in Brazil has been increasing every year. In fact, there is room for 150 instructors in that country alone, Silva claims. BLS class sizes are very large and graduate courses by the Silvas range from 600 to 1000 per course. The SMC success in Brazil is part of the general success in Mexico and Central and South America. These Spanish speaking countries are currently among the fastest growing for SMCI.

According to a number of sources, the SMC success in Latin America countries is attributable to one or a combination of the following factors: (1) the lecturer; (2) the type of follow-up given the graduates; (3) post-graduate activities; and (4) the culture. It is the opinion of a number of top lecturers--both U. S. and foreign--that there is an essential difference between lecturers in North America and those in the Spanish speaking countries. Most lecturers from the latter are not only committed to the Method but also to their students. That commitment extends beyond the forty hours of BLS instruction. The lecturers make themselves available outside of the formal class time and after the class has finished. The students, in turn, capitalize on this by going to the lecturer for advice on programming difficulties, personal matters, and in particular by attending the graduate activities. In Brazil, for example, they have weekly or semi-weekly activities which draw 600 graduates. This, in turn, is closely related to the follow-up support given by the lecturer to her/his graduates. Lecturers in the Spanish speaking countries become more involved with their graduates. They know more about their students' families, problems, and successes. They are, as Juan Silva characterizes them, more like social workers. This degree of involvement by the lecturers results in a strong commitment to them by their graduates. In general, according to SMCI, graduates' first loyalty is always to their BLS lecturer but the degree of loyalty can be dependent upon the lecturer's continued support of those grads. Top lecturers in North America realize this and provide a strong support systems and regular follow-up activities for their graduates. Since a large number of BLS students enroll as the result of referrals from graduates, it is important that graduates are serviced to their satisfaction. These practices have led to success in the Spanish speaking countries and for the top North American lecturers.

A final factor which has contributed to the success of SMC in Mexico and Central and South America is the cultural pre-disposition to believe in the spiritual, the mystical, and non-Western healing techniques (e.g. spiritual healing). Curanderos and folk or traditional healers have been a part of this areas cultural traditions for centuries. Also, in these countries, persons holding degrees occupy a high status. The Silva lecturer is a teacher and as such is afforded not only a great deal of respect but deference as well. These four factors working together account for the growing success of SMC in the Spanish speaking areas.

The importance of graduate follow-up is reflected in the Silva "start-up" policy. Generally, when Laredo decides to begin teaching the BLS in a new country, the first classes are taught in English. This continues until a native speaker becomes a certified lecturer and is able to offer the BLS in the local language. Laredo maintains it will not begin teaching in a new country, however, until there is someone there who can work with the graduates and provide them with necessary follow-up activities.

SMCI claims it has had very few problems in starting a program in any country it has chosen. The only major exceptions are France and the Near East. For the past seven and one half years, Laredo has been trying to start teaching the BLS in France. Supposedly the problem has been that there are three dialects prominent in France. Laredo claims it had problems deciding which of the three to use. Spain, however, which also has major regional dialects did not present a problem. In France, the problem has finally been resolved and Laredo is preparing to offer the BLS. The problem in Arab dominated Moslem countries is the strong influence the Koran has on all aspects of life. Officials in these countries have not yet been convinced, according to Juan Silva, that SMC is not a religion which would conflict with the teachings of the Koran and Islam.

There is very little known about what is happening in the Soviet block countries, according to Juan Silva. Apparently there is a group of Silva graduates in Bulgaria who originally took the course in Venezuela. But, Laredo has not heard from any of them for quite some time.

One way in which Laredo hopes to gain access to countries in which SMC is not yet being taught is through its new course oriented towards business executives. The course, which was still in the planning stage during my fieldwork, is to be a reorganization of the BLS with an emphasis on ways the Silva Method can be used for successful business. A new book entitled The Silva Mind Control Method for Business Managers by José Silva in association with Robert B. Stone. is also a reflection of this new orientation. It is hoped that this course, offered to businesses internationally, will be an effective way to begin teaching the Method in a number of countries.

2. The Annual International Convention

One of the most important events for SMCI is the International Convention held annually in Laredo, Texas. This two day convention is filled with lectures, workshops, informal rap sessions, luncheons, and a gala ball. At the 1983 Convention, there were over 300 people from over 20 countries who attended the festivities. The convention is part of three weeks of activity which includes presentation of the BLS and Ultra Seminar by José Silva, the Graduate Seminar by Harry McKnight and the ten day Lecturer Development Seminar.

The convention activities begin with the arrival of the conventioneers on Friday. The 1983 Convention itself began at 8:45 am on Saturday with a brief opening meditation followed by a half-hour of Mexican music and dancing. The remainder of the two days was composed of rap sessions, workshops, and lectures. The informal hour rap sessions allowed conventioneers to interact with the Silva family and convention speakers. It also provided them the opportunity to take pictures with these individuals--which many chose to do. The rap sessions also function as an intermission during which time people were able to buy the books, tapes, and other items offered for sale by SMCI.

The twelve workshops (six each afternoon) were run by top SMCI lecturers. Topics included using your memory more effectively; playing your hunches; developing your potential; effective case working; and advanced programming. Since the workshops ran concurrently on each day, attending more than one necessitated missing part or all of the others. The special needs of the Spanish speaking conventioneers were met by providing simultaneous translation during the convention and offering Spanish workshops on both Saturday and Sunday.

The Keynote speaker at the 1983 Convention was Sr. Naomi Curtain, SSND. Currently assigned to Guam, Sr. Naomi Curtain has been teaching the Silva Method for nine years. Recipient of the 1982 Silva Mind Control World Cup (see below), she has presented numerous classes and workshops on Guam and taught SMC throughout the U. S. At present, she is in charge of a pilot project in the Guam parochial schools. The Silva Method was introduced in one, 550-student elementary school 1982. The success of this initial program resulted in approval for a second school last year and a third school in the Fall of 1984. Eventually all the parochial schools on Guam will be teaching children the Silva Method. The project, which has the full approval of the Bishop and Sister Curtain's religious order (School Sisters of Nortre Dame), receives financial support from the Guam business community, SMCI, and SIGA (see below).

Other speakers at the convention included Dr. George DeSau (who is working very closely with Sister Naomi) on the current status of SMC research, Rev. David Drew on achieving the ultimate level, Paul Fransella (who is in charge of the SMC business course) on Silva Mind Control in the business world, and Sr. Elizabeth Reis on holistic health.

Lunch, on both days, was provided by SMCI as part of the $150 Convention fee. These lunches afforded additional opportunities for the conventioneers to interact with the Silvas, leading lecturers, convention speakers, and other conventioneers.

The major social event of the convention is the awards presentation and dance on Saturday evening. At the 1983 Convention the outstanding SMCI lecturer was Paul Grivas who received the World Cup--the top award offered by SMCI. The World Cup is awarded to the person who has done the most to bring the Silva Method to the people (translated as the largest number of new BLS students). Grivas, a SMCI lecturer since 1974 and the SMCI Center Director for New

York, has translated the Silva Method into Greek and teaches the BLS in Greece and Trinidad. In 1981 and 1982, Grivas was awarded the President's Cup one of which is given to the outstanding lecturer in the U.S. and another of which is given to the outstanding lecturer in foreign countries.

In 1983, the President's Cup for outstanding U. S. lecturer went to Fr. Justin Belitz. Fr. Belitz has been a SMCI lecturer since 1978 and is currently SMCI Center Director in Indianapolis. The President's Cup for outstanding lecturer in foreign countries was given to Dr. Marcelino Alcala. Dr. Alcala has received this award for three years. He is one of the "largest producers in the organization", having taught the Silva Method to over 10,000 people in the last ten years. Currently SMCI Director of the Caribbean and SMCI Center Director in Miami, Alcala is also responsible for the new graduate magazine, Alpha Amigos. In addition to these awards to top lecturers SMCI also gives awards in the following categories: top lecturer by territory size; outstanding first and second year lecturer, Foreign Director, SMCI Center, SMCI organizer, Graduate Newsletter, and Graduate Activity. Special projects are also acknowledged with awards and those lecturers who have been with the organization for ten years are given Ten Year Service Awards. Some lecturers receive Bachelor, Master and Doctor of Psychorientology Certificates for having taught 20, 40, and 60 classes respectively with at least twenty paying students per class.

F. Silva Mind Control Related Organizations

1. Ecumenical Society of Psychorientology

Peripheral to SMCI are two related, but not officially affiliated organizations. The Ecumenical Society of Psychorientology (E.S.P.) is a non-profit holistic faith healing organization. Founded in 1975, the stated purposes of this international organization are:

1) to scientifically research the effectiveness of prayer, spiritual healing, psychic healing and faith healing;
2) to conduct workshops which will give individuals instructions for training in psychic healing, spiritual healing and prayer or faith healing, supported by scientific research which will be useful to participants in improving or developing their capabilities; and
3) to do this work and this research in conjunction with other organizations and institutions, especially with churches and other religious organizations(E.S.P. brochure).

There are four degrees of membership in E.S.P. with an annual $25 fee. From least to most active involvement, the memberships are:

1) Supporting Psychorientologist: This entitles the applicant to an ID card, the Quarterly Newsletter , and announcements of E. S. P. activities.

2) Student Psychorientologist: This is primarily preparation for becoming a third level member. It affords the same benefits as level one but the applicant also attends lecturers, workshops and developmental programs.

3) Practicing Psychorientologist: This includes all the benefits of levels 1 and 2 but the applicant is

certified as "knowledgeable in the regulation or
balance of energies according to Ecumenical Society
of Psychorientology".

4) Instructing Psychorientologist: Once certified, the
applicant is eligible for training as an
Instructing Psychorientologist to "guide others to
help them become certified." The training is done
by "researchers and scientists associated with"
E.S.P. (Ibid).

Because E.S.P. is a non-profit organization, any
donation is tax deductible. The President of E.S.P. is Anna
Maria Silva Martinez, daughter of José Silva. By being
trained in holistic faith healing and being a member of a
recognized healing society, these psychic healers are
permitted to enter hospitals in certain areas to perform
psychic healings if requested by the patient.

2. Silva International Graduates Organization.

A major problem many BLS grads have faced is follow-up
after the course is finished. In many areas there are few
opportunities for grads to be involved in activities which
keep them using the techniques and in touch with SMC news.
Graduates in some areas have formed cottage (local) groups
which regularly meet to work health cases and practice the
techniques. This is especially likely in areas which do not
have an established center from which the lecturer works.
Graduates without cottage groups or centers or in areas
where the SMC lecturer only occasionally comes to teach,

find themselves isolated after the BLS and frequently stop using the techniques. Recognizing this problem, Neva Davis, (a member of the first lecturer training class in 1969) and a group of graduates formed a graduate association. In November 1982, the first chapter of "Silva International Graduates Association" (SIGA) was formed in Dallas/ Ft. Worth. Nine months later, the number of chapters had risen to thirteen--with one of those on Guam.

The minimum number of graduates necessary to form a chapter is five and the annual membership fee is $40. SIGA is non-profit and in Aug. 1983 had applied for tax-exempt status. Because the membership is still relatively small approximately 2000, most of the $40 fee is used primarily to defray expenses such as mailings and video productions. As membership grows and more contributions are sent from local chapters, SIGA plans to spend increasing money on various research projects. For example, at the 1983 SIGA "mini-convention", the members adopted a resolution to support the research project on Guam. SIGA also is establishing a student exchange. Started by Isabel Silva de las Fuentes, this program will allow SIGA members to host other SIGA members in all parts of the world.

One advantage of having a SIGA chapter in an area is that graduates will be able to keep in touch with SMCI. The SIGA chapter can also request special projects, speakers, and workshops from Laredo and be given priority for their assignment.

Jose Silva is the symbol of Mind Control. Even though he spends 90% of the year teaching the Ultra Seminar and the Healing Workshop throughout the U. S. and select countries, this does not provide sufficient opportunities for everyone who wants to see him. Realizing this, Laredo has produced video recordings of Jose and Juan Silva directed specifically at SIGA members. These tapes are available upon request to local SIGA chapters which in turn, show them to their members.

Michigan has one of the 13 SIGA chapters. It was the fifth to be formed and is chaired by Sanford Math. Currently there are 60 members in this chapter. It, like other SIGA chapters, sponsors individual projects. This SIGA chapter provided financial assistance to the author to enable her to attend the three weeks of activities in Laredo which surrounded the International Convention. Without their support, that segment of fieldwork would not have been possible.

ENDNOTES

[1] For example, see Room at the Top or How to Sell Anything

[2] For example see Think and Grow Rich

[3] As of early 1984, Ms. Goushaw chose to stop teaching Mind Control for personal reasons.

[4] See, for example, the following works by Ayn Rand: The Virtue of Selfishness, For the New Intellectual, or Introduction to Objectivist Epistemology; or The Philosophic Thought of Ayn Rand edited by Douglas Den Uyl and Douglas Rasmussen; or An Answer to Ayn Rand by John Robbins.

CHAPTER SIX

THE MEMBERS

I. INTRODUCTION

There are, according to SMCI, over four million
individuals who have taken the Silva training. Because of
the constraints of the study, it was not possible to reach
even one-half percent of that number. In order to reach as
large a population as the study would permit, questionnaires
were used to supplement the primary technique of
participant-observation (see Chapter Two). These
questionnaires were designed to gain information in four
categories; (1) demographic data, (2) opinion about the BLS
and the Method, (3) ideological orientation, and (4) degree
of involvement with the organization and the Method. The
respondents represent a convenience sample--i.e. those who
were willing to take the time and make the effort to answer
the questionnaires. The sample is divided into four sub-
groups:

    1) Laredo functionaries; Twenty-eight lecturers who
       were in Laredo for the August 1983 Convention and
       LDS.

2) Laredo graduates; Thirty-two SMCI graduates who attended the same convention. Both of these groups answered Questionnaire 3 (see Appendix 7).

3) Metro-Detroit; This is the group with whom I had the most personal interaction, as I attended the classes which brought them to the SMCI Center. One hundred and fourteen answered Questionnaire 1 and nineteen of those returned an open-ended follow-up questionnaire (Questionnaire 2).

4) Indianapolis; These are twelve individuals who were given the Laredo questionnaire by their local lecturer.

This chapter will describe the general study population and, where appropriate, compare the four sub-groups. It will also examine the influence selected variables may have on each other.

The total size of the sample is 188.[1] The response rate was exceptionally high. In Metro-Detroit, of the students in the BLS courses and workshops that I attended, approximately 90% participated by taking a questionnaire and 80% of those questionnaires were returned. At the Ultra Seminar, approximately 42% took a questionnaire of which 56% were returned. These high participation and return rates can be attributed to the same factors: (1) class size; (2) intensity of interaction; and (3) type of person attracted to SMCI. The class size of the BLS was usually about 30 people. As the course progressed through the four, ten hour

days, an esprit de corps developed. Participating as I did,
I became "one of the class" (and hence trusted) as well as
"the person doing the study". I became confidant and
listening board for experiences difficult to speak of
outside of Mind Control circles. Combined with this,
however, was always the fact that I was an "old grad" and
had used the Method. This was important--not only in Metro-
Detroit but in Laredo as well--with both the graduates and
the officials of the organization. This status added to my
credibility and acceptance and contributed, I believe, to
the high return rates for all the questionnaires. Not to be
overlooked, however, is the equally important attitude of
the participants in the BLS courses. With virtually no
exceptions they were friendly, open and anxious to help.
Not only were they responsive to conversations I initiated
but many actively sought me out or waited in line to talk
with me during the breaks. This too is reflected in the
response rates.

The lower participation and response rates from the
Ultra Seminar are also due to the same interaction of
factors. In this case, class size was quite large,
approximately 200 people. Opportunities to interact were
much less and the length of time together was shorter. I
was not, therefore, as familiar to them as to the BLS
students so the perceived obligation to participate was much
less. The rates, nonetheless, are still quite high, which

again is a reflection of the willingness to help from those (in general) attracted to SMCI.

The response rate for the Laredo sub-groups is slightly lower, approximately 33%. This can be attributed to one major factor: time constraints. The questionnaire designed for Laredo included both forced choice and open-ended questions. When I designed it, I was unaware the schedule would be so inflexible. Initially, I thought it could be completed in 30 to 40 minutes. I was later told it was taking an hour and a half or more.

The Laredo population included both conventioneers and LDS participants. Most conventioneers arrived on Friday afternoon and departed on Monday. During that period, the time was filled with convention activities. Most also took advantage of shopping in Mexico which left little time for other endeavors. Time, however, was even more crucial for the LDS participants. Their day began at 9:00am and lasted until 6:00pm or later every evening. With eating, sleeping and visiting old friends (or making new ones) there were few precious moments to just sit, let alone answer the lengthy questionnaire. I believe I was fortunate to achieve the response rate that I did. Part of that rate is attributed to the fact that 48% of the questionnaires returned were mailed to me after all of us had left Laredo.

A second factor that influenced this return rate is that many individuals wanted questionnaires to keep for themselves. This was either for their own use among their graduates or as an extension of my sample to include some of their graduates. Of the five who suggested they would do the latter, only one actually did.[2] The person who followed through with distributing the Laredo questionnaire to his graduates was Fr. Justin Belitz and his staff at the Indianapolis SMCI Center. Their efforts resulted in my forth sub-group.

II DEMOGRAPHIC CHARACTERISTICS

It has been suggested by José Silva that his classes always have more females than males. In fact, as he says, 95% of the first class in Texas was female, as were his first two subjects and the first and second schools in which the Method was taught. Silva believes that females are more spiritually oriented. He says females were created to first control the spiritual dimension and secondly control the biological dimension. He maintains it is the opposite for men. Females are natural psychics, naturally sensitive to the spiritual. Men, on the other hand, must be trained to become aware of their intuitive powers.

The data support the sex ratio claim (see Table 4). Of the 188 respondents, 123 (65.4%) were female while only 65 (34.6%) were male, a nearly 2:1 ratio. The ratio holds true for each of the four sub-groups. Among the Laredo functionaries, 17 (60.7%) were females while 11 (39.3%) were male. For the Laredo graduates there were 22 females (68.7%) and 10 males (31.3%). The Detroit group was composed of 74 females (64.9%) and 40 males (35.1%). The small Indianapolis group also held the ratio with 8 females (66.7%) and 4 males (33.3%).

TABLE 04.

Sex

Sex	Laredo Funct. n=28		Laredo Grads n=32		Metro- Detroit n=114		Indiana- polis n=12		Total n=188	
	n	%	n	%	n	%	n	%	n	%
Female	17	60.7	22	68.7	74	64.9	8	66.7	123	65.4
Male .	11	39.3	10	31.3	40	35.1	4	33.3	65	34.6
Missing	0		0		0		0		0	

It has been suggested by numerous authors that those attracted to cults (which is how some view SMCI) come from the fringes of society, from the dispossessed, or from a specific age strata. The data support none of these observations.

The total respondents range in age from 15 to 76 years with the median age being 44 years (see Table 5). The median age for the Laredo functionaries, who range from 15 to 72 years, was 47 years. The Laredo grads were slightly older with a median age of 52 in a 26-76 year range. Among the Detroit group, whose range was 15-69 years, the median age was 39 years compared with Indianapolis, where the median in the 23 to 64 year span was 50 years.

TABLE 5.

Age

Age	Laredo Funct. n=28	Laredo Grads n=32	Metro-Detroit n=114	Indiana-polis n=12	Total n=188
Range	15-72	26-76	15-69	23-64	15-76
Median	47	52	39	50	44

The income range for the sample was from less than $5,000 to over $60,000 with the mid-ranges almost equally represented. As a result the mean was in the $20,000 to $29,000 range (see Table 6). This was also the mean for the four sub-groups. Among the Laredo functionairies, 42.9% earned between $20,000 and $40,000, while among the Laredo grads 43.8% had incomes in that range. The pattern was similar in Detroit with 43% in that category. The Indianapolis population, however, was evenly distributed across the spectrum. One hundred and forty individuals (78.2% of the total) were employed. This high employment rate held for each of the sub-groups (see Table 7).

While the data indicate that most individuals in the sample were married, the differences between the groups are not that great. Of the 188 respondents, 74 (39.4%) were married, 54 (28.7%) were never married and 56 (29.8%) were either widowed, divorced or separated (see Table 8). The same distribution is found for the other sub-groups with the exception of Indianapolis. Here, 6 (50.0%) were never

TABLE 6.

Income

Income	Laredo Funct. n=25		Laredo Grads n=26		Metro-Detroit n=100		Indiana-polis n=8		Total n=160	
	n	%	n	%	n	%	n	%	n	%
<$5,000 .	1	3.6	1	3.1	1	1.0	1	8.3	4	2.5
5-9,000 .	1	3.6	3	9.4	3	3.0	1	8.3	9	5.6
10-19,000	2	3.6	3	9.4	3	3.0	1	8.3	9	5.6
20-29,000	5	17.9	10	31.3	22	22.0	1	8.3	40	25
30-39,000	7	25.0	4	12.5	21	21.0	1	8.3	33	20.6
40-49,000	3	10.7	0		28	28.0	1	8.3	32	20.0
50-59,000	0		1	3.1	0		1	8.3	2	1.2
>$60,000	3	10.7	3	9.4	0		1	8.3	7	4.3
Missing .	3		6		14		4		28	

TABLE 7.

Employment

Emply	Laredo Funct. n=27		Laredo Grads n=29		Metro-Detroit n=111		Indiana-polis n=12		Total n=179	
	n	%	n	%	n	%	n	%	n	%
Yes . .	19	70.4	20	69.0	88	77.2	11	91.7	140	78.2
No . .	5	18.5	1	3.4	18	15.8	1	8.3	25	14.5
Retired	2	7.4	8	27.6	4	3.5	0		14	7.8
Missing	1		3		3		0		7	

married. This difference, however, is due to the fact that some of these respondents were Catholic nuns.

Of those who responded, 107 (58.2%) had children. Among the Laredo groups 39 respondents, (65.0%) had

TABLE 8.

Marital Status

Status	Laredo Funct. n=28		Laredo Grads n=32		Metro- Detroit n=114		Indiana- polis n=12		Total n=188	
	n	%	n	%	n	%	n	%	n	%
Single . .	6	21.4	7	21.9	34	29.8	6	50.0	54	28.7
Married . .	13	46.4	14	43.8	42	38.6	3	25.0	74	39.4
Wid,div,sep	8	28.6	10	31.3	34	29.8	3	25.0	56	29.8
Living with	1	3.6	0		2	1.7	0		3	1.6
Missing . .	0		0		0		0		0	

children. For both the Detroit and Indianapolis groups, 54%
had children. The number of children ranged from 1 to 8
with an average of 3 (see Table 9).

TABLE 9.

Children

Child	Laredo Funct. n=28		Laredo Grads n=29		Metro- Detroit n=114		Indiana- polis n=11		Total n=184	
	n	%	n	%	n	%	n	%	n	%
Yes . .	19	67.9	20	69.0	62	54.4	6	54.5	107	58.2
No . .	8	28.6	9	31.0	52	45.6	5	45.5	76	41.3
Range .	1-5		1-5		1-8		2-8		1-8	
Mean .	2.52		3.11		3.7		4.3		3.09	
Missing	0		3		0		1		4	

The most obvious skewness in distribution was for the
response on group identity. As Table 10 indicates, 90% of

the total was White. It is only among the Detroit sub-group
that this percentage falls below ninety to 81.5% with four
Blacks (4.6%) and three Hispanics (3.4%) represented.

TABLE 10.

Group Identity

Group Identity	Laredo Funct. n=28		Laredo Grads n=29		Metro-Detroit n=114		Indiana-polis n=12		Total n=185	
	n	%	n	%	n	%	n	%	n	%
White . .	27	96.4	26	81.3	103	81.5	11	91.7	167	90.3
Asian . .	1	3.6	0		0		1	8.3	2	1.0
Afro-Amer	0		2	6.3	4	3.5	0		8	4.3
Hispanic	0		1	3.1	5	4.4	0		6	3.2
Other . .	0		0		2	1.7	0		2	1.0
Missing .	0		3		0		0		3	

One hundred and thirty four respondents (71.8%) had a
public school education³ (see Table 11). Fifty percent
(93) have had some college or received an undergraduate
degree while 18% (34) had graduate degrees⁴. Approximately
the same distribution is found in the sub-groups. The only
exception is found among the Laredo functionaries, where 8
individuals (28.6%) held graduate degrees (see Table 12).

TABLE 11.

Educational Background

Edbk	Laredo Funct. n=28		Laredo Grads n=32		Metro- Detroit n=114		Indiana- polis n=12		Total n=188	
	n	%	n	%	n	%	n	%	n	%
Public . .	21	75.0	24	75.0	83	72.8	5	41.7	135	71.8
Priv-norel	2	7.1	0		8	7.0	0		10	5.3
Priv-rel .	3	10.7	6	18.3	19	16.8	7	58.3	35	18.6
Multiple .	2	7.1	2	6.3	4	3.5	0		8	4.3
Missing .	0		0		0		0		0	

TABLE 12.

Educational Level

Edlev	Laredo Funct. n=28		Laredo Grads n=29		Metro- Detroit n=113		Indiana- polis n=12		Total n=184	
	n	%	n	%	n	%	n	%	n	%
<hi.school .	1	3.6	0		6	5.2	1	8.3	8	4.3
H.S.diploma	2	7.1	4	12.5	14	12.3	2	16.7	23	12.5
Post hi tec	2	7.1	2	6.3	4	3.5	1	8.3	9	4.9
Some college	4	14.3	7	21.9	35	30.7	2	16.7	48	26.1
2 yr grad .	1	3.6	2	6.3	11	9.7	1	8.3	15	8.2
4 yr grad .	6	21.4	6	18.8	24	12.3	4	33.3	30	16.3
Grad sch . .	3	10.7	3	9.4	10	8.8	0		16	8.7
Grad degree	8	28.6	5	15.6	19	16.7	1	8.3	34	18.5
Missing . .	0		3		1		0		4	

III. BLS/METHOD VARIABLES

A. General Frequencies

The first SMC class was taught in 1966 in Amarillo, Texas. There were more than 60 people in that class and two of those were part of the Laredo functionaries group. The first class held outside of Texas was in 1969 and another two of the Laredo functionaries are from that class. Only 53 individuals (28.7%) took the BLS during the seventies decade. The majority of the sample (111 or 60.0%) have taken the BLS since 1980. This distribution is caused by the large number of people in the Detroit sub-group. In comparing the four individual groups a notable difference is found. Among both the Detroit and Indianapolis groups most of the people were relatively new graduates having taken the BLS since 1980 (84 or 75.7% and 7 or 58.3% respectively). Laredo grads were almost equally distributed with 11 (34.4%) from the 70s and 12 (37.5%) from the 80s. As would be expected, it is among the functionaries that one finds the reverse distribution. Here, thirteen individuals (46.4%) took the BLS during the 1970s and only six (21.4%) were from 1980 or later (see Table 13). One also sees from Table 13 that most of the sample (116 or 67%) have taken a graduate course(s).

Many of the remaining variables to be discussed are associated with open-ended questions. This does not affect

TABLE 13.

Courses

Year	Laredo Funct. n=28		Laredo Grads n=32		Metro- Detroit n=100		Indiana- polis n=11		Total n=173	
	n	%	n	%	n	%	n	%	n	%
70s . .	13	46.4	11	34.4	26	23.4	3	25.0	53	28.7
80s . .	6	21.4	12	37.5	84	75.4	7	58.3	111	60.0
Graduate										
No . . .	0		6	18.8	46	40.4	5	45.5	57	32.9
Yes . .	28	100	26	81.3	54	47.4	6	54.5	116	67.1
Missing	0		0		14		1		15	

the Laredo or Indianapolis groups but the size of the Metro-Detroit group changes from 114 to 19 (see Chapter 2).

Of prime importance in understanding the members of SMCI is their perceived motivation for taking the BLS and their impressions of the Method after they have completed the course. During the Intros and the first session of 101 (in the BLS classes I attended), the students were always asked why they were taking the course and what they intended to gain from it. An examination of Table 14 reveals that 25.8% of the people were attracted to SMC for multiple reasons (most of which are included in the other selections). For those who were attracted for only one reason, the two most popular were (1) the development of mind potential or psychic development (17 or 18.3%) and (2) gaining more control of one's self and one's life (11 or 11.8%). The trend holds true for each of the sub-groups.

TABLE 14.

Attraction to SMC

Reasons	Laredo Funct. n=28		Laredo Grads n=31		Metro-Detroit n=19		Indiana-polis n=11		Total n=93	
	n	%	n	%	n	%	n	%	n	%
Control .	3	10.7	3	9.7	4	21.1	0		11	11.8
Self-impr	1	3.6	4	12.9	0		2	9.1	6	6.5
Relax . .	0		1	3.2	0		2	18.2	3	3.2
Mind devel	5	17.9	6	19.4	5	26.3	1	9.1	17	18.3
Philosophy	2	7.1	4	12.9	1	5.3	1	9.1	8	8.6
Healing .	1	3.6	0		1	5.6	0		3	3.2
Multiple .	10	35.7	6	19.4	5	26.3	3	27.3	24	25.8
Friend . .	2	7.1	4	12.9	0		2	18.2	8	8.6
Other . .	4	14.3	2	6.5	2	10.5	1	9.1	9	9.7
Missing .	0		1		0		1		2	

Correspondingly, when asked what part of the BLS was most beneficial, 28% (24) felt they benefited from more than one aspect of the course while 16.5% (14) felt all of the course was beneficial. The other area many felt was beneficial was some aspect of 303 or 404--the parapsychological elements of the course (see Table 15).

When asked to evaluate the BLS, indicating what they did not like about the course, 36 people (38.7%) chose not to respond. Of those who did respond 23 (40.4%) indicated there was nothing they disliked about the course (see Table 16). Again, there were no major deviations in the sub-groups. Asked for their perception of weakspots in the

TABLE 15.

Beneficial Aspects of BLS

Area	Laredo Funct. n=26		Laredo Grads n=27		Metro-Detroit n=111		Indiana-polis n=12		Total n=185	
	n	%	n	%	n	%	n	%	n	%
All	4	15.4	6	22.2	1	6.3	1	8.3	14	16.5
101 and 202	1	3.8	3	11.1	2	12.5	1	8.3	7	8.2
303 and 404	3	11.5	2	7.4	4	25.0	2	16.7	11	12.9
Healing . .	1	3.8	1	3.7	1	6.3	0		3	3.5
Alpha use .	2	7.7	3	11.1	2	12.5	1	8.3	8	9.4
Multiple .	15	57.7	6	22.2	0		3	25.0	24	28.2
Spiritual .	0		1	3.7	0		0		1	1.2
Other . . .	0		3	11.1	4	25.0	3	25.0	10	11.8
A technique	0		2	7.4	0		1	8.3	2	2.4
+ thinking	0		0		2	12.5	0		2	2.4
Missing . .	2		5		3		0		8	

Method, 17 (18.3%) chose not to respond. Of those who did, 31 (40.8%) indicated no weak areas in the Method. Among the functionaries, this response accounted for 16 (64%) of the individuals. One-third of the Detroit group chose not to respond. This may be due to the fact that so many in this group were new graduates and perhaps felt unqualified to criticize . Those that did respond were unsure about what they did not like. Hence, 7 (53.8%) were in the catch-all category of other (see Table 16).

The attempt to understand how the graduates viewed Mind Control and the beliefs that underlie it are summarized in Table 17[5]. A scan reveals that 37.7% (32) of the respondents in the study viewed Mind Control primarily as a means of developing their inner potential, including their

TABLE 16.

BLS Evaluation

Area	Laredo Funct. n=18		Laredo Grads n=18		Metro-Detroit n=11		Indiana-polis n=9		Total n=57	
	n	%	n	%	n	%	n	%	n	%
Follow-up . .	0		1	5.6	0		1	11.1	2	3.5
A technique .	3	16.7	1	5.6	0		0		4	7.0
Other	5	27.8	4	22.2	0		3	33.3	12	21.1
Nothing . . .	10	55.6	8	44.4	0		5	53.6	23	40.4
Time	0		0		9	69.2	0		9	15.8
Too long . .	0		3	16.7	1	7.7	0		5	8.8
Group atms .	0		1	5.6	0		0		1	1.7
Knew material	0		0		1	7.7	0		1	1.7
Missing . . .	10		14		9		3		36	
Weakspot . .	25		24		13		10		76	
Yes	0		1	4.2	2	15.4	0		3	4.0
No	16	64.0	8	33.3	2	15.4	4	40.0	31	40.8
Amt material	0		0		1	7.7	0		1	1.3
Lack practice	1	4.0	2	8.2	0		0		3	4.0
Lack support	1	4.0	3	12.5	1	7.7	0		5	6.6
Other	5	20.0	8	33.3	7	53.8	5	50.0	26	43.2
Teaching . .	2	8.0	1	4.2	0		1	10.0	4	5.3
Missing . . .	3		8		6		2		17	

psychic ability. This is true for both the Laredo grads and
the Detroit group with 9 (36%) and 12 (66.4%) respectively
choosing that response. Among the functionaries, the
responses were equally distributed between "other" and
"development of potential" (9 or 34.6% and 8 or 30.8%
respectively). A few examples of the responses in that
"other" category are: meditation; coordinating the physical,

the mental and the spiritual; centering; and realizing that we are all gods.

When asked what they perceived as the underlying beliefs of SMC, 20 (25%) responded with some variation of the idea "whatever the mind can conceive, it can achieve" (see Table 17). Eleven (13.8%) maintained SMC is based on the belief that everyone has both the responsibility and ability to control themselves and their lives. Thirteen percent also gave multiple ideas upon which they believe SMC is based--most of which are included in the other responses. A large group of responses (25%) had to be classified as "other". These responses included such ideas as using the universal power, helping others, using one's intuition, and that we are all part of the "one". I think the inability to categorize 25% of the functionaries' responses to these two variables reflects the fact that by teaching the course these individuals have given more thought to these subjects and hence, are not as likely to give standard responses.

Table 18 displays the graduates attitude toward Jose Silva'. When asked to give their thoughts about Jose Silva, 41 (48.2%) wrote positive statements such as the following:

> Jose Silva is a 'little big man' who has graced the earth with his presence and shares his genius and love with those of us who were 'lucky enough' to be 'earth bond' during his lifetime. I view him as the Jesus Christ of my lifetime.

> I view Jose Silva as one of the prime movers who will be known to have assisted the human race in moving into and through our next phase of human evolution--the new age of consciousness.

TABLE 17.

Perception of SMC

Perception	Laredo Funct. n=26		Laredo Grads n=25		Metro- Detroit n=18		Indiana- polis n=12		Total n=85	
	n	%	n	%	n	%	n	%	n	%
Whatsit .										
Potential	8	30.8	9	36.0	12	66.4	3	25.0	32	37.7
Love . . .	0		1	4.0	0		0		1	1.2
Self-disc	1	3.8	2	8.0	0		1	8.3	4	4.7
Control .	1	3.8	7	28.0	4	22.2	0		12	14.2
Helping .	3	11.5	2	8.0	0		2	16.7	7	8.2
Other . .	9	34.6	2	8.0	2	11.1	3	25.0	16	18.2
Multiple .	3	11.5	1	4.0	0		1	8.3	6	7.1
Prob solv	0		1	4.0	0		0		1	1.2
Self-impr	1	3.8	0		0		2	8.3	3	3.5
Missing .	2		7		1		0		8	
Underbels	25		23		16		12		80	
Control .	2	8.0	5	21.7	4	25.0	0		11	13.8
Love . . .	0		5	21.7	0		1	8.3	7	8.6
Alpha . .	0		2	8.7	0		0		2	2.5
God w/in .	2	8.0	1	4.3	0		0		3	3.6
Christian	0		2	8.7	0		1	8.3	3	3.6
Multiple .	4	16.0	5	21.7	0		1	8.3	11	13.6
Other . .	10	40.0	0		7	43.8	3	25.0	20	25.0
Tht to act	7	28.0	3	13.0	5	31.3	5	41.7	20	25.0
Missing .	13		9		3		0		13	

I think he is a great man, destined to be the most important and influential personality of this century.

I love him.

I trust him.

The "other" category was also numerous for each of the sub-groups.

The only additional category worth noting is from the Metro-Detroit sub-group. Four individuals (25%) were dissatisfied with Silva. They were dissatisfied with his presentation of self, his style of writing, or his presentation of the material.

TABLE 18.

Thoughts About Silva

Silthts	Laredo Funct. n=27		Laredo Grads n=30		Metro- Detroit n=16		Indiana- polis n=12		Total n=85	
	n	%	n	%	n	%	n	%	n	%
Positive . .	8	59.6	17	58.6	12	75.1	4	33.3	41	48.2
Love humanity	1	3.7	1	3.4	0		2	16.7	4	4.7
Other	18	66.7	11	37.9	0		6	50.0	37	12.9
Negative . .	0		0		4	25.0	0		4	4.7
Missing . . .	1		2		3		0		6	

B. Relationships Amongst Variables

In an attempt to determine influence among variables, crosstabulations were done comparing the reason the individual was attracted to SMC(smcreas), the underlying beliefs (underbels), and what the people think SMC is all about (whatsit). An examination of the data reveals no significant clustering in any of the cells of the tabulation comparing smcreas and underbels (see Appendix 9 for all crosstabulations--"x-tab"). Responses were scattered throughout the cells. The only cell worth noting was of those females attracted to SMC for multiple reasons, five (55.6%) indicated the basic belief which underlies SMC is the power of the mind to achieve whatever it desires (x-Tab 1). In comparing smcreas and whatsit, again there was no clustering. In a comparison of whatsit and underbels no strong relationship was found. The only statistics worth noting are those females who believed SMC is about developing one's potential. Here, 5 (35.7%) felt the underlying belief of SMC was the mind achieving what it desires. Another 5 maintained SMC is based on multiple beliefs. The male responses showed no clustering (x-Tab 2).

Due to the nature of the data, statistics for the crosstabulations were limited to chi square, phi, contingency coefficient, lamda, and uncertainty coefficient. The level of significance for chi square values of each of the crosstabulations was markedly greater than .05. This would seem to indicate that the variables tested were not independent.

IV. IDEOLOGICAL ORIENTATION

A. General Frequencies

Silva Mind Control International teaches a method not an ideology. Nonetheless, there are implicit beliefs which cut through the BLS and the Method itself. This section will examine the religious background and present ideological orientation of the respondents in this study.

An examination of Table 19 reveals definite changes in religion between the individual's family of orientation and the individual's present preference. Seventy-three individuals (40.1%) were raised as Roman Catholics but only 47 (27.6%) still identified themselves as such. The Protestant category' also showed a sharp decrease in religious activity going from 69 active practitioners (37.9%) to 20 (11.8%). Among the sub-groups, the Detroit population has on interesting characteristic. Fifteen (13.2%) were raised atheist. When one looks at present religious orientation, the "other" category demands attention. Of all the responses listed', "Unity" was by far the popular religious orientation. Of the 29 respondents in this category from Metro-Detroit, 12 (41.3%) belonged to Unity. Among the two Laredo sub-groups, 15 of the 28 (53.6%) identified with Unity. This gives a total of 43.5% of the 62 respondents in this category who identified themselves as belonging to Unity.

Informants told me, Unity has many beliefs which are similar to the underlying ideology of SMC. For example, self-responsibility and control and metaphysical (psychic) beliefs are part of both. Although many of those with whom I spoke were dissatisfied with their previous religions, Unity itself is bi-religious. One does not have to abandon a previous religious relief system to belong to Unity. For Silva graduates, Unity may provide the "church atmosphere"--

TABLE 19.

Religious Orientation

Orientation	Laredo Funct. n=26		Laredo Grads n=28		Metro- Detroit n=114		Indiana- polis n=12		Total n=182	
	n	%	n	%	n	%	n	%	n	%
Past rel .										
Roman Cath	8	28.6	8	25.0	47	41.2	9	75.0	73	40.1
Protestant	15	53.6	16	50.0	35	31.6	2	16.7	69	37.9
Other ..	1	3.6	2	6.3	5	4.4	0		9	4.9
Atheist .	0		0		15	13.2	0		15	8.2
Jewish ..	0		2	6.3	6	5.2	0		8	4.4
East Orth	1	3.6	0		1	.8	0		4	2.2
Multiple .	1	3.6	0		0		0		1	.5
Islam ..	0		0		2	1.7	0		2	1.1
East Phil	0		0		0		1	8.3	1	.5
Missing .	2		4		0		0		6	
Pres rel .	25		29		101		12		170	
Roman Cath	2	7.1	5	17.2	33	29.0	7	58.3	47	27.6
Protestant	6	21.4	6	20.7	7	6.1	1	8.3	20	11.8
Other ..	13	46.4	15	51.7	29	25.4	3	25.0	62	36.5
Atheist .	0		0		7	6.1	0		7	4.1
Jewish ..	0		1	3.4	6	5.2	0		7	4.1
East Orth	0		0		10	8.8	0		10	5.9
Multiple .	1	3.6	0		1	.8	0		2	1.2
East Phil	1	3.6	1	3.4	2	1.7	0		4	2.4
Humanist .	2	7.1	1	3.4	6	5.2	1	8.3	10	5.9
Missing .	3		0		13		0		18	

and fulfill the social and individual functions of a church which SMCI does not.

As would be expected from the Church identification of the majority of the group, 62% have been to church for

worship services in the last year. Of those, 42% (79)
attended services at least once a month (see Table 20).

TABLE 20.

Church Attendance

	Laredo Funct. n=28		Laredo Grads n=32		Metro- Detroit n=114		Indiana- polis n=12		Total n=188	
Within Year	n	%	n	%	n	%	n	%	n	%
Yes . . .	19	67.9	21	65.6	63	55.3	12	100	117	62.2
No . . .	9	32.1	11	34.4	51	44.7	0		71	37.8
Frequency										
Daily . .	0		1	3.1	3	2.6	4	33.3	8	4.3
Weekly .	6	21.4	10	31.3	32	28.0	5	41.7	55	29.6
1/mth . .	2	7.1	4	12.5	15	13.2	3	25.0	24	12.8
1-3/yr .	10	35.7	5	15.6	16	14.0	0		31	16.5
<1/yr . .	1	3.6	2	6.3	3	2.6	0		6	3.2
Missing .	0		0		0		0		0	

Because SMC is primarily a method (rather than an
ideology) it appeals to those of many different religious
backgrounds. This universal appeal is a factor of success
for SMCI, as is reflected in the fact that 68.2% (60) of the
whole group experienced no conflict between their religious
belief system and SMC or the Method (see Table 21). In
fact, 22.7% (20) maintained SMC enhanced or clarified what
they believed. Among the Laredo functionairies, 10.7% felt
SMC was better than their previous religion. But 21% (4) of

the Metro-Detroit group suggested SMC conflicted with traditional Christian beliefs.'

TABLE 21.

Religious Conflict

Experience	Laredo Funct. n=28		Laredo Grads n=29		Metro-Detroit n=19		Indiana-polis n=12		Total n=90	
	n	%	n	%	n	%	n	%	n	%
Yes	0		1	3.4	0		0		1	1.1
No	18	69.2	19	65.5	13	68.4	9	75.0	60	68.2
Enhanced . .	7	26.9	8	27.6	2	10.5	2	16.7	20	22.7
conflict w/ P	0		0		4	21.1	0		4	4.4
SMC better .	3	10.7	1	3.4	0		0		4	4.4
Missing . . .	0		3		0		0		4	

Correspondingly, when asked if their religious beliefs had changed as a result of SMC, 27 people (31%) said no, but 28 (32.2%) said their beliefs had been enhanced. The same response rates were found in each of the sub-groups, as is shown in Table 22.

An attempt was made to gain a broader understanding of the ideological orientation (world view or fundamental and important ideas about the nature of the world and reality) of the respondents. In so doing, I asked questions about god, reincarnation and psychic phenomena. Table 23 shows the response rates for the participants' perception of "god". As an examination reveals, only 8 people (9.3%) held traditional Christian beliefs. Thirty-one (36%) viewed god as a principle or energy which exists within everyone and

TABLE 22.

Changed Religious Beliefs

Change	Laredo Funct. n=26		Laredo Grads n=28		Metro-Detroit n=18		Indiana-polis n=12		Total n=87	
	n	%	n	%	n	%	n	%	n	%
Yes	3	11.5	0		3	16.7	1	9.1	8	9.2
No	8	30.8	7	25.0	10	55.6	2	18.2	27	31.0
Idea of god	5	19.2	3	10.7	0		0		8	9.2
Enhanced . .	7	26.0	11	39.3	5	27.8	5	45.5	28	32.0
Rel affil .	0		1	3.6	0		1	9.1	1	1.2
Spirituality	3	11.5	3	10.7	0		0		7	8.1
Explain . .	0		3	10.7	0		2	18.2	6	6.9
Missing . .	2		4		1		1		6	

everything. Fifteen individuals (17.4%) believed god is higher intelligence. All of the sub-groups showed little deviation from these ratios. Both of these responses (god is a higher intelligence existing within everything) are part of the ideology presented in the SMC courses. It would appear that either the graduates have accepted that ideology or have stayed with Mind Control because SMC presents what. they independently believed.

Psychic ability is an important element of SMC. Table 24 shows the respondents interest in parapsychology. The vast majority (151 or 89%) were interested in or believed in psychic events. Thirty-four percent (51) had been interested for life while 52% had been interested from 1 to 64 years. The average length of time interested in psychic phenomena was 14.2 years.

TABLE 23.

Idea of God

Ideas	Laredo Funct. n=28		Laredo Grads n=27		Metro-Detroit n=19		Indiana-polis n=12		Total n=88	
	n	%	n	%	n	%	n	%	n	%
In all . .	11	39.3	11	40.7	4	22.2	5	45.5	31	36.0
Hier intell	3	10.7	5	18.5	7	38.9	0		15	17.4
Christian .	2	7.1	3	11.1	1	5.6	2	18.2	8	9.3
Yes	0		2	7.4	0		0		2	2.3
Other . . .	12	42.9	6	22.2	5	27.8	4	36.4	29	33.7
Multiple .	0		0		1	5.6	0		1	1.2
Missing . .	0		5		0		0		5	

Although SMC claims to teach everyone who takes the course to be a working psychic, only 82 people (46.1%) had never used the services of a psychic. Of those who had, the average frequency was 4.8 times per year (see Table 24).

Even though discussions of reincarnation are not part of the BLS, SMCI has done research in the area. This research, some of which was conducted with Silva's children, is presented in the graduate courses. In fact, one of the graduate techniques learned is age regression which supposedly can take a person to a past life. Given the religious orientation of most of the group and the fact that, traditionally, Western religions do no believe in reincarnation, it was somewhat surprising to find that only 9 people (10%) definitely did not believe in reincarnaticn. Rather, 57 (63.3%) did believe and 21 (23.3%) were undecided about the issue (see Table 25).

TABLE 24.

Parapsychology

ESP	Laredo Funct. n=27		Laredo Grads n=26		Metro- Detroit n=111		Indiana- polis n=12		Total n=168	
	n	%	n	%	n	%	n	%	n	%
Interest										
Yes	27	100	26	100	86	77	12	100	151	89.1
No	0		0		25	19.5	0		25	14.8
Missing	1		6		15		0		17	
Time										
Range- yrs	1-52		1-40		1-64		1-11		1-64	52.8
Life	10		12		25		6		51	34.3
None	0		0		20		0		22	13.1
Mean-yrs	20.9		13.5		14.5		7.3		14.2	
Use of Psychic	25		30		110		11		178	
No	8	32.0	13	43.3	57	51.8	4	36.4	82	46.1
Yes	17	68.0	17	56.7	53	48.1	7	63.6	96	53.9
Missing	3		2		4		1		10	
Freq.										
Range- x/yr	1-52		1-50		1-20		1-7		1-52	
Daily	0		1		1		0		3	
Never	12	7.1	19	59.4	54	29.3	0		85	
mean-yrs	7.2		9.1		3.5		3.2		4.8	

TABLE 25.

Reincarnation

Reincarnation	Laredo Funct. n=28		Laredo Grads n=28		Metro- Detroit n=19		Indiana- polis n=12		Total n=92	
	n	%	n	%	n	%	n	%	n	%
Yes . . .	18	64.3	16	55.2	13	68.4	8	66.7	57	63.3
No . . .	1	3.6	3	10.3	4	21.1	1	8.3	9	10.0
Explain .	0		2	6.9	0		1	8.3	3	3.3
Undecided	9	32.1	8	27.6	2	10.5	2	16.7	21	23.3
Missing .	0		3		0		0		3	

B. Relationships Amongst Variables

In an attempt to determine independence (or lack of it) amongst the ideological variables, crosstabulations were done on selected variables, controlling for sex (see Appendix 9 for the x-tabs). The data reveal that females attracted to SMC for multiple reasons were more likely (43.8%) to have ideas about god that did not fit into one of the major categories (x-Tab 3). Males, who were just as likely to be attracted for multiple reasons (26.7% vs 27.3%), were equally divided in their ideas about god. Fourteen percent believed god exists within all and 14% had ideas difficult to categorize (x-Tab 3).

A comparison of the respondents' perception of the underlying beliefs of SMC and their perception of god, reveals that 40% of the females believed god exists within all and of those, 56% hold multiple or other ideas upon which they believe SMC is based (x-Tab 4). Forty-two percent of the males also believed god exists within all but their underlying beliefs about SMC did not cluster. The majority of both sexes believed in reincarnation (63.4% of females and 55% of males). Of these females, 30.8% (19.5% of the total) held views about SMC that were uncategorizable (x-Tab 5). Likewise, both sexes were interested in parapsychological events (100% both) while 66.7% of the females and 57.9% of the males had used a psychic (x-Tab 6). Sixty-three percent of the females and 73.7% of the males experienced no conflict between SMC and their religious orientation. Of these females, 34.6% maintained that SMC was based on the belief that thought results in action and, desire brings achievement theme.

Crosstabulating ideas about god with select variables reveals that regardless of the particular personal idea about god, the majority of both females and males (77.8% and 65.2%) had attended church services within the last year (x-Tab 7). Females were more likely to attend church weekly and believe god exists within everyone and everything (13.3%) or have uncatoregorizable ideas about god—13.3% (x-Tab 8). Most of the population believed in reincarnation (63.6% of females and 59.1% of males). Of these, 20.5% of the females and 31.8% of the males also believed that god exists in all (x-Tab 9). One also sees that those who held this belief were more likely to use a psychic (26.8% of females, 33.3% of males)—x-Tab 10. In comparing use of a psychic within sex categories, the data reveal that 68.3% of the women had used a psychic, while 31.7% had never done so. The difference was not as marked among the men with 57.1% indicating they had used a psychic and 42.9% maintaining they never had.

V. DEGREE OF INVOLVEMENT

One point of primary interest in this study is the degree of involvement with the Method, the philosophy, and the activities of SMC displayed by the graduates. To ascertain the degree of involvement, questions were designed to uncover the areas of life in which SMC had been most influential. These "way of life" variables, although by no means definitive, deal with changes resulting from contact with SMC and give some indication of the degree of commitment to the Method.

A. General Frequencies

SMC maintains that the Silva Method is a technique that can be applied to any area of life--business, social, personal. To learn to what degree graduates accepted this, respondents were asked the following question, "Do you consider Silva Mind Control a 'way of life' in that you incorporate the Silva Method and beliefs into your daily activities and interactions with others? Or, is Silva Mind Control a technique that you use only for specific purpose such as solving a problem or controlling a habit?" Table 26

shows the response to this question. Sixty-four people
(74.8%) viewed SMC as a way of life and only 15 (17.4%)
stated they used it as a technique for problem solving.
Seven (8.0%) viewed it as both a way of life and a
technique. The "way of life" response was in the 70th or
80th percentile for three of the sub-groups. In the fourth,
the Metro-Detroit follow-up, only 11 (59.7%) responded this
way, while 6 (31.6%) viewed it as a technique.

TABLE 26.

Perception

Percp	Laredo Funct. n=26		Laredo Grads n=29		Metro-Detroit n=18		Indiana-polis n=11		Total n=86	
	n	%	n	%	n	%	n	%	n	%
Way of life	22	84.6	22	75.9	11	59.0	8	72.7	64	74.8
Technique .	2	7.7	4	13.8	6	31.0	3	27.3	15	17.4
Both . . .	2	7.7	3	10.3	1	5.0	0		7	8.0
Missing . .	2		3		1		1		7	

To see if this stated perception held true in other
areas, changes in reading habits, religion and life (as a
result of SMC) were also queried. Table 27 is a summation
of the responses. When asked if their reading habits had
changed as a result of taking the BLS or, if their reading
had lead them to SMC, 37 respondents (42.1%) indicated the
BLS had changed their reading habits. Of the Laredo
functionairies, 15 (57.7%) felt SMC had changed their
reading habits. Seventeen (19.3%) suggested their reading

lead them to SMC and 25 (28.4%) saw no relationship between the two. Among the Detroit population, however, 10 (55.6%) saw no relationship. When asked if their religious beliefs had changed as a result of the BLS, 27 (31%) felt their beliefs were the same as before the BLS while 8 (9.2%) believed they had changed. Twenty-eight people (32.2%), however, felt their religious beliefs were enhanced by SMC. In response to the question concerning changes in their lives because of SMC, 86 people (48.4%) indicated their lives had changed for the better because of SMC. They maintained they had become more relaxed, more understanding, more responsible for themselves, or more productive because of taking the BLS. Only 3 graduates (3.3%) felt their lives had not changed.

One would expect that if SMC had become a "way of life" for the graduates that this would be expressed in their use of the Method. Table 28 shows the programming frequency of the respondents. Ninety-nine (55%) had continued with programming --using the Method--while 78 (43.1%) had not. When asked how frequently they programmed, 108 graduates (66.7%) said daily (or up to 3 times daily).

The degree to which the graduates believe in the Method is partially reflected in whether they have involved their children in SMC. Table 29 indicates the number of graduates with children who have taught their child the Method and the type of course, if any, the child took. One hundred and seven graduates had children; of those, 41

TABLE 27.

Changes Due To BLS

	Laredo Funct. n=26		Laredo Grads n=29		Metro- Detroit n=18		Indiana- polis n=11		Total n=85	
	n	%	n	%	n	%	n	%	n	%
Reading										
SMC rdg	15	57.7	11	39.3	4	22.2	5	45.5	37	43.5
No . . .	5	19.2	7	25.0	10	55.6	3	27.3	27	29.4
Rdg SMC	6	23.1	7	25.0	2	11.1	2	18.2	17	20.0
Other .	0		3	10.8	2	11.1	1	9.1	6	7.1
Missing	2		3		1		1		6	
Religion			28						87	
Yes . .	3	11.5	0		3	16.7	1	9.1	8	9.2
No . . .	8	30.8	7	25.0	10	55.6	2	18.2	27	31.0
Enhanced	7	26.9	11	39.3	5	27.8	5	45.5	28	32.2
Other .	8	30.8	10	35.7	0		3	27.3	22	25.4
Missing	2		4		1		1		6	
Life . .	27				19		12		91	
Yes . .	12	44.4	11	37.9	17	89.5	2	16.7	86	96.6
No . . .	1	3.7	1	3.4	1	5.3	0		3	3.3
Missing	1		3		0		0		4	

(38.3%) had taught their children the Method but 58 (54.2%) had not. Some of these grads, however, indicated their children were too young to teach. Of those who had children, 10 (9.6%) indicated their children had taken a SMC course, 8 indicated their child had taken the Childrens' Course, and 30 (28.9%) said their children had taken the

TABLE 28.

Programming

	Laredo Funct. n=28		Laredo Grads n=32		Metro- Detroit n=106		Indiana- polis n=12		Total n=180	
	n	%	n	%	n	%	n	%	n	%
Cont'd .										
Yes . .	28	100	31	96.9	26	22.9	12	100	99	55.0
No . . .	0		1	3.1	77	67.5	0		78	43.3
Just fin	0		0		3	2.6	0		3	1.7
Missing	0		0		8		0		8	
Freq . .	27		31		88		12		162	
Daily .	25	92.6	23	74.2	51	58.0	9	75.0	108	66.7
2 x/wk .	1	3.7	3	9.7	6	6.8	0		10	6.2
1 x/wk .	0		0		3	3.4	0		3	1.9
1-2/mth	0		0		6	6.8	0		6	3.7
<1/mth .	0		0		1	1.1	0		1	.6
Irreg .	1	3.7	4	12.9	12	12.6	3	25.0	18	11.1
Other .	0		1	3.2	5	5.7	0		6	3.8
Missing	1		1		1		0		5	

BLS. Fifty-six (53.9%) said their children had not taken a SMC course.

SMC maintains it is not an alternative to conventional medical care. At various times throughout the BLS, students are instructed to consult with a physician and warned against diagnosing and treating a person. In addition to the legal necessity of such statements, the phrases also reflect the attitude that the Method is a supplement to Western medicine. The majority of the graduates apparently

TABLE 29.

Children and the Method

Invol	Laredo Funct. n=19 n	%	Laredo Grads n=20 n	%	Metro-Detroit n=60 n	%	Indiana-polis n=6 n	%	Total n=107 n	%
Tautchld										
Yes . .	13	68.4	8	40.0	18	30.0	2	33.3	41	38.3
No . . .	6	31.5	12	60.0	36	60.0	4	66.6	58	54.2
Just fin	0		0		6	10.0	0		6	5.6
Course .			18		61				104	
Yes . .	1	3.6	2	7.4	6	9.8	1	16.7	10	9.6
No . . .	5	17.9	5	18.5	42	68.9	4	66.7	56	53.9
Chldcrs	2	7.1	2	7.4	4	6.5	0		8	7.7
BLS . .	11	39.3	9	33.3	9	14.8	1	16.7	30	28.9

agree. Fifty-one (56.7%) viewed SMC and Western medicine as being complimentary to each other. Twelve (13.3%) saw no relationship but 13 (14.4%) viewed SMC as better (see Table 30).

Some parts of the questionnaires were designed to discover if participation in SMC was part of a "joiner" life pattern for the respondents. Table 31 is a summary of the data. One hundred and fourteen people (64.0%) had taken other self-help, personal growth, hypnosis, or memory courses. Sixty-four (36%) had not taken any related courses. Ninety-five graduates (54.3%) belonged to other formal organizations besides SMC, while 80 (45.7%) did not.

TABLE 30.

SMC and Medicine

View	Laredo Funct. n=28		Laredo Grads n=32		Metro- Detroit n=16		Indiana- polis n=12		Total n=90	
	n	%	n	%	n	%	n	%	n	%
Compl . .	20	71.4	17	63.0	8	50.0	4	33.3	51	56.7
SMC bet'r	2	7.1	5	18.5	3	18.8	3	25.0	13	14.4
No relshp	3	10.7	4	14.8	3	18.8	2	16.7	12	13.3
Undec'd .	0		1	3.7	0		0		1	1.1
Other . .	3	10.7	5	18.5	0		3	25.0	11	12.2
Contra .	0		0		2	12.5	0		2	2.2
Missing .	0		0		3		0		3	

Most people (41 or 38.3%) belonged to more than one organization. The most frequently listed groups in the "other" category were professional organizations. The Laredo groups were more likely to belong to more than one organization while the Detroit group was more likely to fall into the other category. As would be expected, 50% of the Indianapolis population belonged to a religious organization.

B. Relationships Amongst Variables

The crosstabulations for the "way of life" variables are found in Appendix 9. Those females who perceived SMC as a way of life were just as likely to teach their children the Method as not. Thirteen (38.2%) had taught their children while 12 (35.3%) had not. Males, on the other

TABLE 31.

Other Organizations

	Laredo Funct. n=27		Laredo Grads n=31		Metro- Detroit n=107		Indiana- polis n=11		Total n=178	
	n	%	n	%	n	%	n	%	n	%
Courses .										
No . . .	7	25.9	12	38.7	42	39.3	2	18.2	64	36.0
Yes . . .	20	74.1	19	61.3	65	60.7	9	81.8	114	64.0
Missing .	1		1		7		1		10	
Membshp .	25		27		111		10		175	
Yes . . .	15	60.0	16	59.3	55	48.3	7	70.0	95	54.3
No . . .	10	40.0	11	40.7	56	42.1	3	30.0	80	45.7
Missing .	3		5		2		2		12	
Type . .	16		18		56		8		100	
Healing .	1	6.3	2	11.1	4	7.1	0		7	7.0
Psychic .	0		0		2	3.6	0		2	2.0
Self-help	1	6.3	0		5	8.9	1	12.5	8	8.0
Relig . .	1	6.3	0		3	5.4	4	50.0	8	8.0
Other . .	2	12.5	6	33.3	26	46.4	0		34	34.0
Multiple	11	68.8	10	55.6	16	28.6	3	37.5	41	41.0

hand, were more likely to have taught their children the Method if they viewed SMC as a way of life--8 or 42.1% vs 5 or 26.3%--(see x-Tab 11). Females whose children had taken a SMC course were more likely to have had them take the BLS (13 or 40.6%) if they viewed SMC as a way of life (which 78% did). Males were just as likely to have children who had not taken a course as had taken the BLS (4 or 21.1% vs 5 or

26.3%) if they viewed SMC as a way of life (which 72.2% did)(see x-Tab 12).

In comparing perception of SMC and reading habits, females who saw SMC as a way of life were most likely to have had their reading habits change as a result of contact with SMC (21 or 21.8%). Males with the same perception, on the other hand, were just as likely to say their reading led them to SMC as vice versa--6 or 31.6% for both selections (see x-Tab 13). A comparison of life changes and perception (x-Tab 14) shows that 25 females (56.8%) viewed SMC as a way of life and felt their lives had changed in a positive way because of it; twelve males (50%) felt similarly. As would be expected, viewing SMC as a way of life was related to changed religious attitudes for females (x-Tab 15). Ten (29.4%) had their beliefs enhanced and 6 (17.6%) had their idea of god changed. Only 8 (23.5%) experienced no change in their religious belief system. Males with that perspective were most likely to say SMC had enhanced their religious attitudes (8 or 42.1%).

Looking at the relationship between the respondents' perception of SMC and their opinion of the relationship between SMC and medicine, 51.2% of the females viewed SMC as a way of life with the Method and medicine being complimentary. Among the males, 45% held similar views (see x-Tab 16).

As would be expected, those who viewed SMC as a way of life were more likely to engage in activities offered by SMC (x-Tab 17). Sixty-six percent of the females (20 individuals) and 50% of the males (9) in that category engaged in five or more SMC activities.

Finally, in comparing perception with the respondents' idea of what SMC is all about, one finds that 12 (27.9%) of the females viewed SMC as a means to develop the potential of their minds and practiced it as a way of life. Only 4 (21.6%) of the males were in this category. The males were more likely to practice SMC as a way of life but held various ideas about what it is all about (x-Tab 18).

VI. CONCLUSIONS/PROFILE

A close examination of the data reveals that the typical person attracted to Silva Mind Control exhibits characteristics no different from the majority of the general population. The only distinguishing feature is that the Silva groups are somewhat older than the U. S. average of 30.3 years. This section will present a profile of the typical SMC graduate based only upon the data of this study.

The average graduate of the Basic Lecture Series is a white female in her early forties. She is a relatively new graduate, having taken the BLS since 1980--unless she is a lecturer, in which case she took the BLS during the 70s. There was no one primary reason for her taking the course; rather, she was attracted to SMC for multiple reasons. Likewise, she benefited in more than one way from what she learned in the course. In thinking back over the course, there was nothing she was dissatisfied with nor would she change anything. When asked by her friends to describe Silva Mind Control, she tells them it is a means to develop the full potential of their minds, including their innate psychic abilities. The method to do this, (developed by José Silva--for whom she has only warm, positive thoughts) is based on the belief that the mind is capable of achieving anything it truly desires. Married with three children, she is employed and earns between $20,000 and $30,000 per year. She received the majority of her education in the public school system and has had at least some college; she probably holds an undergraduate degree. Although associated with SMC for only a few years, she has, nonetheless, continued with daily use of the Method. In addition to the BLS, she has taken some other self-help, hypnosis or meditation courses and is a member of some other group or formal organization. If she is from Metro-Detroit, it is probably a professional organization.

Ideologically, she was raised a Roman Catholic. Today she is just as likely to still have that religious orientation as to no longer identify with that Church. If she is still a practicing Catholic, she attends Mass weekly. If she no longer identifies herself as such, she probably finds the beliefs of Unity more in line with her thinking. In either case, she experienced no conflict between her past religious beliefs and what was presented to her during the BLS. In fact, her religious beliefs were likely to have been enhanced because of the course. Although raised in a Christian tradition, she views god as a principle or energy that exists in everyone and everything. Although raised in a Western tradition, she believes in reincarnation. And, although she may not speak freely of the idea, she believes in parapsychological events. In fact, she has even used the services of a psychic a few times.

What she has learned in the BLS fits so nicely into her belief system that she views the Silva Method as her way of life. Because of the course, her reading habits have changed to include more on self-development, positive thinking, and the parapsychological. She believes that life has changed for the better due to the BLS. She feels more relaxed, more in control, and more responsive to those around her. Because of the control over her own health and well being she acquired from the BLS, she no longer feels so dependent upon the medical profession and views the two systems as complementary--each addressing the needs the other does not. Interestingly, even with the degree of involvement she has with the Method, she probably has not taught her children the Method nor have they taken a Silva course.

Using these data, one finds nothing exceptional, nothing extraordinary, nothing distinguishing about the individuals attracted to Silva Mind Control. Unlike what would be expected for a group with a belief system that is relatively uncommon, the people who are a part of it are

very common. What sets them apart as a   group   are
qualitative   characteristics: their   openness;   their
friendliness; their willingness to help.

ENDNOTES

¹ The two case discrepancy between the total number and the sum of the four sub-groups is due to the difficulty of including those two in any of the four sub-groups.

² Two of the five, however, were from foreign countries which would have required two translations before I could analyze the data (i.e. Brazil and Germany).

³ These categories refer to the type of school in which the individual received the majority of their education. "Priv-norel" is a private, secular school. "Priv-rel" is a private school with a religious orientation. "Multiple" means the respondent believed her/his education was equally divided between the two categories.

⁴ The educational level responses represent the highest level attained by the respondent.

⁵ "Whatsit" refers to what the respondents believe SMC is all about. "Underbels" refers to the respondents perception of the underlying beliefs of SMC.

⁶ "Silthts" refers to the respondents thoughts about Silva.

⁷ The Pro testant category included the following responses: Presbyterian, Methodist, Episcopalian, Lutheran, Non-denominational, Baptist, ALC, Christian Scientist, Mormon, Pentecostal, Congregationalist, and Fundamentalist.

⁸ The responses in the 'other' category included the following: Quakers, Universal, Agnostic, New Thought, Science of Mind, Western Pagan, and the philosophy of SMC.

⁹ The only exception appears to be some in the "born-again" movement. According to Jose Silva, it is from this group that most of the opposition to SMC has come. They maintain SMC is doing the work of the devil and corrupting the souls of the members.

CHAPTER SEVEN

SUMMARY AND CONCLUSIONS

I. SUMMARY

This study has presented a description of Silva Mind Control International. The focus has been on the structure of the organization, the courses of instruction, and the lecturers and students of the Silva Method.

Silva Mind Control International is a parapsychological, self-help organization which claims to use meditation, self-hypnosis, and guided fantasy in order to achieve relaxation, personal growth, altered states of consciousness, and psychic functioning. The Silva Method of self-mind control is based on the assumption that the brain functions most effectively, for certain tasks, when it is at a brain wave frequency of ten cycles/second. It is also at this frequency, according to José Silva, that the body's immune system is activated and health is improved. Based on this, the Silva Method is designed to train the individual to enter ten cycles/second at will.

The Silva Method is taught in a forty hour course known as the Basic Lecture Series. The lecturers are independent contractors who pay royalties to SMCI by purchasing their necessary BLS kits from the organization.

Although the price for these kits is fixed, the lecturer is free to charge whatever s/he chooses for the BLS course. The Silva Method is copyrighted and during the BLS, must be presented just as it appears in the manuals. The style of presentation, the approach taken and the content of the lectures are determined by each lecturer. In addition to these independent lecturers, there are also regional directors and SMCI Center directors. These directors have other SMC lecturers who work with them in teaching the BLS in their area.

In the span of eighteen years, Silva Mind Control has grown from a local, one-man business to an international, multi-million dollar enterprise. Today, the BLS is taught by 150 lecturers in 61 countries and 14 languages. The International Headquarters is located in Laredo, Texas--the site of the original research which led to the development of the Silva Method. It is from here that SMCI oversees all international affairs, services the Laredo area, and conducts research. It is also here that new lecturers are trained to teach the Silva Method.

Silva Mind Control International is one of five subsidiaries of a larger limited partnership/holding company, owned exclusively by José Silva and his nuclear family. Each of the subsidiaries is located in or near (PSI Building) the International Headquarters and all activities are coordinated from there.

The lecturers and students of the Silva Method are a heterogeneous group. Internationally, of course, they come from many different cultural backgrounds. Presently, the largest numbers are coming from Mexico, Central and South America. In the United States, the growth rate has slowed since the mid and late seventies. Nonetheless, there is still a diversity of backgrounds of the members. They include young and old, poor and affluent, blue collar and professional, nuns and clerics, married and unmarried, and females and males.

The profile that emerged from the questionnaire population of the present study is more specific. In this case the individual is most likely a white female in her early forties, married with three children, and earning between $20,000 and $30,000 annually. She views SMC as a means to develop the full potential of her mind and was satisfied with what she learned in the BLS. She received her education in the public school system and now holds a college degree. Although raised a Roman Catholic, she also believes in reincarnation. She also believed in psychic phenomena and probably has used the services of a professional psychic. Her belief system and the Silva ideology interface so completely that using the Method has become part of her life style.

Locally, SMCI is represented by the Forward Thinking Institute, the SMCI Center for Michigan. Currently, there are two SMCI lecturers and six lecturers in training working with the Center's Director, Mr. Louis Barbone. The Forward Thinking Institute is one of eight SMCI Centers in the United States but it is unique in its philosophical orientation and team orientation approach. Additionally, there is a small number of SMCI lecturers unaffiliated with the FTI who also teach in Michigan.

II. CONCLUSIONS

Although parapsychological phenomena has been studied in the Soviet Union for decades, Western scientists have only recently seriously begun investigating it. There seems little doubt among many researchers that parapsychological phenomena exists[1]. Some government agencies, such as the CIA, are concerned enough that they are one of the major sponsors of parapsychological research--especially remote viewing (Ebon, 1984). What is still unclear is what the phenomena really is; what factors influence its expression; how it works; and whether everyone has the same degree of latent ability to function psychically.

This is important to the present study because psychic functioning is of prime importance to Silva Mind Control. Unless the student limits her/himself to the relaxation techniques, at some point it is necessary to accept the reality of psychic functioning.

Based upon observations and personal experience, I suggest that psychic communication[2] is a qualitatively different form of communication than language. Language is linear and, in itself, non-emotional. Psychic communication/functioning is not. Effective communication in the mental mode is achieved by transmitting the gestalt of the message not the individual words or a simple image. That gestalt includes not only the idea to be communicated but also the emotional context. It is triggered by an all encompassing desire to achieve contact with the target--which involves more than simply saying, "I want". I suggest one of the causes for the variability in parapsychological experimental results is failure to recognize this difference between the verbal and mental modes of communication. Further, in experimental situations, it is extremely difficult to achieve the level of desire necessary to trigger the psychic process.

This is relevant to Silva Mind Control because the primary way the student demonstrates her/his psychic functioning during the BLS is in the 404 health case working. After seeing the demonstration in front of the class of health case working by one of their fellow students, the desire to succeed in their own health case working is extremely high. I suggest that this is the major reason why virtually every student receives correct information on those first health cases worked[3]. After the BLS, two things happen to decrease health case working and success. First, the group opportunities to work become limited and few students continue on their own. Secondly, many students who were very successful during the 404 session, become reluctant to try again. I suggest this is due to one or a combination of the following. Some are reluctant because they want to hold on to their successes without testing the process again--just in case it was a fluke. Others are reluctant because they fear they will succeed again and they do not want that much power. so fear of success and fear of failure keeps some from developing this aspect of the Silva training. Additionally, of course, there are those who do continue to regularly work health cases and those who are simply not interested in doing so.

It has been suggested by various authors that parapsychological functioning may have been an important part of human communication systems during the earlier stages of human evolution. As language developed, parapsychological communication, like gesturing, became less important[4].

I propose that psychic functioning continued but its expression got channeled to religious specialists--shamans. In non-Western societies, it continues to be expressed through shamans, magicians, and traditional healers[5]. I suggest Silva Mind Control represents a Western cultural expression of that phenomena. In both cases, similar feats are achieved. In the West, however, some of the "bizarre" actions associated with shamanic rituals would not be accepted. The Silva Method is reserved, non-emotional, private, and respectable. It allows the person to

experience psychic functioning in a culturally acceptable
manner.

In addition to the parapsychological aspects of SMC,
its other major area of concern, health, is also influenced
by culture. In Mexico, Central and South America, SMC is,
currently an enormous success. One of the major reasons for
this is the areas' cultural predisposition to believe in and
use spiritualist healing and the similarity between that and
the Silva Method.

According to SMC, each person is responsible for
maintaining her/his own state of health and well being.
This idea of individual responsibility for health
maintenance meshes well with the strong, individualistic
orientation of American culture. With health care costs
increasing in quantum leaps, more and more people are
seeking alternatives or supplements to conventional health
care delivery systems. Holistic medicine is becoming
increasingly popular as are health maintenance programs.
Medicine is beginning to appreciate how powerful an agent
the mind is in health maintenance. Unmanaged stress, for
example can have devastating effects on the body leading to
such conditions as hypertension, heart disease, and possibly
cancer. Studies have shown that Transcendental Meditation
works in improving the health and general well being of
those who practice it. The Silva Method is similar to TM in
the state achieved by the practitioner'. As such, the

Silva Method should be equally effective as a relaxation technique and in stress management.

During the decade of the seventies, TM and other meditation techniques became very popular. This is reflected in the growth rate of SMCI during that time. Since the eighties, however, there has been a decline in BLS enrollment. This may be due to a shift in emphasis in the media from "esoteric" concerns to practical economic matters and the resultant shift in attitude among the general public. I suggest, however, that it is due more to problems within SMCI. It is a paternalistic, nepotistic organization which is run like a small family business--not like an international enterprise. The decline of the regional concept and the prominence of independent lecturers has resulted in numerous problems--which Laredo is attempting to correct by the resurgence of the regional concept once again. Secondly, there is virtually no public relations and advertising. This is primarily due to the fact that the Method is taught by independent lecturers who are expected to be responsible for those things in their areas. In reality, they fall short in the promotion and hence, the number of people they are able to reach. If Laredo were to launch a nationwide advertising campaign, their numbers would probably increase significantly. Finally, there appears to be a lack of commitment by many of the SMCI lecturers (compared to the Spanish Speaking lecturers). If those lecturers do not use the Method, do not believe in what they teach, do not support their graduates, or are just "in it" for the money they end up in a self-defeating situation of decreasing enrollment.

According to Robert Ellwood (1973), a cult is a group

derived from the experiences of one or a few individuals who are able to enter...a superior, ecstatic state of consciousness in which contact and rapport with all reaches of a non-historical and impersonal universe are possible...(p.5).

He further suggests that cults in the U.S. have 15 specific characteristics (pp.28-31). Using Ellwood's criteria, Silva Mind Control International would have to be classified as a cult. Not only does José Silva enter an altered state of consciousness in which the conventional limits of time and space do not exist, but so do the practitioners of the Silva Method. Likewise, in comparing SMCI to Ellwood's typology of American cults, one finds that the majority of the characteristics apply. Nonetheless, I do not view SMCI as a cult for the following reasons. In the United States, the word "cult" has mostly negative connotations. This is primarily due to the well publicized, exclusionist cults such as Jim Jones and his People's Temple, the Reverend Sun Myung Moon and his Unification Church, the Children of God, and Scientology. To link SMCI with that would be inaccurate and unfair. There is no "brainwashing" in SMCI as one finds in many of the well publicized cults nor is there a surrender of self-control. On the contrary, SMCI repeatedly tells the students that they are responsible for their own lives and that they must take charge of their lives. Unlike "est", however, the aggressive coercion to do so is not present. Likewise, in the mental training exercises there are numerous statements reinforcing the person's self-control over all aspects of her/his life.

Secondly, SMC is a methodology not an ideology. A person can practice the Method for relaxation and some problem solving without accepting the underlying belief system. If, however, they practice it in its fullest sense, the ideology must become incorporated into their belief systems.

Finally, SMCI is a broad spectrum appeal group. Most cults draw their membership from the alienated, the marginal, or the dispossessed individuals of society. SMCI does not. Related to this, however, is the appeal SMC appears to have for females.

In this society, women have made some gains in the last decade in the amount of power and position they may achieve. Nonetheless, females are still disadvantaged in this culture (for e.g women earn .52 for every $1 a man earns in a comparable position). This may explain why females are more attracted to SMC than are males. Or, as others suggest, the sex ratio difference may be due to cultural permissiveness. Females are more likely to express psychic ability because this culture expects females to be intuitive.

The sex ratio difference may also be an expression of a theme that is present in virtually every culture--ritual power acts as a substitute for the lack of political power. In non-Western societies, women have very little political power. Ritually, however, they often are very powerful. This theme is not limited to females. In chiefdom level societies, the divine chief is both a political and a religious leader. In any particular chiefdom, however, one often finds that the politically weak divine chief is ritually very powerful and vice verca (e.g. Shilluk vs. the Nyoro in East Africa). In the United States, the high percentage of females attracted to SMC may be an attempt (consciously or unconsciously) to gain "ritual" power in a politically disadvantaged situation.

By the study of parapsychology, consciousness research and culture, anthropologists are able to gain a greater understanding of human experience. Well known phenomena in anthropology take on expanded meaning with a psi perspective. Divination, in addition to traditional explanations, is seen as a form of telepathy, precognition, clairvoyance, or PK. Magic, beyond the functional explanations, becomes an expression of numerous psi processes. The shaman can be viewed as an individual with controlled psychic power. Voodoo death can be seen as a negative application of PK. In fact, Eisenbud (1977) submits that illness itself can result directly from a psychokinetic mechanism, independent of cultural taboos or fears, stress, or other forces usually associated with psychosomatic illness. Likewise, healing and psychic surgery can be viewed as a beneficial application of PK. As we learn more about psi processes, we can expect more of the things we take for granted to acquire a new meaning. As Margaret Mead points out (1977), it is not a question of belief or disbelief but rather it is an area that must be considered by anthropologists in their study of culture.

In these times of increasing social unrest, competition for dwindling resources, economic crises, and increased feelings of powerlessness, it is common for people to turn to a variety of different methods and choices for resolution, relaxation, comfort, and escape. Among these options, SMC claims to be a viable alternative. It allows for access to the limitless potential of the human mind. The Silva Method, like the growing interest in psi or the the holistic health movement, is symbolic of a paradigm shift in the West--a recognition of the validity of the subjective. That is, it is a realization that the subjective realm (psi) can be studied objectively (scientifically). The power of the mind, as an agent in influencing health and life circumstances, is being recognized by an ever increasing number of individuals.

Although this perspective is becoming accepted by increasing number of people, the idea is not new. The basic

tenet of the Silva Method was written in   the   <u>Bhagavad-Gita</u>
3,000 years ago:

Man is made by his beliefs...As he believes, so he is.

ENDNOTES

[1] For example see: Mead 1977; Rao 1977, 1978 1979; Ransom 1976; Staniford 1977; Ehrenwald 1978; Hansel 1980; Leeds and Murphy 1980; LeShan 1969; Long 1977; Mitchell 1974; Wolman 1977; cf. Moore 1977.

[2] This includes telepathy, psychokinesis, clairvoyance or precognition, and other phenomena generally included under the term "psi".

[3] As mentioned earlier, the student chooses only three areas of concern. The probability of choosing the correct three or even two areas which are a problem out of the possible hundreds of maladies that can afflict the human body, by chance alone is very low. Case working, from my observations, is not a guessing game. The student seems to focus in on the problem area(s) almost immediately.

[4] For example see: Bourguignon 1974, 1977; Campbell 1977; Eisenbud 1976, 1977; Rao 1979.

[5] For example see: Boshier 1974, 1976; Dobkin de Rios 1978; Ehrenwald 1977; Foster 1943; Frank 1980; Long 1977; Pope 1953; Reichbart 1978; Rose 1951; Shiels 1978; Singer and Ankenbrandt 1980; Winkelman 1980; Van de Castle 1970.

[6] It differs in that TM is passive meditation (the person simply repeats their mantra for 15 minutes) while SMC is active meditation (the person is mentally active).

APPENDICES

APPENDIX 1

SILVA FAMILY KINSHIP CHART

KINSHIP CHART OF JOSE AND PAULA SILVA

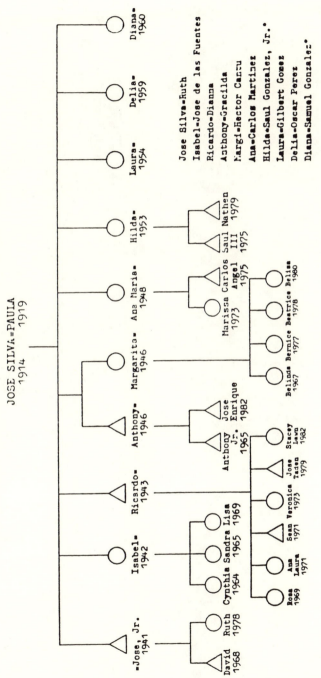

JOSE SILVA=PAULA
1914   1919

Jose Silva=Ruth
Isabel=Jose de las Fuentes
Ricardo=Dianna
Anthony=Gracilda
Margi=Hector Cantu
Ana=Carlos Martinez
Hilda=Saul Gonzalez, Jr.*
Laura=Gilbert Gomez
Delia=Oscar Perez
Diana=Samuel Gonzalez*

*Brothers

APPENDIX 2

CORRESPONDENCE

MIND SCIENCE FOUNDATION
414 L.. Mulberry
San Antonio, Texas

March 24, 1965

Dr. Everett F. Dagle
Cambridge Research Laboratories
Office of Aerospace Research
Hanscom Field, Bedford, Mass.

Dear Dr. Dagle:

Your letter of 5 June, 1964 to Mr. Jose Silva (R), president of the Laredo Parapsychology Foundation, stimulated my interest in the possibility of demonstrating some features of psychic operations by trained sensitives. The orbital flight of Grissom and Young was selected as an occasion to make clairvoyant observations and psychic suggestions which could be checked against known facts. The Mind Science Foundation has been observing the work of the Laredo Group for about one year and feels that there are many valid parapsychological phenomena exhibited at will by these dedicated workers. Detailed analysis by qualified researchers has not been made of their experiments and in an effort to arouse interest in this possibility I am sending you with this letter a brief summary of some of the events recorded on tape during an hour and a half session with three different sensitives this morning during the flight. Each sensitive was tested apart from the others and I am prepared to certify that the experiment was valid.

It is certainly not to be expected that the majority of the psychic manipulations reported in this experiment have caused ascertainable results. Rather, it would be of the greatest interest to us if you would take it upon yourself to check all the data available to you in order to determine if any of the observations or suggestions are ESP phenomena. There are so many other tests that can be made and with nine more such flights planned a great opportunity exists for future work on which we would appreciate your comments and suggestions.

If any correlation is found between the data enclosed and observed facts I am sure that you, as well as we, will wish to review the whole taped session in detail and seek the most effective means for further defining telepathic and clairvoyant communication.

Sincerely yours,

Wm. R. Gray, Consultant
(M.A., U. of Tex., 1942)

Copy - Original in files

HEADQUARTERS
AIR FORCE CAMBRIDGE RESEARCH LABORATORIES
OFFICE OF AEROSPACE RESEARCH
UNITED STATES AIR FORCE
LAURENCE G HANSCOM FIELD   BEDFORD MASSACHUSETTS

REPLY TO
ATTN OF CRBG   April 9, 1965

SUBJECT: Laredo ESP Experiment

   TO: Mr. William F. Gray
       212 Soledad Street
       San Antonio, Texas

   Dear Mr. Gray:

   Thank you for sending the data from the March 23 experiment by
   members of the Laredo Parapsychology Foundation.

   The data looks quite interesting, and I now have two sources
   trying to look into it. I have no idea when I will hear from
   my sources, but you may rest assured that I will notify you as
   soon as I have anything definite.

   Thank you again for allowing me to check into the matter, and I
   do hope we find a high percentage of hits.

                    Sincerely,

                    Everett F. Dagle
                    Research Engineer

COPY

1110 Cedar Avenue
Laredo, Texas 78040
August 11, 1965

Hon. Lyndon B. Johnson
President of the United States
Washington, D.C.

Dear Mr. President:

I approach you as a humble citizen sincerely stating that I am not seeking
material gains nor glory.

My name is Jose Silva. I am 51 years of age, born at Laredo, Texas. I have
a wife and ten children, three boys and seven girls. I am self-employed and
an electronics technician by profession.

I am what is known as a layman scientist. My interest in scientific research
for the past twenty-one years has been in the field of para-normal activities
of the human mind. I use what is known as hypnosis quite extensively in my
research work, which is done on a strictly scientific basis. I have found that
by using my research experience I can develop in the human mind the ability to
perceive and discern information through means other than the normal senses.
A person trained to use his mind in this manner is known as a sensitive, a
clairvoyant or a seer.

I will now quote from a letter directed to me from a research scientist from
the headquarters of the Air Force Cambridge Research Laboratories, Bedford, Mass.:

> "I have felt all along that the training of sensitives is the key
> to the 'repeatable experiment' which the conventional scientist
> will demand. A significant success in this area could be the break-
> through of all time."

I feel that the time is now, because now we can produce the 'repeatable experiment.' We can train the mind to operate at a special level which will enable it
to produce para-normal results in many areas. For higher accuracy, a team of
sensitives can be trained to work on a particular project producing results never
before obtained by the best natural born sensitives. Because of this, all fields
of science could be affected, including warfare.

I feel that it is my duty to God and my country and to all humanity to turn over
to you, or to persons assigned by you, all information accumulated to date, relative to the knowledge of how to develop the para-normal faculties of the human
mind.

I await your further instructions in this matter.

May God again guide you as He has always in the past.

Very truly yours,

Jose Silva

JS:lap

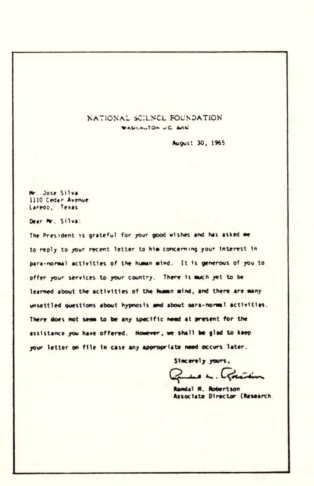

NATIONAL SCIENCE FOUNDATION
WASHINGTON DC 20550

August 30, 1965

Mr. Jose Silva
1110 Cedar Avenue
Laredo, Texas

Dear Mr. Silva:

The President is grateful for your good wishes and has asked me
to reply to your recent letter to him concerning your interest in
para-normal activities of the human mind. It is generous of you to
offer your services to your country. There is much yet to be
learned about the activities of the human mind, and there are many
unsettled questions about hypnosis and about para-normal activities.
There does not seem to be any specific need at present for the
assistance you have offered. However, we shall be glad to keep
your letter on file in case any appropriate need occurs later.

Sincerely yours,

Randal M. Robertson
Associate Director (Research)

APPENDIX 3

COUNTRIES AND LANGUAGES FOR THE BLS

COUNTRIES

1. Abu-Dabi; 2. Argentina; 3. Australia; 4. Austria;
5. Bahamas; 6. Belgium; Bolivia; 8. Borneo; 9. Brazil;
10. Canada; 11. Chile; 12. Colombia; 13. Costa Rica;
14. Dominican Republic; 15. DuBai; 16. Ecuador; 17. El
Salvador; 18. England; 19. France; 20. Germany; 21. Greece;
22. Guam; 23. Guatemala; 24. Holland; 25. Honduras;
26. India; 27. Indonesia; 28. Ireland; 29. Isreal;
30. Italy; 31. Japan; 32. Kenya; 33. Korea; 34. Kuwait;
35. Malaysia; 36. Mexico; 37. New Zealand; 38. Nicaragua;
39. Nigeria; 40. Pakistan; 41. Panama; 42. Paraguay;
43. Peru; 44. Philippines; 45. Portugal; 46. Puerto Rico;
47. Republic of Lesotho; 48. Saudi Arabia; 49. Scotland;
50. Singapore; 51. South Africa; 52. Spain; 53. Sri Lanka;
54. Switzerland 55. Thailand. 56. Taiwan; 57. Trinidad;
58. Tunisia; 59. U.S.A. 60. Uruguary; 61; Venezuela.

LANGUAGES

1. Chamorro; 2. Chinese Mandarian dialect; 3. Dutch;
4. English; 5. French 6. German; 7. Greek; 8. Hebrew;
9. Italian; 10. Japanese; 11. Korean; 12. Malay;
13. Portuqese; 14. Spanish.

APPENDIX 4

BRAIN WAVE FREQUENCY CHART

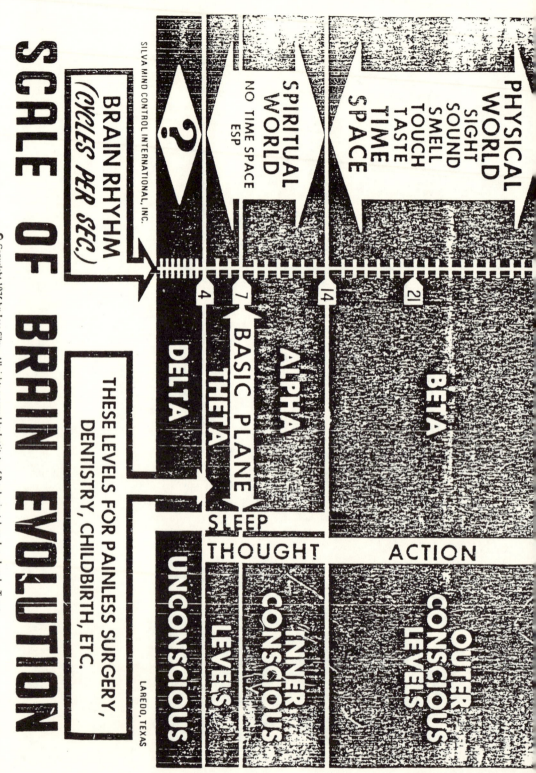

SCALE OF BRAIN EVOLUTION

SILVA MIND CONTROL INTERNATIONAL, INC.

BRAIN RHYHM
(CYCLES PER SEC.)

THESE LEVELS FOR PAINLESS SURGERY,
DENTISTRY, CHILDBIRTH, ETC.

LAREDO, TEXAS

PHYSICAL WORLD
SIGHT
SOUND
SMELL
TOUCH
TASTE
TIME
SPACE

SPIRITUAL WORLD
NO TIME SPACE
ESP

?

4   7   14   21

DELTA   THETA   BASIC PLANE   ALPHA   BETA

SLEEP

THOUGHT   ACTION

UNCONSCIOUS   LEVELS   INNER CONSCIOUS   OUTER CONSCIOUS LEVELS

APPENDIX 5

GUARANTEE

Forward Thinking Institute
17000 W. Eight Mile Road, Suite 175
Southfield, Michigan 48075

Money-Back Guarantee

This is to certify that you, as a participant in the Silva Mind Control Basic Lecture Series, are guaranteed satisfaction for the time, effort, and money invested.

THE INSTITUTE GUARANTEES TO REFUND 100% OF THE FEE upon completion of the series if you are not satisfied with the results and benefits obtained in self-improvement.

In order to exercise the guarantee, simply make your wishes known to the instructor before accepting your certificate and return the manual in serviceable condition.

To keep the guarantee in effect you must do the following:
1. Attend sessions.
2. Participate in mental training exercises.

Louis H. Barbone
Director

APPENDIX 6

BLS CERTIFICATES

No. 107009

MIND CONTROL ⚡ INSTITUTE INC.

LAREDO, TEXAS

This is to Certify that *Amaline Marie Powers*

has satisfactorily completed our specialized course in all phases of
Psychic Operation and has been examined at *Marine City, Mich.*
(CITY)   (STATE)
and found duly qualified in the subjects of this course and is hereby awarded this

Diploma

and the title of Psi Operator (Psi Op.)
as an acknowledgement of thorough knowledge and proficiency and in recognition
of accomplishments.

In Witness Whereof, I hereunto affix my signature
and seal, this 26 day of *January* 19 74

MIND CONTROL INSTITUTE, INC.

Rita A. Sigridson
INSTRUCTOR

Jose Silva
DIRECTOR

APPENDIX 7

QUESTIONNAIRES

QUESTIONNAIRE NUMBER ONE

GENERAL BACKGROUND QUESTIONNAIRE

ALL INFORMATION FROM THIS QUESTIONNAIRE IS CONFIDENTIAL

1. When did you take the Basic Lecture Series? (write in month and year)
   _____

2. Have you taken any training beyond the Basic Lecture Series?
   ___ no   ___ yes

3. If yes, please indicate the following:
   ___ (type)   ___ (when)
   ___ (lecturer)

4. Have you continued with activities offered by the Forward Thinking Institute or other activities offered by Silva Mind Control? (check one)
   ___ does not apply--just completed basic course
   ___ yes   ___ no

5. If yes, which activities have you been involved with? (check all that apply)
   ___ grad workshops   ___ repeat of basic course
   ___ seminars   ___ repeat of grad course
   ___ hear speakers   ___ other (specify) _____
   ___ special activities

6. Since you completed the Basic Lecture Series, have you continued with your programing?
   ___ does not apply--just finished course
   ___ yes   ___ no

7. If yes, how frequently do you program or go to level? (check one)
   ___ daily   ___ less than once a week
   ___ twice weekly   ___ irregularly
   ___ once a week   ___ other (write in) _____
   ___ 1 or 2 times a month

8. In what type of school did you receive the majority of you education? (check one)
   ___ public   ___ private, religious
   ___ private, non-religious

9. Except for baptism, weddings, or funerals have you attended religious services in the last year? (check one)
___ yes   ___ no

10. If yes, about how frequently do you attend? (check one)
___ daily   ___ 1-3 times a year
___ weekly   ___ less than once a year
___ once a month

11. Which of the following best describes the religious orientation of the family you were raised in? (please check one)
___ Roman Catholic   ___ Jewish
___ Islam   ___ Humanist
___ Aetheist   ___ Eastern Orthodox
                                    Christian
___ Protestant (denomination) _____
___ Eastern Philosophy/Religion (specify) _____
___ Other (write in) _____

12. Which of the following best describes your religious preference or orientation at this time? (please check one)
___ Roman Catholic   ___ Jewish
___ Islam   ___ Humanist
___ Aetheist   ___ Eastern Orthodox
                                    Christian
___ Protestant (denomination) _____
___ Eastern Philosophy/Religion (specify) _____
___ Other (write in) _____

13. What is your sex?
___ female   ___ male

14. How old were you on your last birthday? Enter age in years.
_____ years old.

15. What is your marital status? (check one)
___ single (never married)   ___ widowed, divorced, separated
___ currently married   ___ living with some as a couple

16. Which of the following best describes your ethnic background?
___ White   ___ Afro-American or Black
___ Asian   ___ Hispanic
___ other (specify) _____

17. Approximately, what was your family's income last year?
___ under $5,000   ___ $20,000-29,999
___ $5,000-9,999   ___ $30,000-39,999

___ $10,000-19,999   ___ $40,000 or more

18. Do you have children?
    ___ yes   ___ no

19. If yes, how many?
    _____ (enter number)

20. Have you taught your children the Silva Method?
    ___ yes   ___ no   ___ just finished

21. Have your children taken the Silva courses?--Children's
    Course or Basic Sequence.
    ___ yes   ___ no
    ___ Children's Course   ___ Basic Lecture Series

22. What is the highest educational level you have
    achieved? (check one)
    ___ less than high school diploma
    ___ high school diploma
    ___ post high school technical training'
    ___ some college
    ___ college graduate--two year program
    ___ college graduate--four year program
    ___ some graduate school
    ___ graduate degree(s)

23. Are you currently a student?
    ___ no   ___ yes (where) _____

24. What is the highest educational level your father
    achieved? (check one)
    ___ less than high school diploma
    ___ high school diploma
    ___ post high school technical training'
    ___ some college
    ___ college graduate--two year program
    ___ college graduate--four year program
    ___ some graduate school
    ___ graduate degree(s)

25. What is (was) your father's main occupation? Please
    write in. If retired indicate from where.
    _____

26. Are you currently employed?
    ___ yes   ___ no   ___ retired

27. If employed, what is your main occupation? Please be
    specific by indicating some details of your job. For
    example dental assistant, engineer in a small firm.
    _____

28. If unemployed, how long? Write in months or years.

29. If retired, how long? Write in months or years.

30. If unemployed or retired, what was your main occupation? Please write in.

31. Do you belong to any other formal organization or group? (other than Silva). ___ yes ___ no

32. If yes, what type of group or organization is it?
    ___ healing   ___ religious
    ___ parapsychological or ESP   ___ other (specify) _____
    ___ self-help or personal growth

33. How much time do you devote to this other group or organization? (write in)

34. If you are interested in parapsychology or ESP, how long have you had that interest? Please write in length or time.

35. Have you ever used the services of a psychic?
    ___ yes   ___ no

36. If yes, how often? (write in)

37. Where were you born? (write in)

38. How far did you have to travel, from your home, to come here today? (write in miles)

39. Which of the following best describes the community you live in?
    ___ urban/city   ___ rural
    ___ small town   ___ other (specify) _____
    ___ suburban

40. Approximately, what is the population size of the community you live in?
    ___ under 1,500 inhabitants   ___ 25,001-100,000
    ___ 1,501-5,000   "   ___ 100,000-250,000
    ___ 5,000-25,000   "   ___ above 250,000

41. Have you taken any other self-help, personal growth, hypnosis, or memory courses?
    ___ no   ___ yes (specify) _____

42. Are you a member of SIGA--Silva International Graduates Association?
    ___ no   ___ yes

43. Why are you at the Center today?
    ___ to take the basic course sequence (first time)
    ___ to repeat the basic course or a part of it
    ___ to take a graduate course
    ___ for a graduate workshop
    ___ other (specify) _____

44. If I have additional questions, is it all right to contact you?
    ___ yes   ___ no

THANK YOU FOR YOU HELP IN THIS STUDY

QUESTIONNAIRE NUMBER TWO

DETROIT FOLLOW-UP

1. What attracted you the most about Silva Mind Control?

2. Do you think your life has changed since taking the Silva course(s)? If so, how?

3. Have your religious attitudes or beliefs about life changed since taking the Silva course(s)? If so how?

4. Have your reading habits changed as a result of contact with SMCI? If so how? Or, did your reading lead you into SMC? How?

5. Do you consider Silva Mind Control a "way of life" in that you incorporate the Silva Method and beliefs into your daily activities and interactions with others? Or, is Silva Mind Control a technique that you use only for specific purposes such as solving a problem or controlling a habit? Please explain.

6. Have you experienced any conflict between your past or present religious beliefs and your participation in SMC or the use of the Silva Method? Please explain.

7. What are your beliefs about God?

8. Do you believe in reincarnation? Please explain.

9. Successfully working health cases involves psychically receiving correct information about the ill person. Have you successfully worked health cases, either during the 404 session or at some time after the basic lecture series? When?

How often do you successfully work health cases?

Do you think working health cases is important? Why?

10. Did you ever have any non-traditional healing experiences (psychic, spiritual) before you went through the Silva training? Please explain.

Have you had any non-traditional healing experiences since the Silva training? Please explain.

11. In your opinion, what is the relationship between the Silva Method and traditional medicine?

12. What part of the Silva course--BLS--was most beneficial or helpful or important to you? Why? What about the graduate course and/or the Ultra Seminar? Please explain.

13. Do you think there are any weak areas in the method? What are they? Please explain.

14. What didn't you like about the course(s) or method? Please explain.

15. In your opinion, what is Silva Mind Control really all about?

16. In your opinion, what are the basic beliefs that underlie the Silva Method?

17. Since you originally took the BLS, how often have you reviewed all or a portion of the that course?

18. In the last year, how often have you used the Silva Method?

19. In what ways do you use the Method?

20. Do you sue all of the techniques or are there certain ones you rely on more often? If so, which ones are they and why?

21. What other members of your family have taken the Silva BLS? When did they take it?

22. Have they taken the graduate course(s)? If so, when?

23. Were you responsible for getting them interested in the
    Silva Method?

24. Have any of your friends taken the BLS because of your
    advice?

25. If you are not programming regularly, or using the
    method regularly, what are your reasons for not doing
    so?

26. Are you interested in or do you believe in ESP or
    parapsychology or psychic events?

    How long have you been interested?

    Were you interested in these things before you took the
    Silva training?

    Did you consider yourself psychic <u>before</u> the Silva
    training?

    Did you ever have any psychic experiences before you
    went through the Silva training. Explain.

27. What are your thoughts about Jose Silva?

PLEASE INCLUDE THE FOLLOWING FOR MY RECORDS.   AGAIN   <u>ALL</u>
INFORMATION IS STRICTLY CONFIDENTIAL

Name _____   Date _____

Address _____Phone _____
_____

THANK YOU FOR YOUR HELP IN THIS STUDY

QUESTIONNAIRE NUMBER THREE

EXTENSIVE LAREDO QUESTIONNAIRE

1. When did you take the Basic Lecture Series? (write in month and year)
   _____

2. Have you taken any training beyond the Basic Lecture Series?
   ___ no   ___ yes

3. If yes, please indicate the following:
   ___ (type)   ___ (when)
   ___ (lecturer)

4. Have you continued with activities offered by your Silva Mind Control center or SMCI?
   ___ does not apply--just completed basic course
   ___ yes   ___ no

5. If yes, which activities have you been involved with? (check all that apply)
   ___ grad workshops   ___ repeat of basic course
   ___ seminars   ___ repeat of grad course
   ___ hear speakers   ___ other (specify) _____
   ___ special activities

6. Since you completed the Basic Lecture Series, have you continued with your programing?
   ___ does not apply--just finished course
   ___ yes   ___ no

7. If yes, how frequently do you program or go to level? (check one)
   ___ daily   ___ less than once a week
   ___ twice weekly   ___ irregularly
   ___ once a week   ___ other (write in) _____
   ___ 1 or 2 times a month

8. In what type of school did you receive the majority of you education? (check one)
   ___ public   ___ private, religious
   ___ private, non-religious

9. Except for baptism, weddings, or funerals have you attended religious services in the last year? (check one)
   ___ yes   ___ no

10. If yes, about how frequently do you attend? (check one)
___ daily   ___ 1-3 times a year
___ weekly   ___ less than once a year
___ once a month

11. Which of the following best describes the religious
    orientation of the family you were raised in? (please
    check one)
    ___ Roman Catholic   ___ Jewish
    ___ Islam   ___ Humanist
    ___ Aetheist   ___ Eastern   Orthodox
    Christian
    ___ Protestant (denomination) _____
    ___ Eastern Philosophy/Religion (specify) _____
    ___ Other (write in) _____

12. Which of the following best describes your religious
    preference or orientation at this time? (please check
    one)
    ___ Roman Catholic   ___ Jewish
    ___ Islam   ___ Humanist
    ___ Aetheist   ___ Eastern   Orthodox
    Christian
    ___ Protestant (denomination) _____
    ___ Eastern Philosophy/Religion (specify) _____
    ___ Other (write in) _____

13. What is your sex?
    ___ female   ___ male

14. How old were you on your last birthday? Enter age in
    years.
    _____ years old.

15. What is your marital status? (check one)
    ___ single (never married)   ___ widowed, divorced,
    separated
    ___ currently married   ___ living with some as a
    couple

16. Which of the following best describes your ethnic
    background?
    ___ White   ___ Afro-American or Black
    ___ Asian   ___ Hispanic
    ___ other (specify) _____

17. Approximately, what was your family's income last year?
    ___ under $5,000   ___ $20,000-29,999
    ___ $5,000-9,999   ___ $30,000-39,999
    ___ $10,000-19,999   ___ $40,000 or more

18. Do you have children?
    ___ yes   ___ no

19. If yes, how many?
    _____ (enter number)

20. Have you taught your children the Silva Method?
    ___ yes   ___ no   ___ just finished

21. Have your children taken the Silva courses?--Children's
    Course or Basic Sequence.
    ___ yes   ___ no
    ___ Children's Course   ___ Basic Lecture Series

22. What is the highest educational level you have
    achieved? (check one)
    ___ less than high school diploma
    ___ high school diploma
    ___ post high school technical training'
    ___ some college
    ___ college graduate--two year program
    ___ college graduate--four year program
    ___ some graduate school
    ___ graduate degree(s)

23. Are you currently a student?
    ___ no   ___ yes (where) _____

24. Are you currently employed?
    ___ yes   ___ no   ___ retired

25. If employed, what is your main occupation? Please be
    specific by indicating some details of your job. For
    example dental assistant, engineer in a small firm.
    _____

26. If unemployed, how long? Write in months or years.
    _____

27. If retired, how long? Write in months or years.
    _____

28. If unemployed or retired, what was your main occupation?
    Please write in.
    _____

29. Do you belong to any other formal organization or
    group? (other than Silva). ___ yes ___ no

30. If yes, what type of group or organization is it?
    ___ healing   ___ religious
    ___ parapsychological or ESP   other (specify) _____
    ___ self-help or personal growth

31. How much time do you devote to this other group or
    organization? (write in)
    _____

32. Have you ever used the services of a psychic?
    ___ no   ___ yes (how often) _____

33. Where is your home located? _____(city and state)

34. Have you taken any other self-help, personal growth, hypnosis, or memory courses?
    ___ no   ___ yes (specify) _____

35. Are you a member of SIGA--Silva International Graduates Association?
    ___ no ?   ___ yes

36. Why are you here today?
    ___ convention activities   ___ repeat of BLS
    ___ repeat of grad course   ___ instructor training
    ___ other (specify) _____

THE FOLLOWING QUESTIONS ARE TO BE ANSWERED IN
THE SPACE PROVIDED BETWEEN EACH

37. What attracted you the most about Silva Mind Control?

38. Do you think your life has changed since taking the Silva course(s)? If so, how?

39. Have your religious attitudes or beliefs about life changed since taking the Silva course(s)? If so how?

40. Have your reading habits changed as a result of contact with SMCI? If so how? Or, did your reading lead you into SMC? How?

41. Do you consider Silva Mind Control a "way of life" in that you incorporate the Silva Method and beliefs into your daily activities and interactions with others? Or, is Silva Mind Control a technique that you use only for specific purposes such as solving a problem or controlling a habit? Please explain.

42. Have you experienced any conflict between your past or present religious beliefs and your participation in SMC or the use of the Silva Method? Please explain.

43. What are your beliefs about God?

44. Do you believe in reincarnation? Please explain.

45. Successfully working health cases involves psychically receiving correct information about the ill person. Have you successfully worked health cases, either during the 404 session or at some time after the basic lecture series? When?

How often do you successfully work health cases?

Do you think working health cases is important?   Why?

46. Did you ever have any non-traditional healing
     experiences (psychic, spiritual) before you went
     through the Silva training? Please explain.

     Have you had any non-traditional healing experiences
     since the Silva training? Please explain.

47. In your opinion, what is the relationship between the
     Silva Method and traditional medicine?

48. What part of the Silva course--BLS--was most beneficial
    or helpful or important to you? Why? What about the
    graduate course and/or the Ultra Seminar? Please
    explain.

49. Do you think there are any weak areas in the method?
     What are they? Please explain.

50. What didn't you like about the course(s) or method?
    Please explain.

51. In your opinion, what is Silva Mind Control really all about?

52. In your opinion, what are the basic beliefs that underlie the Silva Method?

53. If you are not programming regularly, or using the method regularly, what are your reasons for not doing so?

54. Are you interested in or do you believe in ESP or parapsychology or psychic events?

How long have you been interested?

Were you interested in these things before you took the Silva training?

Did you consider yourself psychic before the Silva training?

Did you ever have any psychic experiences before you went through the Silva training? Explain.

55. What are your thoughts about Jose Silva?

56. If I have any additional questions, is it all right to
    contact you?
    ___ yes   ___ no

     In   either   case,   please   include the following for my
records. Again, all information is strictly confidential.

Name   _____   Date _____

Address _____   Phone _____
        _____

THANK YOU FOR YOUR HELP IN THIS.

Are you a SMC instructor?
     ___ no   ___ yes--if so, how long _____yrs.

APPENDIX 8

CROSSTABULATIONS

28 NOV 84   SPSS-X RELEASE 2.0A FOR MTS
17:42:32   Wayne State University

- - - - - - - - - - - - - C R O S S T A B U L A T I O N   O F - - - - - - - - - - - - -
SMCREAS   ATTRACTION TO SMC   BY UNDERBEL   UNDERLYING BELIEFS
CONTROLLING FOR..
  SEX   SEX   VALUE =   1. FEMALE   PAGE 1 OF 2

CROSSTABULATION # ONE

UNDERBEL

COUNT ROW PCT COL PCT TOT PCT	1	2	3	5	6	7	8	ROW TOTAL
SMCREAS 1	1 25.0 25.0 2.4	1 25.0 16.7 2.4			1 25.0 11.1 2.4		1 25.0 11.1 2.4	4 9.8
2		1 25.0 16.7 2.4			2 50.0 22.2 4.9	1 25.0 10.0 2.4		4 9.8
3	1 50.0 25.0 2.4						1 50.0 11.1 2.4	2 4.9
5		1 20.0 16.7 2.4	1 20.0 100.0 2.4			2 40.0 20.0 4.9	1 20.0 11.1 2.4	5 12.2
7		2 66.7 33.3 4.9			1 33.3 11.1 2.4			3 7.3
8					1 100.0 11.1 2.4			1 2.4
10	2 16.7 50.0 4.9	1 8.3 16.7 2.4		2 16.7 100.0 4.9	1 8.3 11.1 2.4	1 8.3 10.0 2.4	5 41.7 55.6 12.2	12 29.3
COLUMN TOTAL	4 9.8	6 14.6	1 2.4	2 4.9	9 22.0	10 24.4	9 22.0	41 100.0

(CONTINUED)

```
28 NOV 84    SPSS-X RELEASE 2.0A FOR MTS
17:42:32     Wayne State University

- - - - - - - - - - - - - - - - -  C R O S S T A B U L A T I O N  O F  - - - - - - - - - - - - - - - - -
  SMCREAS   ATTRACTION TO SMC                      BY UNDERBEL  UNDERLYING BELIEFS
CONTROLLING FOR..
  SEX       SEX                                    VALUE =      1.  FEMALE              PAGE  2 OF  2
- - - - - - - - - -
```

	UNDERBEL								
COUNT ROW PCT COL PCT TOT PCT	1	2	3	5	6	7	8		ROW TOTAL
SMCREAS									
11					3 50.0 33.3 7.3	3 50.0 30.0 7.3			6 14.6
12					3 75.0 30.0 7.3	3 75.0 30.0 7.3	1 25.0 11.1 2.4		4 9.8
COLUMN TOTAL	4 9.8	6 14.6	1 2.4	2 4.9	9 22.0	10 24.4	9 22.0		41 100.0

```
CHI-SQUARE      D.F.     SIGNIFICANCE       MIN E.F.      CELLS WITH E.F.< 5
- - - - - -      - - -    - - - - - - - -    - - - - -     - - - - - - - - - - -

53.56193        48       0.2694             0.024         63 OF  63 (100.0%)


              STATISTIC            SYMMETRIC        WITH SMCREAS      WITH UNDERBEL
              - - - - - - -        - - - - - -      DEPENDENT         DEPENDENT
                                                    - - - - - - -     - - - - - - - -

LAMBDA                            0.26667          0.20690           0.32258
UNCERTAINTY COEFFICIENT          0.34902          0.32714           0.37405


              STATISTIC            VALUE            SIGNIFICANCE
              - - - - - - -        - - - - -        - - - - - - - -

CRAMER'S V                        0.46662
CONTINGENCY COEFFICIENT          0.75261
```

28 NOV 84   SPSS-X RELEASE 2.OA FOR MTS
17:42:32   Wayne State University

- - - - - SMCREAS   ATTRACTION TO SMC - - - - - C R O S S T A B U L A T I O N   O F - - - - -
CONTROLLING FOR..   BY UNDERBEL UNDERLYING BELIEFS
      SEX   SEX   VALUE =   2. MALE   PAGE 1 OF 1

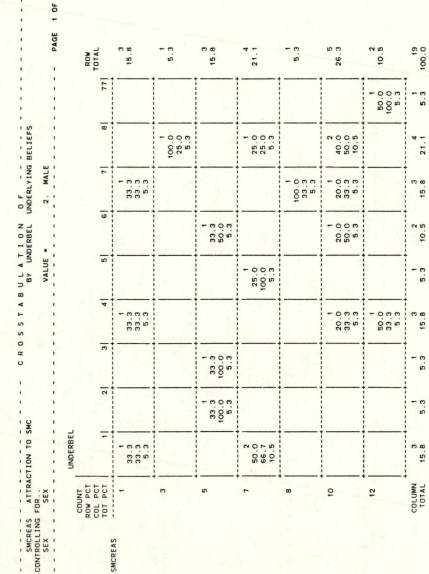

UNDERBEL

SMCREAS		COUNT ROW PCT COL PCT TOT PCT	1	2	3	4	5	6	7	8	77	ROW TOTAL
1			1 33.3 33.3 5.3			1 33.3 33.3 5.3			1 33.3 33.3 5.3			3 15.8
3										1 100.0 25.0 5.3		1 5.3
5				1 33.3 100.0 5.3	1 33.3 100.0 5.3			1 33.3 50.0 5.3				3 15.8
7			2 50.0 66.7 10.5				1 25.0 100.0 5.3			1 25.0 25.0 5.3		4 21.1
8									1 100.0 33.3 5.3			1 5.3
10						1 20.0 33.3 5.3		1 20.0 50.0 5.3	1 20.0 33.3 5.3	2 40.0 50.0 10.5		5 26.3
12						1 50.0 33.3 5.3					1 50.0 100.0 5.3	2 10.5
COLUMN TOTAL			3 15.8	1 5.3	1 5.3	3 15.8	1 5.3	2 10.5	3 15.8	4 21.1	1 5.3	19 100.0

28 NOV 84   SPSS-X RELEASE 2.0A FOR MTS
17:42:32   Wayne State University

CHI-SQUARE	D.F.	SIGNIFICANCE	MIN E.F.	CELLS WITH E.F. < 5
47.42083	48	0.4965	0.053	63 OF 63 (100.0%)

STATISTIC	SYMMETRIC	WITH SMCREAS DEPENDENT	WITH UNDERBEL DEPENDENT
LAMBDA	0.37931	0.42857	0.33333
UNCERTAINTY COEFFICIENT	0.55314	0.59137	0.51955

STATISTIC	VALUE	SIGNIFICANCE
CRAMER'S V	0.64496	
CONTINGENCY COEFFICIENT	0.84495	

NUMBER OF MISSING OBSERVATIONS =   147

CROSSTABULATION * TWO

- - - - - - - - - - - C R O S S T A B U L A T I O N   O F - - - - - - - - - - -
SMCREAS   ATTRACTION TO SMC   BY WHATSIT   WHAT IS SMC ABOUT
CONTROLLING FOR..
  SEX   SEX   VALUE =   1. FEMALE   PAGE   1 OF 2

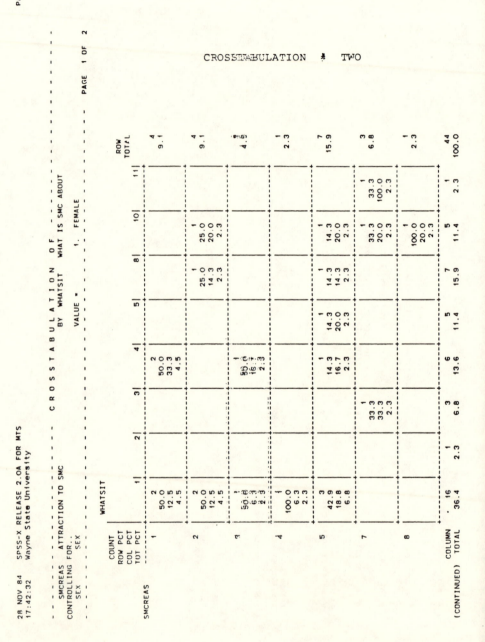

- - - - - - - - - - - - - - - C R O S S T A B U L A T I O N   O F - - - - - - - - - - - - - - - - - - -

SMCREAS   ATTRACTION TO SMC   BY WHATSIT   WHAT IS SMC ABOUT

CONTROLLING FOR..

SEX   VALUE =   1. FEMALE - - - - - - - PAGE   2 OF 2

| | WHATSIT | | | | | | | | |
COUNT ROW PCT COL PCT TOT PCT	1	2	3	4	5	8	10	11	ROW TOTAL
SMCREAS **10**	3 25.0 18.8 6.8	1 8.3 100.0 2.3	1 8.3 33.3 2.3	1 8.3 16.7 2.3	4 33.3 80.0 9.1	1 8.3 14.3 2.3	1 8.3 20.0 2.3		12 27.3
11	3 50.0 18.8 6.8		1 16.7 33.3 2.3	1 16.7 16.7 2.3		1 16.7 14.3 2.3			6 13.6
12	1 25.0 6.3 2.3					3 75.0 42.9 6.8			4 9.1
COLUMN TOTAL	16 36.4	1 2.3	3 6.8	6 13.6	5 11.4	7 15.9	5 11.4	1 2.3	44 100.0

CHI-SQUARE	D.F.	SIGNIFICANCE	MIN E.F.	CELLS WITH E.F. < 5
63.90351	63	0.4445	0.023	80 OF 80 (100.0%)

STATISTIC	SYMMETRIC	WITH SMCREAS DEPENDENT	WITH WHATSIT DEPENDENT
LAMBDA	0.15000	0.12500	0.17857
UNCERTAINTY COEFFICIENT	0.30418	0.28309	0.32866

STATISTIC	VALUE	SIGNIFICANCE
CRAMER'S V	0.45550	
CONTINGENCY COEFFICIENT	0.76956	

28 NOV 84   SPSS-X RELEASE 2.0A FOR MTS
17:42:32   Wayne State University

- - - - - - - - - - - - - - - C R O S S T A B U L A T I O N   O F - - - - - - - - - - - - - - -
SMCREAS   ATTRACTION TO SMC   BY WHATSIT   WHAT IS SMC ABOUT
CONTROLLING FOR...
SEX   SEX   VALUE =   2. MALE   PAGE 1 OF 1
- - - - - - - - - - - - - -

	COUNT ROW PCT COL PCT TOT PCT	WHATSIT 1	3	4	5	8	10	12	ROW TOTAL
SMCREAS 1		1 / 33.3 / 25.0 / 5.3				2 / 66.7 / 28.6 / 10.5			3 / 15.8
3		1 / 100.0 / 25.0 / 5.3							1 / 5.3
5		1 / 25.0 / 25.0 / 5.3		1 / 25.0 / 50.0 / 5.3		2 / 50.0 / 28.6 / 10.5			4 / 21.1
7			1 / 25.0 / 100.0 / 5.3	1 / 25.0 / 50.0 / 5.3	1 / 25.0 / 50.0 / 5.3			1 / 25.0 / 50.0 / 5.3	4 / 21.1
10					1 / 20.0 / 50.0 / 5.3	2 / 40.0 / 28.6 / 10.5	1 / 20.0 / 100.0 / 5.3	1 / 20.0 / 50.0 / 5.3	5 / 26.3
12		1 / 50.0 / 25.0 / 5.3				1 / 50.0 / 14.3 / 5.3			2 / 10.5
COLUMN TOTAL		4 / 21.1	1 / 5.3	2 / 10.5	2 / 10.5	7 / 36.8	1 / 5.3	2 / 10.5	19 / 100.0

CHI-SQUARE	D.F.	SIGNIFICANCE	MIN E.F.	CELLS WITH E.F. < 5
22.60774	30	0.8310	0.053	42 OF 42 (100.0%)

28 NOV 84   SPSS-X RELEASE 2.0A FOR MTS
17:42:33   Wayne State University

STATISTIC	SYMMETRIC	WITH SMCREAS DEPENDENT	WITH WHATSIT DEPENDENT
---------	---------	----------------------	----------------------
LAMBDA	0.19231	0.21429	0.16667
UNCERTAINTY COEFFICIENT	0.40029	0.40337	0.39726

STATISTIC	VALUE	SIGNIFICANCE
---------	-----	------------
CRAMER'S V	0.48783	
CONTINGENCY COEFFICIENT	0.73713	

NUMBER OF MISSING OBSERVATIONS = 144

260

- - - - - - - - - - - - - - - C R O S S T A B U L A T I O N   O F -
    SMCREAS   ATTRACTION TO SMC   BY GOD   BELIEFS ABOUT GOD
CONTROLLING FOR:
    SEX   SEX   VALUE =   1. FEMALE   PAGE 1 OF 2
- -

CROSSTABULATION # THREE

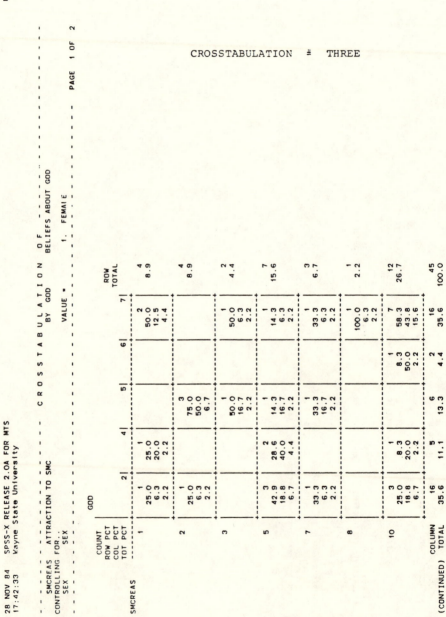

COUNT / ROW PCT / COL PCT / TOT PCT	GOD 2	4	5	6	7	ROW TOTAL
SMCREAS 1	1 / 25.0 / 6.3 / 2.2	1 / 25.0 / 20.0 / 2.2			2 / 50.0 / 12.5 / 4.4	4 / 8.9
2	1 / 25.0 / 6.3 / 2.2		3 / 75.0 / 50.0 / 6.7			4 / 8.9
3			1 / 50.0 / 16.7 / 2.2		1 / 50.0 / 6.3 / 2.2	2 / 4.4
5	3 / 42.9 / 18.8 / 6.7	2 / 28.6 / 40.0 / 4.4	1 / 14.3 / 16.7 / 2.2		1 / 14.3 / 6.3 / 2.2	7 / 15.6
7	1 / 33.3 / 6.3 / 2.2		1 / 33.3 / 16.7 / 2.2		1 / 33.3 / 6.3 / 2.2	3 / 6.7
8					1 / 100.0 / 6.3 / 2.2	1 / 2.2
10	3 / 25.0 / 18.8 / 6.7	1 / 8.3 / 20.0 / 2.2		1 / 8.3 / 50.0 / 2.2	7 / 58.3 / 43.8 / 15.6	12 / 26.7
COLUMN TOTAL	16 / 35.6	5 / 11.1	6 / 13.3	2 / 4.4	16 / 35.6	45 / 100.0

(CONTINUED)

28 NOV 84   SPSS-X RELEASE 2.0A FOR MTS
17:42:33   Wayne State University

- - - - - - - - - - - - - - - C R O S S T A B U L A T I O N   O F - - - - - - - - - - - - - - -
  SMCREAS   ATTRACTION TO SMC   BY GOD   BELIEFS ABOUT GOD
CONTROLLING FOR..
  SEX   SEX   VALUE =   1. FEMALE   PAGE 2 OF 2
- -

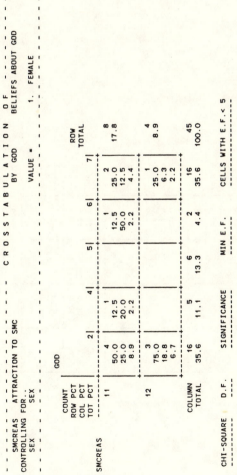

	GOD						ROW
COUNT							ROW TOTAL
ROW PCT							
COL PCT							
TOT PCT	2	4	5	6	7		
SMCREAS							
11	4	1		1	2		8
	50.0	12.5		12.5	25.0		17.8
	25.0	20.0		50.0	12.5		
	8.9	2.2		2.2	4.4		
12	3				1		4
	75.0				25.0		8.9
	18.8				6.3		
	6.7				2.2		
COLUMN	16	5	6	2	16		45
TOTAL	35.6	11.1	13.3	4.4	35.6		100.0

CHI-SQUARE   D.F.   SIGNIFICANCE   MIN E.F.   CELLS WITH E.F.< 5
- - - - - -   - - -   - - - - - - -   - - - - -   - - - - - - - - - -
35.13838   32   0.3217   0.044   45 OF   45 (100.0%)

       STATISTIC   SYMMETRIC   WITH SMCREAS   WITH GOD
       - - - - - - -   - - - - - -   DEPENDENT   DEPENDENT
                                              - - - - - - - -   - - - - - -
LAMBDA   0.22581   0.15152   0.31034
UNCERTAINTY COEFFICIENT   0.22992   0.19474   0.28062

       STATISTIC   VALUE   SIGNIFICANCE
       - - - - - - -   - - - - -   - - - - - - - -
CRAMER'S V   0.44183
CONTINGENCY COEFFICIENT   0.66217

- - - - - - - - - - - - - - - C R O S S T A B U L A T I O N   O F - - - - - - - - - - - - - - -
SMCREAS   ATTRACTION TO SMC   BY GOD   BELIEFS ABOUT GOD
CONTROLLING FOR..
SEX   SEX   VALUE =   2. MALE   PAGE 1 OF 2
- -

SMCREAS	COUNT ROW PCT COL PCT TOT PCT	GOD				ROW TOTAL
		2	4	5	7	
1		1 33.3 9.1 4.5			2 66.7 25.0 9.1	3 13.6
2		1 50.0 9.1 4.5			1 50.0 12.5 4.5	2 9.1
3					1 100.0 12.5 4.5	1 4.5
5		3 75.0 27.3 13.6	1 25.0 100.0 4.5			4 18.2
7		1 25.0 9.1 4.5		2 50.0 100.0 9.1	1 25.0 12.5 4.5	4 18.2
8		1 100.0 9.1 4.5				1 4.5
10		3 50.0 27.3 13.6			3 50.0 37.5 13.6	6 27.3
COLUMN TOTAL		11 50.0	1 4.5	2 9.1	8 36.4	22 100.0

(CONTINUED)

```
- - - - - - - - - - - - - -  C R O S S T A B U L A T I O N   O F  - - - - - - - - - - - - - - - - - - -
  SMCREAS    ATTRACTION TO SMC                     BY GOD    BELIEFS ABOUT GOD
CONTROLLING FOR..
  SEX        SEX                                    VALUE =      2.  MALE          - - -    PAGE  2 OF  2
- - - - - - - - - - - - - - -
```

```
              GOD
       COUNT  |
       ROW PCT|                                              ROW
       COL PCT|  2|    4|    5|    7|                        TOTAL
       TOT PCT|                                              
SMCREAS -------+-----+-----+-----+-----+                      1
        12    |   1 |     |     |     |                       4.5
              |100.0|     |     |     |
              |  9.1|     |     |     |
              |  4.5|     |     |     |
       -------+-----+-----+-----+-----+
       COLUMN    11     2     1     8                          22
       TOTAL    50.0   9.1   4.5  36.4                       100.0
```

CHI-SQUARE	D.F.	SIGNIFICANCE	MIN E.F.	CELLS WITH E.F. < 5
20.77083	21	0.4730	0.045	32 OF 32 (100.0%)

STATISTIC	SYMMETRIC	WITH SMCREAS DEPENDENT	WITH GOD DEPENDENT
LAMBDA	0.22222	0.18750	0.27273
UNCERTAINTY COEFFICIENT	0.29935	0.23485	0.41269

STATISTIC	VALUE	SIGNIFICANCE
CRAMER'S V	0.56099	
CONTINGENCY COEFFICIENT	0.69687	

NUMBER OF MISSING OBSERVATIONS =   140

CROSSTABULATION # FOUR

- - - UNDERBEL UNDERLYING BELIEFS - - - - - - - C R O S S T A B U L A T I O N   O F - - - - - - -
CONTROLLING FOR..   BY GOD   BELIEFS ABOUT GOD
   SEX   SEX   VALUE =   1. FEMALE
-     PAGE 1 OF 1

GOD

UNDERBEL	COUNT / ROW PCT / COL PCT / TOT PCT	2	4	5	6	7	ROW TOTAL
1		1 / 25.0 / 6.3 / 2.5			1 / 25.0 / 100.0 / 2.5	2 / 50.0 / 13.3 / 5.0	4 / 10.0
2		1 / 16.7 / 6.3 / 2.5	1 / 16.7 / 33.3 / 2.5	2 / 33.3 / 40.0 / 5.0		2 / 33.3 / 13.3 / 5.0	6 / 15.0
3		1 / 100.0 / 6.3 / 2.5					1 / 2.5
5		1 / 100.0 / 6.3 / 2.5					1 / 2.5
6		4 / 44.4 / 25.0 / 10.0	1 / 11.1 / 33.3 / 2.5	1 / 11.1 / 20.0 / 2.5		3 / 33.3 / 20.0 / 7.5	9 / 22.5
7		5 / 50.0 / 31.3 / 12.5	1 / 10.0 / 33.3 / 2.5	1 / 10.0 / 20.0 / 2.5		3 / 30.0 / 20.0 / 7.5	10 / 25.0
8		3 / 33.3 / 18.8 / 7.5		1 / 11.1 / 20.0 / 2.5		5 / 55.6 / 33.3 / 12.5	9 / 22.5
COLUMN TOTAL		16 / 40.0	3 / 7.5	5 / 12.5	1 / 2.5	15 / 37.5	40 / 100.0

28 NOV 84   SPSS-X RELEASE 2.0A FOR MTS
17:42:34   Wayne State University

CHI-SQUARE	D.F.	SIGNIFICANCE	MIN E.F.	CELLS WITH E.F. < 5
19.10278	24	0.7465	0.025	35 OF 35 (100.0%)

STATISTIC	SYMMETRIC	WITH UNDERBEL DEPENDENT	WITH GOD DEPENDENT
LAMBDA	0.14815	0.13333	0.16667
UNCERTAINTY COEFFICIENT	0.13417	0.11712	0.15703

STATISTIC	VALUE	SIGNIFICANCE
CRAMER'S V	0.34553	
CONTINGENCY COEFFICIENT	0.56852	

- - - - UNDERBEL UNDERLYING BELIEFS - - - - - - C R O S S T A B U L A T I O N   O F - - - - - - - - - - - - - - - - - -
CONTROLLING FOR..   BY GOD
    SEX   SEX   BELIEFS ABOUT GOD
-     VALUE =   2. MALE - - - - - - - - - - - - - - -   PAGE 1 OF 2

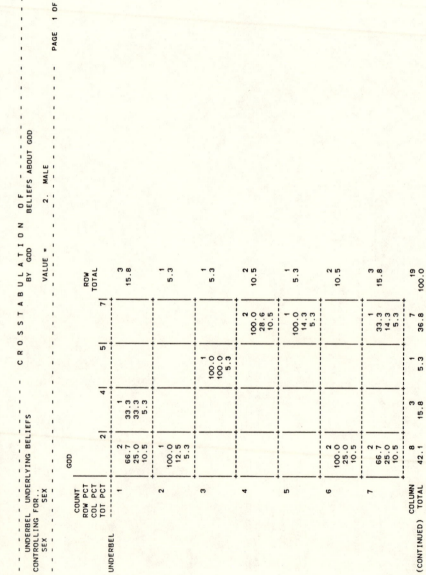

		GOD				
	COUNT ROW PCT COL PCT TOT PCT	2	4	5	7	ROW TOTAL
UNDERBEL	1	2 66.7 25.0 10.5	1 33.3 33.3 5.3			3 15.8
	2	1 100.0 12.5 5.3				1 5.3
	3			1 100.0 100.0 5.3		1 5.3
	4				2 100.0 28.6 10.5	2 10.5
	5				1 100.0 14.3 5.3	1 5.3
	6	2 100.0 25.0 10.5				2 10.5
	7	2 66.7 25.0 10.5			1 33.3 14.3 5.3	3 15.8
	COLUMN TOTAL	8 42.1	3 15.8	1 5.3	7 36.8	19 100.0

(CONTINUED)

-   C R O S S T A B U L A T I O N   O F   -
UNDERBEL UNDERLYING BELIEFS   BY GOD   BELIEFS ABOUT GOD
CONTROLLING FOR..
SEX   SEX   VALUE =   2. MALE
-   PAGE   2 OF 2

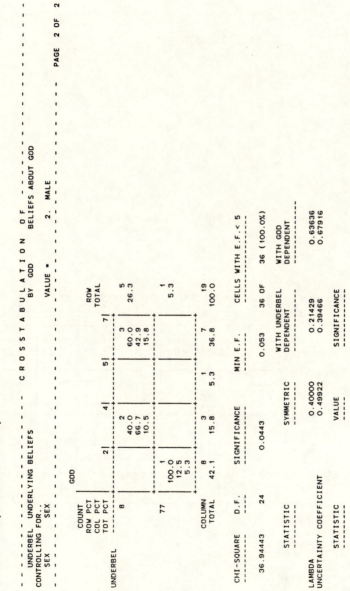

	GOD					ROW TOTAL
COUNT ROW PCT COL PCT TOT PCT	2	4	5	7		
UNDERBEL						
8		2 40.0 66.7 10.5	3 60.0 42.9 15.8			5 26.3
77	1 100.0 12.5 5.3					1 5.3
COLUMN TOTAL	8 42.1	3 15.8	1 5.3	7 36.8		19 100.0

CHI-SQUARE	D.F.	SIGNIFICANCE	MIN E.F.	CELLS WITH E.F. < 5
36.94443	24	0.0443	0.053	36 (100.0%)

STATISTIC	SYMMETRIC	WITH UNDERBEL DEPENDENT	WITH GOD DEPENDENT
LAMBDA	0.40000	0.21429	0.63636
UNCERTAINTY COEFFICIENT	0.49922	0.39466	0.67916

STATISTIC	VALUE	SIGNIFICANCE
CRAMER'S V	0.80508	
CONTINGENCY COEFFICIENT	0.81264	

NUMBER OF MISSING OBSERVATIONS =   148

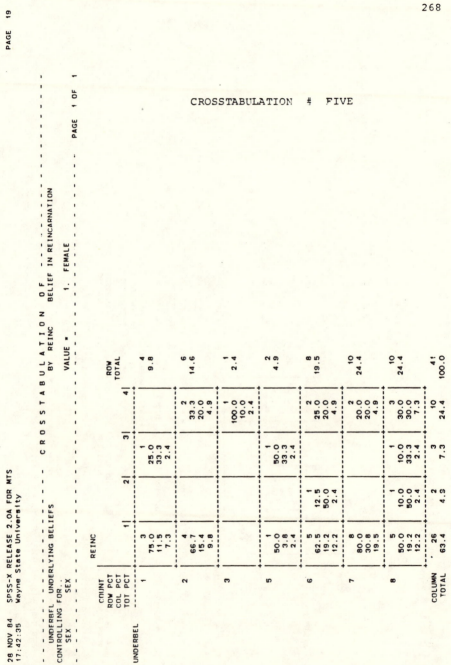

- - - - UNDERBEL UNDERLYING BELIEFS - - - - C R O S S T A B U L A T I O N   O F - - - - - - - - - - -
CONTROLLING FOR..   BY REINC   BELIEF IN REINCARNATION
    SEX   SEX   VALUE =   1. FEMALE   PAGE 1 OF 1
- -

CROSSTABULATION # FIVE

REINC

COUNT ROW PCT COL PCT TOT PCT UNDERBEL	1	2	3	4	ROW TOTAL
1	3 75.0 11.5 7.3		1 25.0 33.3 2.4		4 9.8
2	4 66.7 15.4 9.8			2 33.3 20.0 4.9	6 14.6
3				1 100.0 10.0 2.4	1 2.4
5	1 50.0 3.8 2.4		1 50.0 33.3 2.4		2 4.9
6	5 62.5 19.2 12.2	1 12.5 50.0 2.4		2 25.0 20.0 4.9	8 19.5
7	8 80.0 30.8 19.5			2 20.0 20.0 4.9	10 24.4
8	5 50.0 19.2 12.2	1 10.0 50.0 2.4	1 10.0 33.3 2.4	3 30.0 30.0 7.3	10 24.4
COLUMN TOTAL	26 63.4	2 4.9	3 7.3	10 24.4	41 100.0

28 NOV 84   SPSS-X RELEASE 2.0A FOR MTS
17:42:35   Wayne State University

CHI-SQUARE	D.F.	SIGNIFICANCE	MIN E.F.	CELLS WITH E.F. < 5
-------	----	------------	--------	-------------------
16.94667	18	0.5268	0.049	25 OF 28 (89.3%)

STATISTIC	SYMMETRIC	WITH UNDERBEL	WITH REINC
---------	---------	DEPENDENT	DEPENDENT
		-------------	-----------
LAMBDA	0.08696	0.09677	0.06667
UNCERTAINTY COEFFICIENT	0.15206	0.11816	0.21322

STATISTIC	VALUE	SIGNIFICANCE
---------	-----	------------
CRAMER'S V	0.37118	
CONTINGENCY COEFFICIENT	0.54079	

28 NOV 84   SPSS-X RELEASE 2.0A FOR MTS
17:42:35   Wayne State University

- - - - - - - - - - - - - -   C R O S S T A B U L A T I O N   O F   -
UNDERBEL UNDERLYING BELIEFS   BY REINC   BELIEF IN REINCARNATION
CONTROLLING FOR..
SEX   SEX   VALUE =   2. MALE   PAGE   1 OF 2
- - - - - - - - - - - - - -

	REINC				
COUNT					ROW
ROW PCT					TOTAL
COL PCT					
TOT PCT	1	2	4		
UNDERBEL					
1	2	1			3
	66.7	33.3			15.0
	18.2	50.0			
	10.0	5.0			
2	1				1
	100.0				5.0
	9.1				
	5.0				
3	1	1			1
		100.0			5.0
		50.0			
		5.0			
4	1		2		3
	33.3		66.7		15.0
	9.1		28.6		
	5.0		10.0		
5	1				1
	100.0				5.0
	9.1				
	5.0				
6	1		1		2
	50.0		50.0		10.0
	9.1		14.3		
	5.0		5.0		
7	1		2		3
	33.3		66.7		15.0
	9.1		28.6		
	5.0		10.0		
COLUMN	11	2	7		20
TOTAL	55.0	10.0	35.0		100.0

(CONTINUED)

- - - UNDERBEL UNDERLYING BELIEFS - - - C R O S S T A B U L A T I O N   O F -
CONTROLLING FOR..   BY REINC   BELIEF IN REINCARNATION
    SEX   SEX   VALUE =   2. MALE   PAGE 2 OF 2
- -

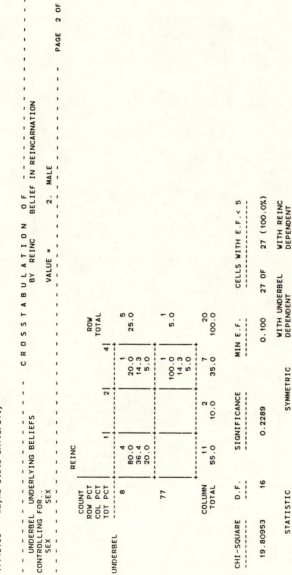

```
              REINC
        COUNT  |
      ROW PCT  |                                      ROW
      COL PCT  |                                      TOTAL
      TOT PCT  |    1|    2|    4|
UNDERBEL     --+-----+-----+-----+
           8 |   4 |     |   1 |     5
             | 80.0|     | 20.0|  25.0
             | 36.4|     | 14.3|
             | 20.0|     |  5.0|
           --+-----+-----+-----+
          77 |     |   2 |   1 |     1
             |     |100.0|100.0|   5.0
             |     | 14.3| 14.3|
             |     | 10.0|  5.0|
           --+-----+-----+-----+
      COLUMN    11     2     7     20
      TOTAL   55.0  10.0  35.0  100.0
```

CHI-SQUARE   D.F.   SIGNIFICANCE   MIN E.F.   CELLS WITH E.F. < 5
----------   ----   ------------   --------   -------------------

19.80953   16   0.2289   0.100   27 OF   27 (100.0%)

    STATISTIC   SYMMETRIC   WITH UNDERBEL   WITH REINC
    ---------   ---------   DEPENDENT   DEPENDENT
                                            ------------   ----------

LAMBDA   0.25000   0.13333   0.44444
UNCERTAINTY COEFFICIENT   0.30151   0.21957   0.48101

    STATISTIC   VALUE   SIGNIFICANCE
    ---------   -----   ------------

CRAMER'S V   0.70373
CONTINGENCY COEFFICIENT   0.70541

NUMBER OF MISSING OBSERVATIONS =   146

272

CROSSTABULATION # SIX

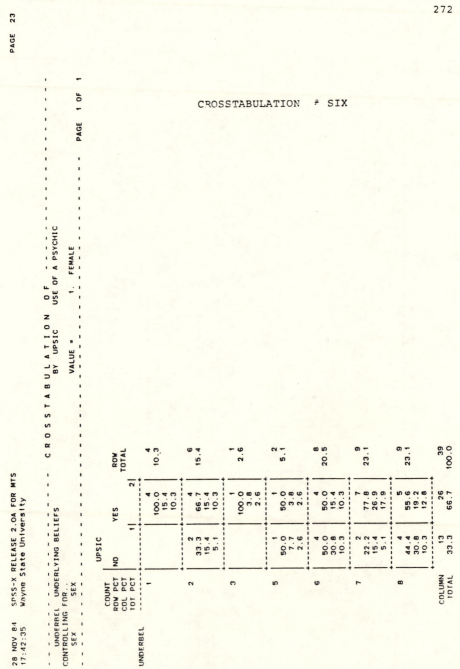

- - - - - - - - - - C R O S S T A B U L A T I O N   O F -
    UNDERBEL UNDERLYING BELIEFS   BY UPSIC   USE OF A PSYCHIC
CONTROLLING FOR..
    SEX   SEX   VALUE =   1. FEMALE   PAGE 1 OF 1

	UPSIC		
COUNT			
ROW PCT	NO	YES	ROW
COL PCT			TOTAL
TOT PCT	1	2	
UNDERBEL			
1		100.0 / 15.4 / 10.3	4 / 10.3
2	33.3 / 15.4 / 5.1	66.7 / 15.4 / 10.3	6 / 15.4
3		100.0 / 3.8 / 2.6	1 / 2.6
5	50.0 / 7.7 / 2.6	50.0 / 3.8 / 2.6	2 / 5.1
6	50.0 / 30.8 / 10.3	50.0 / 15.4 / 10.3	8 / 20.5
7	22.2 / 15.4 / 5.1	77.8 / 26.9 / 17.9	9 / 23.1
8	44.4 / 30.8 / 10.3	55.6 / 19.2 / 12.8	9 / 23.1
COLUMN TOTAL	13 / 33.3	26 / 66.7	39 / 100.0

28 NOV 84   SPSS-X RELEASE 2.0A FOR MTS
17:42:35   Wayne State University

CHI-SQUARE	D.F.	SIGNIFICANCE	MIN E.F.	CELLS WITH E.F. < 5
4.75000	6	0.5763	0.333	11 OF 14 (78.6%)

STATISTIC	SYMMETRIC	WITH UNDERBEL DEPENDENT	WITH UPSIC DEPENDENT
LAMBDA	0.04651	0.06667	0.0
UNCERTAINTY COEFFICIENT	0.06657	0.04526	0.12583

STATISTIC	VALUE	SIGNIFICANCE
CRAMER'S V	0.34899	
CONTINGENCY COEFFICIENT	0.32950	

- - - UNDERBEL UNDERLYING BELIEFS - - - C R O S S T A B U L A T I O N   O F - - - - - - - - - - - - - - - - - - -
CONTROLLING FOR: BY UPSIC   USE OF A PSYCHIC
    SEX   SEX   VALUE =   2. MALE   PAGE 1 OF 2

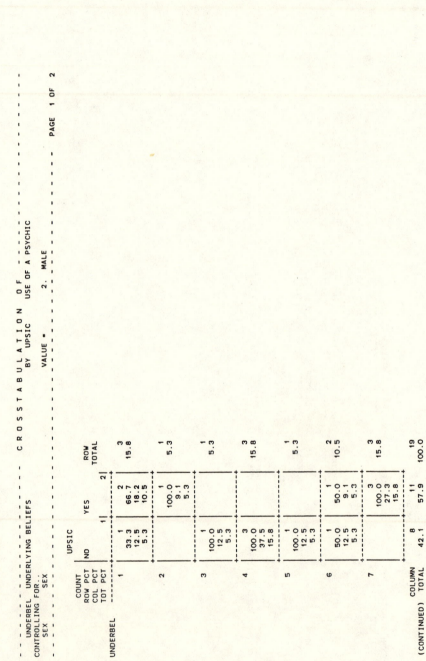

		UPSIC		
COUNT		NO	YES	ROW
ROW PCT				TOTAL
COL PCT				
TOT PCT		1	2	
UNDERBEL	1	33.3 12.5 5.3	2 66.7 18.2 10.5	3 15.8
	2	1 100.0 12.5 5.3	1 100.0 9.1 5.3	1 5.3
	3	3 100.0 37.5 15.8	1 100.0 9.1 5.3	1 5.3
	4	3 100.0 37.5 15.8		3 15.8
	5	1 100.0 12.5 5.3		1 5.3
	6	1 50.0 12.5 5.3	1 50.0 9.1 5.3	2 10.5
	7		3 100.0 27.3 15.8	3 15.8
COLUMN TOTAL		8 42.1	11 57.9	19 100.0

(CONTINUED)

```
- - - UNDERBEL  UNDERLYING BELIEFS - - - C R O S S T A B U L A T I O N   O F - - - - - - - - - - - - - - - - - - - - -
CONTROLLING FOR..                                 BY UPSIC    USE OF A PSYCHIC
     SEX    SEX                                      VALUE =    2. MALE        - - - - -   PAGE 2 OF 2
- - - - - - - - - - - - - - - - - - - - - - - - - - - - - - - - - - - - - - - - - - - - - - - - - - - - - - - -

                   UPSIC
          COUNT  |
          ROW PCT| NO      YES     ROW
          COL PCT|                 TOTAL
          TOT PCT|      1 |     2 |
UNDERBEL  --------+--------+--------+
             8   |    1   |    3   |    4
                 | 25.0   | 75.0   | 21.1
                 | 12.5   | 27.3   |
                 |  5.3   | 15.8   |
          --------+--------+--------+
            77   |        |    1   |    1
                 |        |100.0   |  5.3
                 |        |  9.1   |
                 |        |  5.3   |
          --------+--------+--------+
          COLUMN      8       11       19
          TOTAL     42.1     57.9    100.0
```

CHI-SQUARE	D.F.	SIGNIFICANCE	MIN E.F.	CELLS WITH E.F. < 5
11.13731	8	0.1940	0.421	18 OF 18 (100.0%)

STATISTIC	SYMMETRIC	WITH UNDERBEL DEPENDENT	WITH UPSIC DEPENDENT
LAMBDA	0.30435	0.13333	0.62500
UNCERTAINTY COEFFICIENT	0.28379	0.18880	0.57120

STATISTIC	VALUE	SIGNIFICANCE
CRAMER'S V	0.76562	
CONTINGENCY COEFFICIENT	0.60791	

NUMBER OF MISSING OBSERVATIONS =   149

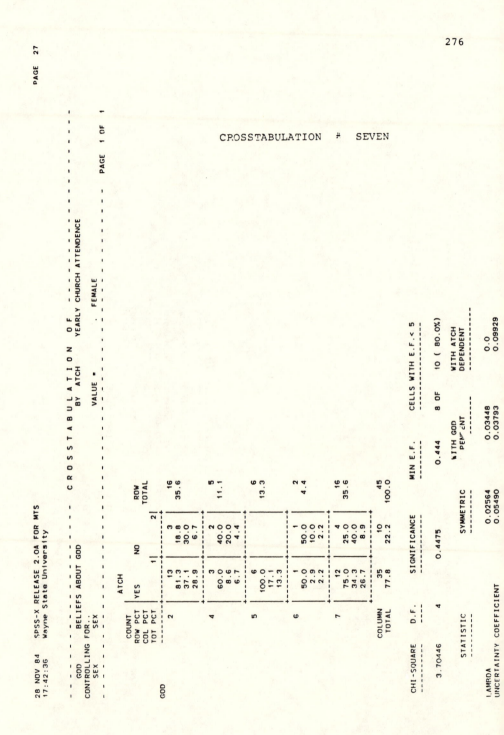

CROSSTABULATION # SEVEN

28 NOV 84   SPSS-X RELEASE 2.0A FOR MTS
17:42:36   Wayne State University

PAGE 27

- - - - - - - - - - C R O S S T A B U L A T I O N   O F - - - - - - - - - - - -
     GOD   BELIEFS ABOUT GOD   BY ATCH   YEARLY CHURCH ATTENDENCE
CONTROLLING FOR..
     SEX   SEX   VALUE =   . FEMALE   PAGE 1 OF 1

GOD	ATCH			
COUNT ROW PCT COL PCT TOT PCT	YES 1	NO 2	ROW TOTAL	
GOD				
2	13 81.3 37.1 28.9	3 18.8 30.0 6.7	16 35.6	
4	3 60.0 8.6 6.7	2 40.0 20.0 4.4	5 11.1	
5	6 100.0 17.1 13.3		6 13.3	
6	1 50.0 2.9 2.2	1 50.0 10.0 2.2	2 4.4	
7	12 75.0 34.3 26.7	4 25.0 40.0 8.9	16 35.6	
COLUMN TOTAL	35 77.8	10 22.2	45 100.0	

CHI-SQUARE	D.F.	SIGNIFICANCE	MIN E.F.	CELLS WITH E.F. < 5
--------	----	------------	--------	-------------------
3.70446	4	0.4475	0.444	8 OF 10 (80.0%)

STATISTIC	SYMMETRIC	WITH GOD PERCENT	WITH ATCH DEPENDENT
---------	---------	--------	---------
LAMBDA	0.02564	0.03448	0.0
UNCERTAINTY COEFFICIENT	0.05490	0.03793	0.09929

28 NOV 84   SPSS-X RELEASE 2.0A FOR MTS
17:42:36   Wayne State University

STATISTIC   VALUE   SIGNIFICANCE
---------   -----   ------------

CRAMER'S V   0.28692
CONTINGENCY COEFFICIENT   0.27579

- - - - - - - - - -   C R O S S T A B U L A T I O N   O F - - - - - - - - - - - - - - -
   GOD   BELIEFS ABOUT GOD   BY ATCH   YEARLY CHURCH ATTENDENCE
CONTROLLING FOR..
   SEX   SEX   VALUE =   2. MALE   PAGE 1 OF 1
- - - - - - - - - -

```
            ATCH
     COUNT  |
     ROW PCT|YES       NO       ROW
     COL PCT|                  TOTAL
     TOT PCT|     1 |     2 |
GOD         +-------+-------+
         2  |    6  |    5  |   11
            |  54.5 |  45.5 |  47.8
            |  40.0 |  62.5 |
            |  26.1 |  21.7 |
            +-------+-------+
         4  |    2  |    1  |    3
            |  66.7 |  33.3 |  13.0
            |  13.3 |  12.5 |
            |   8.7 |   4.3 |
            +-------+-------+
         5  |    1  |       |    1
            | 100.0 |       |   4.3
            |   6.7 |       |
            |   4.3 |       |
            +-------+-------+
         7  |    6  |    2  |    8
            |  75.0 |  25.0 |  34.8
            |  40.0 |  25.0 |
            |  26.1 |   8.7 |
            +-------+-------+
   COLUMN       15       8      23
    TOTAL     65.2    34.8   100.0
```

CHI-SQUARE   D.F.   SIGNIFICANCE   MIN E.F.   CELLS WITH E.F. < 5
----------   ----   ------------   --------   -------------------
1.42588   3   0.6995   0.348   6 OF 8 (75.0%)

     STATISTIC   SYMMETRIC   WITH GOD   WITH ATCH
                                       DEPENDENT   DEPENDENT
     ---------   ---------   ---------   ---------
LAMBDA   0.0   0.0   0.0
UNCERTAINTY COEFFICIENT   0.04292   0.03382   0.05873

     STATISTIC   VALUE   SIGNIFICANCE
     ---------   -----   ------------
CRAMER'S V   0.24899
CONTINGENCY COEFFICIENT   0.24161

28 NOV 84   SPSS-X RELEASE 2.0A FOR MTS   PAGE 30
17:42:36   Wayne State University

- - - - - - - GOD BELIEFS ABOUT GOD - - - - - C R O S S T A B U L A T I O N   O F   -
CONTROLLING FOR..   BY CHFREQ FREQUENCY PER YEAR
      SEX   SEX   VALUE =   1. FEMALE   PAGE 1 OF 1
- -

CROSSTABULATION # EIGHT

Cell contents: COUNT / ROW PCT / COL PCT / TOT PCT

GOD	CHFREQ 0	1	2	3	4	5	ROW TOTAL
2	2 / 12.5 / 22.2 / 4.4	2 / 12.5 / 40.0 / 4.4	6 / 37.5 / 40.0 / 13.3	4 / 25.0 / 40.0 / 8.9	1 / 6.3 / 20.0 / 2.2	1 / 6.3 / 100.0 / 2.2	16 / 35.6
4	2 / 40.0 / 22.2 / 4.4			3 / 60.0 / 30.0 / 6.7			5 / 11.1
5		1 / 16.7 / 20.0 / 2.2	2 / 33.3 / 13.3 / 4.4	2 / 33.3 / 20.0 / 4.4	1 / 16.7 / 20.0 / 2.2		6 / 13.3
6	1 / 50.0 / 11.1 / 2.2		1 / 50.0 / 6.7 / 2.2				2 / 4.4
7	4 / 25.0 / 44.4 / 8.9	2 / 12.5 / 40.0 / 4.4	6 / 37.5 / 40.0 / 13.3	1 / 6.3 / 10.0 / 2.2	3 / 18.8 / 60.0 / 6.7		16 / 35.6
COLUMN TOTAL	9 / 20.0	5 / 11.1	15 / 33.3	10 / 22.2	5 / 11.1	1 / 2.2	45 / 100.0

CHI-SQUARE	D.F.	SIGNIFICANCE	MIN E.F.	CELLS WITH E.F.< 5
16.56875	20	0.6808	0.044	28 OF 30 (93.3%)

STATISTIC	SYMMETRIC	WITH GOD DEPENDENT	WITH CHFREQ DEPENDENT
LAMBDA	0.11864	0.13793	0.10000
UNCERTAINTY COEFFICIENT	0.15469	0.16633	0.14457

28 NOV 84   SPS-X RELEASE 2.0A FOR MTS
17:42:36   Wayne State University

STATISTIC	VALUE	SIGNIFICANCE
CRAMER'S V	0.30340	
CONTINGENCY COEFFICIENT	0.51876	

28 NOV 84   SPSS-X RELEASE 2.0A FOR MTS
17:42:36   Wayne State University

- - - - - - - - - - - - - C R O S S T A B U L A T I O N   O F -
      GOD   BELIEFS ABOUT GOD   BY CHFREQ   FREQUENCY PER YEAR
CONTROLLING FOR..
   SEX   SEX   VALUE =   2. MALE   PAGE 1 OF 1

```
                CHFREQ
         COUNT  |
         ROW PCT|                                                                ROW
         COL PCT|                                                               TOTAL
         TOT PCT|     0|     2|     3|     4|     5|
GOD      --------+------+------+------+------+------+
            2    |    5 |    2 |    3 |      |    1 |   11
                 | 45.5 | 18.2 | 27.3 |      |  9.1 | 47.8
                 | 62.5 | 50.0 | 60.0 |      | 50.0 |
                 | 21.7 |  8.7 | 13.0 |      |  4.3 |
         --------+------+------+------+------+------+
            4    |    1 |      |    1 |    1 |      |    3
                 | 33.3 |      | 33.3 | 33.3 |      | 13.0
                 | 12.5 |      | 25.0 | 50.0 |      |
                 |  4.3 |      |  4.3 |  4.3 |      |
         --------+------+------+------+------+------+
            5    |      |    1 |      |      |      |    1
                 |      |100.0 |      |      |      |  4.3
                 |      | 25.0 |      |      |      |
                 |      |  4.3 |      |      |      |
         --------+------+------+------+------+------+
            7    |    2 |    1 |    2 |    2 |    1 |    8
                 | 25.0 | 12.5 | 25.0 | 25.0 | 12.5 | 34.8
                 | 25.0 | 25.0 | 40.0 | 50.0 | 50.0 |
                 |  8.7 |  4.3 |  8.7 |  8.7 |  4.3 |
         --------+------+------+------+------+------+
         COLUMN       8      4      5      4      2     23
          TOTAL     34.8   17.4   21.7   17.4    8.7   100.0
```

CHI-SQUARE   D.F.   SIGNIFICANCE   MIN E.F.   CELLS WITH E.F. < 5
----------   ----   ------------   --------   -------------------
11.13845   12   0.5171   0.087   20 OF   20 (100.0%)

                    SYMMETRIC   WITH GOD   WITH CHFREQ
   STATISTIC   DEPENDENT   DEPENDENT
   ---------   ---------   ---------   -----------
LAMBDA   0.11111   0.16667   0.06667
UNCERTAINTY COEFFICIENT 0.18824   0.21454   0.15839

   STATISTIC   VALUE   SIGNIFICANCE
   ---------   -----   ------------
CRAMER'S V   0.40178
CONTINGENCY COEFFICIENT 0.57120

NUMBER OF MISSING OBSERVATIONS =   139

CROSSTABULATION # NINE

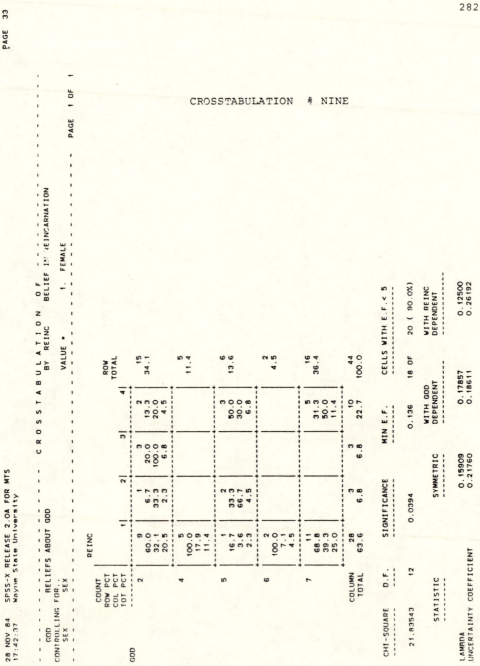

- - -   GOD   RELIEFS ABOUT GOD   - - - - - -   C R O S S T A B U L A T I O N   O F   -
CONTROLLING FOR..   BY REINC   BELIEF IN REINCARNATION
    SEX   SEX   VALUE =   1. FEMALE   PAGE   1 OF 1
- - - - - - - - - - - -

		REINC					
	COUNT						ROW
	ROW PCT						TOTAL
	COL PCT						
	TOT PCT	1	2	3	4		
GOD	2	9	1	3	2		15
		60.0	6.7	20.0	13.3		34.1
		32.1	33.3	100.0	20.0		
		20.5	2.3	6.8	4.5		
	4	5					5
		100.0					11.4
		17.9					
		11.4					
	5	1	2		3		6
		16.7	33.3		50.0		13.6
		3.6	66.7		30.0		
		2.3	4.5		6.8		
	6	2					2
		100.0					4.5
		7.1					
		4.5					
	7	11			5		16
		68.8			31.3		36.4
		39.3			50.0		
		25.0			11.4		
COLUMN		28	3	3	10		44
TOTAL		63.6	6.8	6.8	22.7		100.0

CHI-SQUARE	D.F.	SIGNIFICANCE	MIN E.F.	CELLS WITH E.F.< 5
21.83543	12	0.0394	0.136	18 OF 20 (90.0%)

STATISTIC	SYMMETRIC	WITH GOD DEPENDENT	WITH REINC DEPENDENT
LAMBDA	0.15909	0.17857	0.12500
UNCERTAINTY COEFFICIENT	0.21760	0.18611	0.26192

28 NOV 84   SPSS-X RELEASE 2.0A FOR MTS
17:42:37   Wayne State University

STATISTIC   VALUE   SIGNIFICANCE
---------   -----   ------------

CRAMER'S V   0.40672
CONTINGENCY COEFFICIENT   0.57591

- - - - - G O D   B E L I E F S   A B O U T   G O D - - - - - - C R O S S T A B U L A T I O N   O F - - - - - - - - - - - - - - - - - - -
CONTROLLING FOR: BY REINC   BELIEF IN REINCARNATION
   SEX   SEX   VALUE =   2. MALE   PAGE 1 OF 1

```
                    REINC
          COUNT  |
          ROW PCT|
          COL PCT|                                        ROW
          TOT PCT|    1 |    2 |    4 |                   TOTAL
GOD           ---+------+------+------+
           2     |    7 |    4 |      |                     11
                 | 63.6 | 36.4 |      |                   50.0
                 | 53.8 | 57.1 |      |
                 | 31.8 | 18.2 |      |
              ---+------+------+------+
           4     |    2 |      |    1 |                      3
                 | 66.7 |      | 33.3 |                   13.6
                 | 15.4 |      | 50.0 |
                 |  9.1 |      |  4.5 |
              ---+------+------+------+
           5     |      |    1 |    1 |                      1
                 |      |100.0 |100.0 |                    4.5
                 |      | 50.0 | 50.0 |
                 |      |  4.5 |  4.5 |
              ---+------+------+------+
           7     |    4 |    3 |      |                      7
                 | 57.1 | 42.9 |      |                   31.8
                 | 30.8 | 42.9 |      |
                 | 18.2 | 13.6 |      |
              ---+------+------+------+
          COLUMN     13      2      7                        22
          TOTAL    59.1    9.1   31.8                     100.0
```

CHI-SQUARE   D.F.   SIGNIFICANCE   MIN E.F.   CELLS WITH E.F. < 5
----------   ----   ------------   --------   -------------------

  14.94192   6   0.0207   0.091   11 OF 12 (91.7%)

    STATISTIC   SYMMETRIC   WITH GOD   WITH REINC
    ---------   ---------   DEPENDENT   DEPENDENT
                                             ---------   ---------

LAMBDA   0.10000   0.09091   0.11111
UNCERTAINTY COEFFICIENT   0.25928   0.23274   0.29264

    STATISTIC   VALUE   SIGNIFICANCE
    ---------   -----   ------------

CRAMER'S V   0.58274
CONTINGENCY COEFFICIENT   0.63598

NUMBER OF MISSING OBSERVATIONS = 141

28 NOV 84   SPSS-X RELEASE 2.0A FOR MTS
17:42:37   Wayne State University

- - - - - - - - - - - - C R O S S T A B U L A T I O N   O F -
   GOD   BELIEFS ABOUT GOD   BY UPSIC   USE OF A PSYCHIC
CONTROLLING FOR..
   SEX   SEX   VALUE =   1. FEMALE   PAGE 1 OF

CROSSTABULATION # TEN

	UPSIC		
COUNT			
ROW PCT	NO	YES	ROW
COL PCT			TOTAL
TOT PCT	1	2	
GOD			
2	4	11	15
	26.7	73.3	36.6
	30.8	39.3	
	9.8	26.8	
4	3	1	4
	75.0	25.0	9.8
	23.1	3.6	
	7.3	2.4	
5	3	2	5
	60.0	40.0	12.2
	23.1	7.1	
	7.3	4.9	
6		2	2
		100.0	4.9
		7.1	
		4.9	
7	3	12	15
	20.0	80.0	36.6
	23.1	42.9	
	7.3	29.3	
COLUMN	13	28	41
TOTAL	31.7	68.3	100.0

CHI-SQUARE	D.F.	SIGNIFICANCE	MIN E.F.	CELLS WITH E.F. < 5
7.36461	4	0.1178	0.634	8 OF 10 (80.0%)

STATISTIC	SYMMETRIC	WITH GOD DEPENDENT	WITH UPSIC DEPENDENT
LAMBDA	0.10256	0.03846	0.23077
UNCERTAINTY COEFFICIENT	0.09287	0.06766	0.14804

28 NOV 84   SPSS-X RELEASE 2.OA FOR MTS
17:42:37   Wayne State University

STATISTIC   VALUE   SIGNIFICANCE
---------   -----   ------------

CRAMER'S V   0.42382
CONTINGENCY COEFFICIENT   0.39022

- - - - - - - - - - - - - - C R O S S T A B U L A T I O N   O F -
　　GOD   BELIEFS ABOUT GOD   BY UPSIC   USE OF A PSYCHIC
CONTROLLING FOR..
　　SEX   SEX   VALUE =   2. MALE
-        PAGE   1 OF 1

```
                       UPSIC
            COUNT  |
            ROW PCT|  NO     YES       ROW
            COL PCT|                  TOTAL
            TOT PCT|    1|     2|
         GOD -------+------+------+
                2  |   4  |   7  |   11
                   | 36.4 | 63.6 |  52.4
                   | 44.4 | 58.3 |
                   | 19.0 | 33.3 |
                   +------+------+
                4  |   1  |   2  |    3
                   | 33.3 | 66.7 |  14.3
                   | 11.1 | 16.7 |
                   |  4.8 |  9.5 |
                   +------+------+
                5  |   1  |      |    1
                   |100.0 |      |   4.8
                   | 11.1 |      |
                   |  4.8 |      |
                   +------+------+
                7  |   3  |   3  |    6
                   | 50.0 | 50.0 |  28.6
                   | 33.3 | 25.0 |
                   | 14.3 | 14.3 |
                   +------+------+
          COLUMN        9     12       21
           TOTAL      42.9   57.1    100.0
```

CHI-SQUARE	D.F.	SIGNIFICANCE	MIN E.F.	CELLS WITH E.F.< 5
1.75884	3	0.6239	0.429	7 OF 8 (87.5%)

STATISTIC	SYMMETRIC	WITH GOD DEPENDENT	WITH UPSIC DEPENDENT
LAMBDA	0.05263	0.0	0.11111
UNCERTAINTY COEFFICIENT	0.05613	0.04518	0.07408

STATISTIC	VALUE	SIGNIFICANCE
CRAMER'S V	0.28940	
CONTINGENCY COEFFICIENT	0.27800	

NUMBER OF MISSING OBSERVATIONS =   145

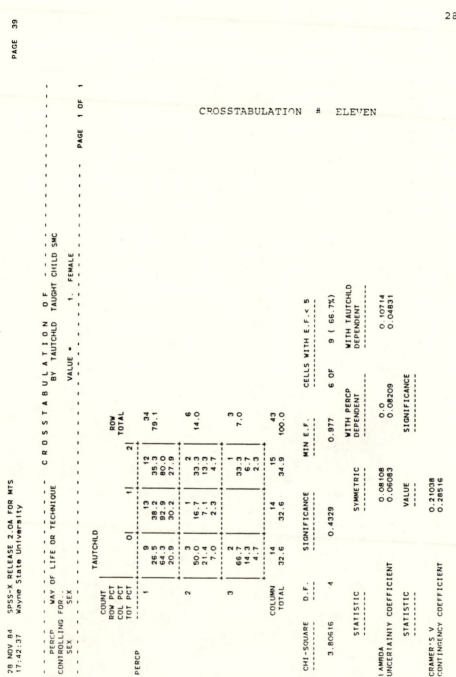

CROSSTABULATION # ELEVEN

```
 - - - - - - - - - - - - - - -  C R O S S T A B U L A T I O N   O F  - - - - - - - - - - - - - - - - -
   PERCP   WAY OF LIFE OR TECHNIQUE          BY TAUTCHLD  TAUGHT CHILD SMC
CONTROLLING FOR..
   SEX    SEX                               VALUE =    2.  MALE          PAGE  1 OF  1
 - - - - - - - - - - - - - - - - - - - - - - - - - - - - - - - - - - - - - - - - - - - - - - - - - - -

                TAUTCHLD
          COUNT  |
          ROW PCT|
          COL PCT|                                    ROW
          TOT PCT|    0|     1|     2|               TOTAL
PERCP     -------+------+------+------+
        1 |    6 |    8 |    5 |                        19
          | 31.6 | 42.1 | 26.3 |                      79.2
          | 75.0 | 88.9 | 71.4 |
          | 25.0 | 33.3 | 20.8 |
          +------+------+------+
        2 |    2 |      |      |                         2
          |100.0 |      |      |                       8.3
          | 25.0 |      |      |
          |  8.3 |      |      |
          +------+------+------+
        3 |      |    1 |    2 |                         3
          |      | 33.3 | 66.7 |                      12.5
          |      | 11.1 | 28.6 |
          |      |  4.2 |  8.3 |
          +------+------+------+
   COLUMN      8      9      7                          24
    TOTAL    33.3   37.5   29.2                       100.0
```

CHI-SQUARE	D.F.	SIGNIFICANCE	MIN E.F.	CELLS WITH E.F.< 5
6.63826	4	0.1563	0.583	6 OF 9 (66.7%)

STATISTIC	SYMMETRIC	WITH PERCP DEPENDENT	WITH TAUTCHLD DEPENDENT
LAMBDA	0.15000	0.0	0.20000
UNCERTAINTY COEFFICIENT	0.18243	0.24419	0.14560

STATISTIC	VALUE	SIGNIFICANCE
CRAMER'S V	0.37188	
CONTINGENCY COEFFICIENT	0.46547	

NUMBER OF MISSING OBSERVATIONS =   140

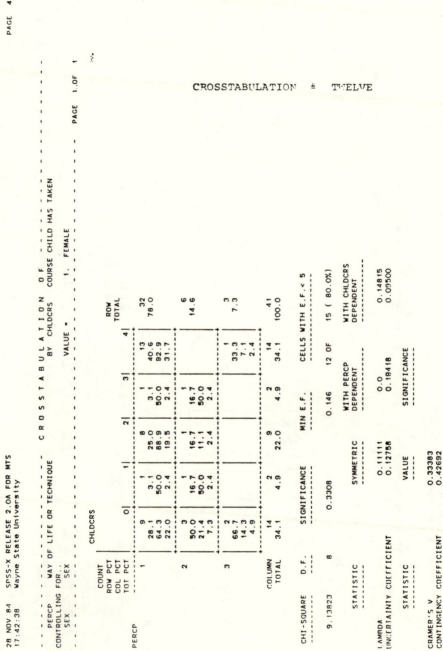

CROSSTABULATION # TWELVE

PERCP - WAY OF LIFE OR TECHNIQUE - CROSSTABULATION OF COURSE CHILD HAS TAKEN
CONTROLLING FOR..   BY CHLDCRS
SEX   SEX   VALUE = 1. FEMALE   PAGE 1.OF 1

CHLDCRS

COUNT ROW PCT COL PCT TOT PCT	0	1	2	3	4	ROW TOTAL
PERCP						
1	9 28.1 64.3 22.0	2 3.1 50.0 2.4	8 25.0 88.9 19.5	1 3.1 50.0 2.4	13 40.6 92.9 31.7	32 78.0
2	3 50.0 21.4 7.3	1 16.7 50.0 2.4	1 16.7 11.1 2.4	1 16.7 50.0 2.4		6 14.6
3	2 66.7 14.3 4.9			1 33.3 7.1 2.4		3 7.3
COLUMN TOTAL	14 34.1	2 4.9	9 22.0	2 4.9	14 34.1	41 100.0

CHI-SQUARE	D.F.	SIGNIFICANCE	MIN E.F.	CELLS WITH E.F.< 5
9.13823	8	0.3308	0.146	12 OF 15 (80.0%)

STATISTIC	SYMMETRIC	WITH PERCP DEPENDENT	WITH CHLDCRS DEPENDENT
LAMBDA	0.11111	0.0	0.14815
UNCERTAINTY COEFFICIENT	0.12758	0.18418	0.09500

STATISTIC	VALUE	SIGNIFICANCE
CRAMER'S V	0.33383	
CONTINGENCY COEFFICIENT	0.42692	

```
- - - - - - - - - - - - - - - - - - - -   C R O S S T A B U L A T I O N   O F   - - - - - - - - - - - - - - - - - - - -
  PERCP   WAY OF LIFE OR TECHNIQUE                            BY CHLDCRS    COURSE CHILD HAS TAKEN
CONTROLLING FOR..
  SEX       SEX                                              VALUE =     2.  MALE
- - - - - -                                                                       PAGE 1 OF 1
```

	CHLDCRS					
COUNT						ROW
ROW PCT						TOTAL
COL PCT						
TOT PCT	0	1	2	3	4	
PERCP						
1	6	2	4	2	5	19
	31.6	10.5	21.1	10.5	26.3	79.2
	75.0	100.0	80.0	100.0	71.4	
	25.0	8.3	16.7	8.3	20.8	
2	2					2
	100.0					8.3
	25.0					
	8.3					
3			1		2	3
			33.3		66.7	12.5
			20.0		28.6	
			4.2		8.3	
COLUMN	8	2	5	2	7	24
TOTAL	33.3	8.3	20.8	8.3	29.2	100.0

CHI-SQUARE	D.F.	SIGNIFICANCE	MIN E.F.	CELLS WITH E.F.< 5
7.46165	8	0.4877	0.167	13 OF 15 (86.7%)

STATISTIC	SYMMETRIC	WITH PERCP DEPENDENT	WITH CHLDCRS DEPENDENT
LAMBDA	0.09524	0.0	0.12500
UNCERTAINTY COEFFICIENT	0.17537	0.28493	0.12667

STATISTIC	VALUE	SIGNIFICANCE
CRAMER'S V	0.39427	
CONTINGENCY COEFFICIENT	0.48700	

NUMBER OF MISSING OBSERVATIONS =   142

28 NOV 84   SPSS-X RELEASE 2.0A FOR MTS   PAGE 43
17:42:38   Wayne State University

- - PERCP   WAY OF LIFE OR TECHNIQUE - - - - - C R O S S T A B U L A T I O N   O F - - - - - READING HABITS HAVE CHANGED
CONTROLLING FOR..   BY CHGREAD
   SEX   SEX   VALUE =   1. FEMALE   PAGE 1 OF 1

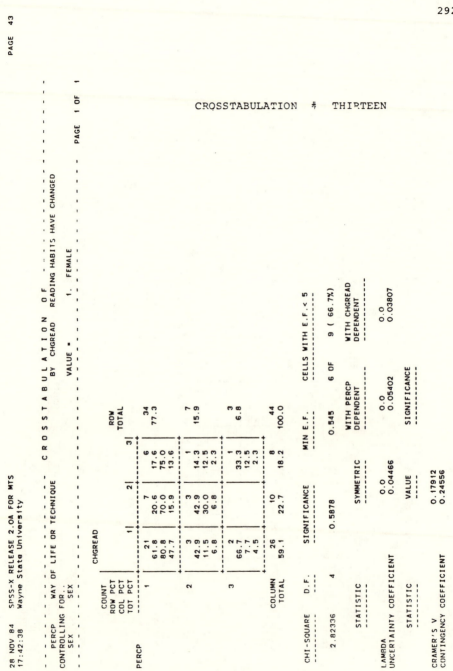

CROSSTABULATION # THIRTEEN

		CHGREAD			
	COUNT ROW PCT COL PCT TOT PCT	1	2	3	ROW TOTAL
PERCP	1	21 61.8 80.8 47.7	7 20.6 70.0 15.9	6 17.6 75.0 13.6	34 77.3
	2	3 42.9 11.5 6.8	3 42.9 30.0 6.8	1 14.3 12.5 2.3	7 15.9
	3	2 66.7 7.7 4.5	1 33.3 12.5 2.3		3 6.8
	COLUMN TOTAL	26 59.1	10 22.7	8 18.2	44 100.0

CHI-SQUARE	D.F.	SIGNIFICANCE	MIN E.F.	CELLS WITH E.F. < 5
2.82336	4	0.5878	0.545	6 OF 9 (66.7%)

STATISTIC	SYMMETRIC	WITH PERCP DEPENDENT	WITH CHGREAD DEPENDENT
LAMBDA	0.04466	0.0	0.0
UNCERTAINTY COEFFICIENT	0.04466	0.05402	0.03807

STATISTIC	VALUE	SIGNIFICANCE
CRAMER'S V	0.17912	
CONTINGENCY COEFFICIENT	0.24556	

28 NOV 84   SPSS-X RELEASE 2.0A FOR MTS
17:42:39   Wayne State University

- - - PERCP   WAY OF LIFE OR TECHNIQUE - - - - - - C R O S S T A B U L A T I O N   O F -
CONTROLLING FOR..   BY CHGREAD   READING HABITS HAVE CHANGED
    SEX   SEX   VALUE =   2. MALE   PAGE 1 OF 1

                          CHGREAD

COUNT ROW PCT COL PCT TOT PCT	1	2	3	4	5	6	8	ROW TOTAL
PERCP 1	6 31.6 85.7 26.1	4 21.1 80.0 17.4	6 31.6 85.7 26.1	1 5.3 100.0 4.3		1 5.3 100.0 4.3	1 5.3 100.0 4.3	19 82.6
PERCP 2	1 50.0 20.0 4.3				1 50.0 100.0 4.3			2 8.7
PERCP 3		1 50.0 14.3 4.3	1 50.0 14.3 4.3					2 8.7
COLUMN TOTAL	7 30.4	5 21.7	7 30.4	1 4.3	1 4.3	1 4.3	1 4.3	23 100.0

CHI-SQUARE	D.F.	SIGNIFICANCE	MIN E.F.	CELLS WITH E.F. < 5
14.04211	12	0.2980	0.087	19 OF 21 (90.5%)

STATISTIC	SYMMETRIC	WITH PERCP DEPENDENT	WITH CHGREAD DEPENDENT
LAMBDA	0.10000	0.25000	0.06250
UNCERTAINTY COEFFICIENT	0.20530	0.38478	0.14000

STATISTIC	VALUE	SIGNIFICANCE
CRAMER'S V	0.55251	
CONTINGENCY COEFFICIENT	0.61570	

NUMBER OF MISSING OBSERVATIONS = 140

CROSSTABULATION # FOURTEEN

- - - - - PERCP   WAY OF LIFE OR TECHNIQUE - - - C R O S S T A B U L A T I O N   O F - - - - - - - - - - -
CONTROLLING FOR..   BY CHGLIFE   LIFE HAS CHANGED
- - - - SEX   SEX - VALUE =   1. FEMALE - - - - PAGE 1 OF 1

CHGLIFE

PERCP	COUNT / ROW PCT / COL PCT / TOT PCT	1	2	3	4	5	6	8	ROW TOTAL
1		10 / 29.4 / 76.9 / 22.7	2 / 5.9 / 100.0 / 4.5	15 / 44.1 / 93.8 / 34.1	1 / 2.9 / 100.0 / 2.3	3 / 8.8 / 100.0 / 6.8		3 / 8.8 / 37.5 / 6.8	34 / 77.3
2		2 / 28.6 / 15.4 / 4.5					1 / 14.3 / 100.0 / 2.3	4 / 57.1 / 50.0 / 9.1	7 / 15.9
3		1 / 33.3 / 7.7 / 2.3		1 / 33.3 / 6.3 / 2.3				1 / 33.3 / 12.5 / 2.3	3 / 6.8
COLUMN TOTAL		13 / 29.5	2 / 4.5	16 / 36.4	1 / 2.3	3 / 6.8	1 / 2.3	8 / 18.2	44 / 100.0

CHI-SQUARE	D.F.	SIGNIFICANCE	MIN E.F.	CELLS WITH E.F.< 5
18.04328	12	0.1144	0.068	18 OF 21 (85.7%)

STATISTIC	SYMMETRIC	WITH PERCP DEPENDENT	WITH CHGLIFE DEPENDENT
LAMBDA	0.15789	0.20000	0.14286
UNCERTAINTY COEFFICIENT	0.18984	0.31065	0.13688

STATISTIC	VALUE	SIGNIFICANCE
CRAMER'S V	0.45281	
CONTINGENCY COEFFICIENT	0.53928	

```
- - - -   PERCP   WAY OF LIFE OR TECHNIQUE   - - -   C R O S S T A B U L A T I O N   O F   - - - - -
CONTROLLING FOR..                                       BY CHGLIFE    LIFE HAS CHANGED
        SEX    - - - - - - - - - - - - - - - - - -        VALUE =     2.   MALE      - - - -   PAGE  1 OF  1
```

```
                    CHGLIFE
             COUNT  |                                                              ROW
           ROW PCT  |                                                            TOTAL
           COL PCT  |
           TOT PCT  |    1 |    3 |    4 |    6 |    7 |    8 |
PERCP             -+------+------+------+------+------+------+
              1    |    9 |    3 |    1 |      |    1 |    5 |   19
                   | 47.4 | 15.8 |  5.3 |      |  5.3 | 26.3 | 79.2
                   | 90.0 | 75.0 | 50.0 |      |100.0 | 83.3 |
                   | 37.5 | 12.5 |  4.2 |      |  4.2 | 20.8 |
                  -+------+------+------+------+------+------+
              2    |      |      |    1 |    1 |    1 |      |    2
                   |      |      | 50.0 | 50.0 | 50.0 |      |  8.3
                   |      |      |100.0 |100.0 | 16.7 |      |
                   |      |      |  4.2 |  4.2 |  4.2 |      |
                  -+------+------+------+------+------+------+
              3    |    1 |    1 |      |      |      |      |    3
                   | 33.3 | 33.3 |      |      |      |      | 12.5
                   | 10.0 | 25.0 |      |      |      |      |
                   |  4.2 |  4.2 |      |      |      |      |
                  -+------+------+------+------+------+------+
          COLUMN       10      4      2      1      6      6       24
           TOTAL      41.7   16.7    8.3    4.2   25.0   25.0   100.0
```

CHI-SQUARE	D.F.	SIGNIFICANCE	MIN E.F.	CELLS WITH E.F.< 5
17.03158	10	0.0737	0.083	17 OF 18 (94.4%)

STATISTIC	SYMMETRIC	WITH PERCP DEPENDENT	WITH CHGLIFE DEPENDENT
LAMBDA	0.10526	0.20000	0.07143
UNCERTAINTY COEFFICIENT	0.23654	0.38711	0.17031

STATISTIC	VALUE	SIGNIFICANCE
CRAMER'S V	0.59567	
CONTINGENCY COEFFICIENT	0.64427	

NUMBER OF MISSING OBSERVATIONS =   139

CROSSTABULATION # FIFTEEN

```
28 NOV 84    SPSS-X RELEASE 2.0A FOR MTS
17:42:39     Wayne State University

- - - - - - - - - -  C R O S S T A B U L A T I O N   O F  - - - - - - - - - - - - - - - - - -
  PERCP   WAY OF LIFE OR TECHNIQUE              BY CHGREL   RELIGIOUS BELIEFS HAVE CHANGED
CONTROLLING FOR..
  SEX     SEX                                    VALUE =    1. FEMALE        PAGE  1 OF  1
- - - - - - - - - -
```

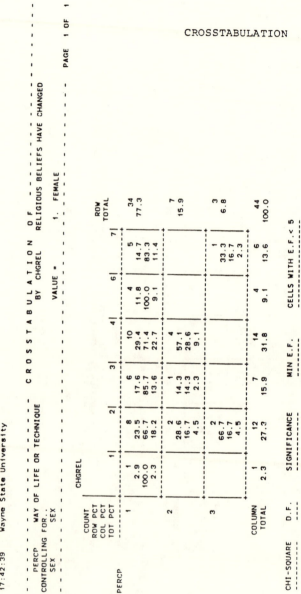

PERCP								
	COUNT	CHGREL						ROW
	ROW PCT							TOTAL
	COL PCT							
	TOT PCT	1	2	3	4	6	7	
1		1	8	6	10	4	5	34
		2.9	23.5	17.6	29.4	11.8	14.7	77.3
		100.0	66.7	85.7	71.4	100.0	83.3	
		2.3	18.2	13.6	22.7	9.1	11.4	
2			2	1	4			7
			28.6	14.3	57.1			15.9
			16.7	14.3	28.6			
			4.5	2.3	9.1			
3			2				1	3
			66.7				33.3	6.8
			16.7				16.7	
			4.5				2.3	
COLUMN		1	12	7	14	4	6	44
TOTAL		2.3	27.3	15.9	31.8	9.1	13.6	100.0

CHI-SQUARE	D.F.	SIGNIFICANCE	MIN E.F.	CELLS WITH E.F.< 5
8.17407	10	0.6118	0.068	18 (83.3%)

STATISTIC	SYMMETRIC	WITH PERCP DEPENDENT	WITH CHGREL DEPENDENT
LAMBDA	0.05000	0.0	0.06667
UNCERTAINTY COEFFICIENT	0.10713	0.17952	0.07634

STATISTIC	VALUE	SIGNIFICANCE
CRAMER'S V	0.30477	
CONTINGENCY COEFFICIENT	0.39581	

28 NOV 84   SPSS-X RELEASE 2.0A FOR MTS
17:42:39   Wayne State University

- - - - - PERCP   WAY OF LIFE OR TECHNIQUE - - - - - C R O S S T A B U L A T I O N   O F - - - - - - - - - - - - - - - - -
CONTROLLING FOR..   BY CHGREL   RELIGIOUS BELIEFS HAVE CHANGED
- - - - SEX   SEX - VALUE =   2. MALE - - - - - - PAGE 1 OF 1

	CHGREL						
COUNT ROW PCT COL PCT TOT PCT	1	2	3	4	5	6	ROW TOTAL
PERCP							
1	4 21.1 100.0 17.4	3 15.8 60.0 13.0	1 5.3 100.0 4.3	8 42.1 88.9 34.8	1 5.3 100.0 4.3	2 10.5 66.7 8.7	19 82.6
2		1 50.0 20.0 4.3		1 50.0 11.1 4.3			2 8.7
3		1 50.0 20.0 4.3				1 50.0 33.3 4.3	2 8.7
COLUMN TOTAL	4 17.4	5 21.7	1 4.3	9 39.1	1 4.3	3 13.0	23 100.0

CHI-SQUARE	D.F.	SIGNIFICANCE	MIN E.F.	CELLS WITH E.F.< 5
6.37544	10	0.7828	0.087	17 OF 18 (94.4%)

STATISTIC	SYMMETRIC	WITH PERCP DEPENDENT	WITH CHGREL DEPENDENT
LAMBDA	0.05556	0.0	0.07143
UNCERTAINTY COEFFICIENT	0.14734	0.26860	0.10152

STATISTIC	VALUE	SIGNIFICANCE
CRAMER'S V	0.37229	
CONTINGENCY COEFFICIENT	0.46587	

NUMBER OF MISSING OBSERVATIONS =   140

CROSSTABULATION # SIXTEEN

- - - - - - - - - - - - C R O S S T A B U L A T I O N   O F -
PERCP   WAY OF LIFE OR TECHNIQUE   BY SMCMED   RELATIONSHIP BETWEEN SMC AND MEDICINE
CONTROLLING FOR:
SEX   SEX   VALUE =   1. FEMALE   PAGE 1 OF 1

PERCP	COUNT ROW PCT COL PCT TOT PCT	SMCMED 1	2	3	5	6	ROW TOTAL
1		22 66.7 78.6 51.2	5 15.2 71.4 11.6	2 6.1 66.7 4.7	1 3.0 100.0 2.3	3 9.1 75.0 7.0	33 76.7
2		4 57.1 14.3 9.3	1 14.3 14.3 2.3	1 14.3 33.3 2.3		1 14.3 25.0 2.3	7 16.3
3		2 66.7 7.1 4.7	1 33.3 14.3 2.3				3 7.0
COLUMN TOTAL		28 65.1	7 16.3	3 7.0	1 2.3	4 9.3	43 100.0

CHI-SQUARE	D.F.	SIGNIFICANCE	MIN E.F.	CELLS WITH E.F. < 5
2.21604	8	0.9737	0.070	13 OF 15 (86.7%)

STATISTIC	SYMMETRIC	WITH PERCP DEPENDENT	WITH SMCMED DEPENDENT
LAMBDA	0.0	0.0	0.0
UNCERTAINTY COEFFICIENT	0.03526	0.04517	0.02892

STATISTIC	VALUE	SIGNIFICANCE
CRAMER'S V	0.16052	
CONTINGENCY COEFFICIENT	0.22138	

- - - - - - - - - - - - - C R O S S T A B U L A T I O N   O F - - - - - - - - - - - - -
  PERCP   WAY OF LIFE OR TECHNIQUE   BY SMCMED   RELATIONSHIP BETWEEN SMC AND MEDICINE
CONTROLLING FOR..
  SEX   VALUE =   2. MALE
- PAGE   1 OF 1

```
                    SMCMED
           COUNT  |
           ROW PCT|
           COL PCT|
           TOT PCT|                                              ROW
                  |    1 |    2 |    3 |    6 |                  TOTAL
PERCP      -------+------+------+------+------+
              1   |    9 |    1 |    4 |    2 |                    16
                  | 56.3 |  6.3 | 25.0 | 12.5 |                  80.0
                  | 81.8 | 50.0 | 80.0 |100.0 |
                  | 45.0 |  5.0 | 20.0 | 10.0 |
                  +------+------+------+------+
              2   |    1 |    1 |      |      |                     2
                  | 50.0 | 50.0 |      |      |                  10.0
                  |  9.1 | 50.0 |      |      |
                  |  5.0 |  5.0 |      |      |
                  +------+------+------+------+
              3   |    1 |      |    1 |      |                     2
                  | 50.0 |      | 50.0 |      |                  10.0
                  |  9.1 |      | 20.0 |      |
                  |  5.0 |      |  5.0 |      |
                  +------+------+------+------+
           COLUMN     11      2      5      2                      20
           TOTAL    55.0   10.0   25.0   10.0                   100.0
```

CHI-SQUARE   D.F.   SIGNIFICANCE   MIN E.F.   CELLS WITH E.F. < 5
-----------   ----   ------------   --------   -------------------
5.14773   6   0.5250   0.200   11 OF   12 (91.7%)

                     STATISTIC   SYMMETRIC   WITH PERCP   WITH SMCMED
                     ---------   ---------   DEPENDENT   DEPENDENT
                                                         ----------   ----------
LAMBDA   0.0   0.0   0.0
UNCERTAINTY COEFFICIENT   0.12905   0.17922   0.10082

                     STATISTIC   VALUE   SIGNIFICANCE
                     ---------   -----   ------------
CRAMER'S V   0.35874
CONTINGENCY COEFFICIENT   0.45244

NUMBER OF MISSING OBSERVATIONS =   144

CROSSTABULATION # SEVENTEEN

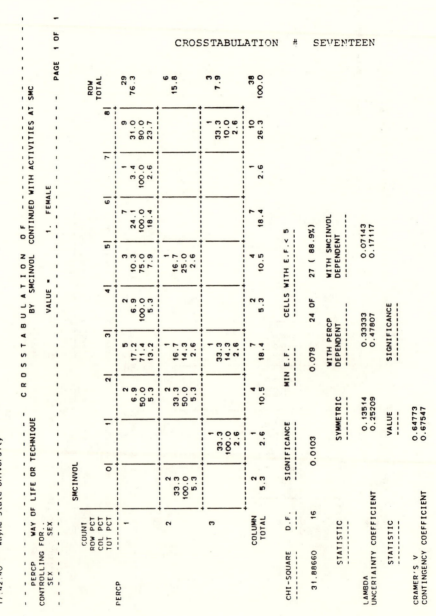

28 NOV 84   SPSS-X RELEASE 2.0A FOR MTS
17:42:40   Wayne State University

- - - - - - - - - - - - - - -   C R O S S T A B U L A T I O N   O F   - - - - - - - - - - - - - - -
  PERCP   WAY OF LIFE OR TECHNIQUE   BY SMCINVOL   CONTINUED WITH ACTIVITIES AT SMC
CONTROLLING FOR:
  SEX   SEX   VALUE =   1. FEMALE   PAGE 1 OF 1

		SMCINVOL									ROW TOTAL
COUNT ROW PCT COL PCT TOT PCT		0	1	2	3	4	5	6	7	8	
PERCP 1				2 6.9 50.0 5.3	5 17.2 71.4 13.2	2 6.9 100.0 5.3	3 10.3 75.0 7.9	7 24.1 100.0 18.4	1 3.4 100.0 2.6	9 31.0 90.0 23.7	29 76.3
2		2 33.3 100.0 5.3	2 6.9 50.0 5.3	2 33.3 50.0 5.3	1 16.7 14.3 2.6	1 16.7 25.0 2.6				6 15.8
3		1 33.3 100.0 2.6		1 33.3 14.3 2.6					1 33.3 10.0 2.6	3 7.9
COLUMN TOTAL		2 5.3	1 2.6	4 10.5	7 18.4	2 5.3	4 10.5	7 18.4	1 2.6	10 26.3	38 100.0

CHI-SQUARE	D.F.	SIGNIFICANCE	MIN E.F.	CELLS WITH E.F.< 5
-------	----	------------	--------	------------------
31.88660	16	0.0103	0.079	24 OF 27 (88.9%)

STATISTIC	SYMMETRIC	WITH PERCP DEPENDENT	WITH SMCINVOL DEPENDENT
---------	---------	--------------------	-----------------------
LAMBDA	0.13514	0.33333	0.07143
UNCERTAINTY COEFFICIENT	0.25209	0.47807	0.17117

STATISTIC	VALUE	SIGNIFICANCE
---------	-----	------------
CRAMER'S V	0.64773	
CONTINGENCY COEFFICIENT	0.67547	

28 NOV 84   SPSS-X RELEASE 2.0A FOR MTS
17:42:40   Wayne State University

- - - - - PERCP WAY OF LIFE OR TECHNIQUE - - - - - - C R O S S T A B U L A T I O N O F - - - - - - - - - - - - - -
CONTROLLING FOR..   BY SMCINVOL CONTINUED WITH ACTIVITIES AT SMC
   SEX   SEX   VALUE =   2. MALE
-                                    PAGE 1 OF 1

```
               SMCINVOL
       COUNT  |
     ROW PCT  |
     COL PCT  |                                                                      ROW
     TOT PCT  |    0|    2|    3|    4|    6|    7|    8|                           TOTAL
PERCP  -------+-----+-----+-----+-----+-----+-----+-----+
          1   |  1  |  3  |  1  |  4  |  2  |  4  |  3  |     18
              | 5.6 |16.7 | 5.6 |22.2 |11.1 |22.2 |16.7 |   78.3
              |50.0 |100.0|50.0 |100.0|66.7 |80.0 |75.0 |
              | 4.3 |13.0 | 4.3 |17.4 | 8.7 |17.4 |13.0 |
              +-----+-----+-----+-----+-----+-----+-----+
          2   |  1  |     |  1  |     |     |     |     |      2
              |50.0 |     |50.0 |     |     |     |     |    8.7
              |50.0 |     |50.0 |     |     |     |     |
              | 4.3 |     | 4.3 |     |     |     |     |
              +-----+-----+-----+-----+-----+-----+-----+
          3   |     |     |     |     |  1  |  1  |  1  |      3
              |     |     |     |     |33.3 |33.3 |33.3 |   13.0
              |     |     |     |     |33.3 |20.0 |25.0 |
              |     |     |     |     | 4.3 | 4.3 | 4.3 |
              +-----+-----+-----+-----+-----+-----+-----+
      COLUMN     2     3     2     4     3     5     4       23
       TOTAL    8.7  13.0   8.7  17.4  13.0  21.7  17.4    100.0
```

CHI-SQUARE   D.F.   SIGNIFICANCE   MIN E.F.   CELLS WITH E.F. < 5

13.39537   12   0.3410   0.174   21 OF   21 (100.0%)

       STATISTIC   SYMMETRIC   WITH PERCP   WITH SMCINVOL
       ---------   ---------   DEPENDENT   DEPENDENT
                                              ---------   ---------

LAMBDA   0.04348   0.0   0.05556
UNCERTAINTY COEFFICIENT   0.20243   0.38774   0.13697

       STATISTIC   VALUE   SIGNIFICANCE
       ---------   -----   ------------

CRAMER'S V   0.53963
CONTINGENCY COEFFICIENT   0.60667

NUMBER OF MISSING OBSERVATIONS =   146

CROSSTABULATION # EIGHTEEN

```
28 NOV 84    SPSS-X RELEASE 2.0A FOR MTS
17:42:40     Wayne State University

- - - - -  PERCP   WAY OF LIFE OR TECHNIQUE  -  C R O S S T A B U L A T I O N   O F   WHATSIT   WHAT IS SMC ABOUT
CONTROLLING FOR..                                          BY WHATSIT
     SEX     SEX                                     VALUE =        1.   FEMALE                                PAGE   1 OF   1
```

PERCP	WHATSIT	1	2	3	4	5	8	10	11	12	ROW TOTAL
COUNT / ROW PCT / COL PCT / TOT PCT											
1		12 / 35.3 / 75.0 / 27.9	1 / 2.9 / 100.0 / 2.3	3 / 8.8 / 100.0 / 7.0	6 / 17.6 / 100.0 / 14.0	2 / 5.9 / 50.0 / 4.7	5 / 14.7 / 71.4 / 11.6	3 / 8.8 / 75.0 / 7.0	1 / 2.9 / 100.0 / 2.3	1 / 2.9 / 100.0 / 2.3	34 / 79.1
2		3 / 42.9 / 18.8 / 7.0				2 / 28.6 / 50.0 / 4.7	1 / 14.3 / 14.3 / 2.3	1 / 14.3 / 25.0 / 2.3			7 / 16.3
3		1 / 50.0 / 6.3 / 2.3					1 / 50.0 / 14.3 / 2.3				2 / 4.7
COLUMN TOTAL		16 / 37.2	1 / 2.3	3 / 7.0	6 / 14.0	4 / 9.3	7 / 16.3	4 / 9.3	1 / 2.3	1 / 2.3	43 / 100.0

```
CHI-SQUARE     D.F.     SIGNIFICANCE        MIN E.F.      CELLS WITH E.F.< 5
--------       ----     ------------        --------      ------------------
 8.61258        16        0.9285             0.047         27 ( 92.6%)

STATISTIC              SYMMETRIC           WITH PERCP           WITH WHATSIT
---------             -----------          DEPENDENT            DEPENDENT
                                           ----------           ----------
LAMBDA                  0.0                 0.0                  0.0
UNCERTAINTY COEFFICIENT 0.09456             0.18581              0.06341

STATISTIC              VALUE               SIGNIFICANCE
---------             -------              ------------
CRAMER'S V             0.31646
CONTINGENCY COEFFICIENT 0.40850
```

```
- - - -  PERCP  WAY OF LIFE OR TECHNIQUE  - - -  C R O S S T A B U L A T I O N  O F  - - - - - - - - - - - - - - - - - -
CONTROLLING FOR..                                       BY WHATSIT  WHAT IS SMC ABOUT
  SEX       SEX                                                VALUE =        2.  MALE
- - - - - - - - - - - - - - - - - - - - - - - - - - - - - - - - - - - - - - - - - - -   PAGE   1 OF   1
```

                    WHATSIT

COUNT ROW PCT COL PCT TOT PCT	1	3	4	5	8	12	ROW TOTAL
PERCP							
1	4 26.7 80.0 21.1	1 6.7 100.0 5.3		2 13.3 100.0 10.5	6 40.0 85.7 31.6	2 13.3 100.0 10.5	15 78.9
2			2 100.0 100.0 10.5				2 10.5
3	1 50.0 20.0 5.3				1 50.0 14.3 5.3		2 10.5
COLUMN TOTAL	5 26.3	1 5.3	2 10.5	2 10.5	7 36.8	2 10.5	19 100.0

```
CHI-SQUARE     D.F.     SIGNIFICANCE     MIN E.F.     CELLS WITH E.F. < 5
---------      ----     ------------     --------     -------------------
20.15809       10         0.0278          0.105       18 ( 94.4%)  17 OF


STATISTIC               SYMMETRIC      WITH PERCP       WITH WHATSIT
---------                              DEPENDENT         DEPENDENT
                                     -------------     ------------
LAMBDA                   0.25000        0.50000          0.16667
UNCERTAINTY COEFFICIENT  0.33647        0.57192          0.23834


STATISTIC               VALUE          SIGNIFICANCE
---------               -----          ------------
CRAMER'S V              0.72834
CONTINGENCY COEFFICIENT 0.71749

NUMBER OF MISSING OBSERVATIONS =    145
```

REFERENCES CITED

Ackerknecht, E. "Psychopathology, Primitive Medicine, and Primitive Culture." Bulletin of the History of Medicine. 14(1943):30-67.

Adler, Herbert and Van Buren Hammet. "Crises, Conversion and Cult Formation: An Examination of a Common Psychological Sequence." American Journal of Psychiatry. 130(1973):861-64.

Aquirre Beltran, Gonzalo. "Training in Intercultural Aspects of Medicine." In Modern Medicine and Medical Anthropology in the U.S.--Mexican Border Populations. Edited by B. Velimirovic. Washington, D.C.: Pan American Health Organization, Scientific Publication PAHO No. 359. 1978.

Balch, Robert and David Taylor. "Salvation in a UFO." Psychology Today, 10(October 1976).

Balswick, Jack. "The Jesus People Movement: A General Interpretation". Journal of Social Issues 30(1974):23-42.

Barkun, Michael. "Millenarian Change: Movements of Total Transformation." American Behavioral Scientist 10(1972):145-288.

Beckford, James. "Explaining Religious Movements." International Social Science Journal 29(1977):235-249.

Belshaw, C. S. "The Significance of Modern Cults in Melanesian Development." In Reader in Comparative Religion: An Anthropological Approach, 3rd edition, pp. 523-527. Edited by W. A. Lessa and E. Z. Vogt. N.Y.: Harper and Row, 1972.

Boshier, Adrian. "African Apprenticeship." In Parapsychology and Anthropology. Edited by Allan Angoff and Diana Barth. New York: Parapsychology Foundation, Inc., 1974.

Bourguignon, Erika. "Dreams and Altered States of Consciousness in Anthropological Research." In Psychological Anthropology. Edited by F. Hsu. Cambridge, Mass.: Schenkman. 1972.

____, ed. Religion, Altered States of Consciousness, and Social Change. Columbus: Ohio State University Press. 1973.

____. "Cross-Cultural Perspectives on the Religious Uses of Altered States of Consciousness." In Religious Movements in Contemporary America, pp. 228-243. Edited by Irving Zaretsky and Mark Leone. Princeton, N.J.: Princeton University Press. 1974.

____. "Culture and Varieties of Consciousness." Addison-Wesley Module in Anthropology. No. 47. 1974.

____. "ASC Within a General Evolutionary Perspective: A Holocultural Analysis." Behavior Science Research 12(1977):196-216.

Bremner, F., V. Benigus, and F. Moritz. "EEG Correlates in Humans." Neuropsychiatry 10(1972):307-312.

Bremner, F. and F. Moritz. "Internal Focus as a Subset of Attention." Neuropsychiatry 10(1972):467-469.

Brier, Robert, Gertrude Schmeidler, and Berry Savits. "Three experiments with Silva Mind Control Graduates." Journal of the American Society for Psychical Research 69(1975):236-271.

Brown, Barbara. New Mind, New Body; Biofeedback: New Directions for the Mind New York: Harper and Row, 1974.

____. The Biofeedback Syllabus. Springfield, Illinois: Thomas, 1975.

Brown, Barbara and Jay Klug. The Alpha Syllabus. Springfield, Illinois: Thomas, 1974.

Campbell, Ronald. "Emergent Cultural Systems: The Psychocultural Evolution of Man." Pheonix. 1(1977):17-26.

Caroll, J. W. "Transcendence and Mystery in the Counter-Culture." Religion in Life 42(1973):361-75.

Cochrane, ?. "Big Men and Cargo Cults." In Reader in Comparative Religion, 4th edition. Edited by Lessa and Vogt. N.Y.: Harper and Row, 1979.

Coue, Emile. Self-Mastery Through Conscious Autosuggestion. London: Allen and Unwin, 1922.

Devereux, George. "Normal and Abnormal: The Key Problem of Psychiatric Anthropology." In Some Uses of Anthropology: Theoretical and Applied. Edited by J. B. Cassagrande and T. Gladwin, pp. 23-44. Washington, D.C.: Anthropological Society of Washington, 1956.

Den Uyl, Douglas and D. Rasmussen. Philosophical Thought of Rand. Urbana, Illinois: University of Illinois, 1984.

Dobkin de Rios, Marlene. "A Psi Approach to Love Magic, Witchcraft and Psychedelics in the Peruvian Amazon." Phoenix: New Directions in the Study of Man 2(1978):22-37.

Ebon, Martin. Psychic Warfare: Threat or Illusion. New York: McGraw Hill, 1984.

Ehrenwald, Jan. "Psi, Psychotherapy, and Psychoanalysis." In Handbook of Parapsychology, pp. 529-540. Edited by Benjamin Wolman. New York: Van Nostrand Reinhold Co. 1977.

_____. The ESP Experience A Psychiatric Validation. New York: Basic Books, 1978.

Eisenbud, Jule. "Perception of Subliminal Visual Stimuli in Relation to ESP." International Journal of Parapsychology. 70(1976):35-53.

_____. "Evolution and Psi." Journal of the American Society for Psychical Research. 70(1976):35-53.

_____. "Perspectives on Anthropology and Parapsychology." In Extrasensory Ecology: Parapsychology and Anthropology, pp. 28-44. Edited by Joseph Long. Metuchen, N.J.: Scarecrow Press. 1977.

Ellwood, Robert. One-Way: The Jesus Movement and Its Meaning. Englewood Cliffs, N.J.: Prentice-Hall, 1973a.

_____. Religious and Spiritual Groups in Modern America. Englewood Cliffs, N.J.: Prentice-Hall, 1973b.

Eliade, M. Shamanism: Archaic Techniques of Ecstasy. N.Y.: Bollingen Foundation--Pantheon Books, 1964.

Fabrega, H. and D. Silver. "Some Social and Psychological Properties of Zinacanteco Shamans." Behavioral Science 15(1970):471-486.

Foster, A. "ESP Tests with American Indian Children." Journal of Parapsychology. 7(1943):94-103.

Foster, George and B. Anderson. Medical Anthropology.
N.Y.: John Wiley and Sons, 1978.

Fradkin, Arlene. "Christian Science: A Religion and a Way
of Life." The Florida Anthropologist 28(1975):117-
122.

Frank, Walter. "Paranormal Healing in Africa and Asia."
Phoenix: New Directions in the Study of Man.
4(1980):58-60.

Furst, Bruno. How to Remember. A Practical Method of
Improving Your Memory and Powers of Concentration.
New York: Greenberg, 1944.

Gillin, J. "Magical Fright." Psychiatry 11(1948):387-400.

Glock, Charles and Robert Bellah, eds. The New Religious
Consciousness. Berkeley: University of Berekely
Press, 1976.

Goldman, Bert. Better and Better. Laredo: Institute of
Psychorientology, 1974. Guzman, Emilio. Mind Control
New Directions in Human Thought. Laredo, Texas:
Institute of Psychorientology, 1975.

Hansel, C. E. M. ESP and Parapsychology: A Critical
Reevaluation. Buffalo, New York: Prometheus Books,
1980.

Hill, Napoleon. Think and Grow Rich. 1954.

Kearny, M. "Espiritualismo as an Alternative Medical
Tradition in the Border Area." In Modern Medicine and
Medical Anthropology in the U.S.-Mexican Border
Population. Edited by Velimirovic, 1978.

Landy, David. "Role Adaptation: Traditional Curers Under
the Impact of Western Medicine." American Ethnologist
1(1974):103-127.

Lantis, M. Eskimo Childhood and Interpersonal Relationship.
Seatle: University of Washington Press. 1960.

Lawrence, Jodi. Alpha Brain Waves. Los Angeles: Nash Pub.,
1972.

Leeds, Morton and Gardner Murphy. The Paranormal and the
Normal A Historical, Philosophical and Theoretical
Perspective. Metuchen, New Jersey: Scarecrow Press,
1980.

LeShan, Lawrence. Toward a General Theory of the
Paranormal. New York: Putnam's Sons, 1969.

Linton, Ralph. "Nativistic Movements." American Anthropologist 45(1943):230-240.

Lofland, J. Doomsday Cult: A Study in Conversion, Proselytization and Maintenance of Faith. Englewood Cliffs, N.J.: Prentice-Hall, 1973.

Long, Joseph, ed. Extrasensory Ecology: Parapsychology and Anthropology. Metuchen, New Jersey: Scarecrow Press, 1977.

____. "Shamanism, Voodoo Death: Stress Theory in Medical Anthropology." In Extrasensory Ecology: Parapsychology and Anthropology, pp.257-270.

____. "Verification of PSI in Ethnographic Fieldwork." In Extrasensory Ecology: Parapsychology and Anthropology, pp. 243-256.

Macklin, June. "Folk Saints, Healers and Spiritualist Cults in Northern Mexico." Revista Interamericana Review 3(1974):351-367.

Marty, Martin. " The Occult Establishment." Social Research 37(1970):212-230.

Mead, Margaret. "An Anthropological Approach to Different Types of Communication and the Importance of Differences in Human Temperaments." In Extrasensory Ecology: Parapsychology and Anthropology, pp. 45-52. Edited by Joseph Long. Metuchen, N. J.: Scarecrow Press, 1977.

Mitchell, Edgar D. ed. Psychic Exploration: A Challenge for Science. New York: Putnam's Sons, 1974.

Moore, R. Lawrence. In Search of White Crows: Spiritualism, Parapsychology, and American Culture. New York: Oxford University Press, 1977.

Needleman, Jacob. The New Religions. N.Y.: Doubleday. 1970.

Nelson, Geoffry. Spiritualism and Society. N.Y.: Schocken Books, 1969.

Newsweek. "Lord Krishna's Children." July 8, p. 50. 1974.

Nicholi, Armond. "A New Dimension in Youth Culture." American Journal of Psychiatry 13(1974):369-401.

Ornstein, Robert. The Psychology of Consciousness. San Francisco, Calif.: W. H. Freeman and Co., 1972.

Penner, Wes. "Hippies' Attraction to Mysticism."
     Adolescence 7(1972):199-210.

Podmore, Frank. From Mesmer to Christian Science. New Hyde
     Park, N.Y.: University Books, 1963.

Pope,, D. "ESP Tests with Primitive People."
     Parapsychological Bulletin. 30(1953):1-3.

Rao, K. Ramakrishna. "The Bidirectionality of Psi."
     Journal of Parapsychology 29(1965):230-250.

____. "On the Nature of Psi." Journal of Parapsychology
     41(1977):294-351.

____. Theories of Psi." In Advances in Parapsychological
     Research 2 Extrasensory Perception, pp. 245-295.
     Edited by Stanley Krippner. New York: Plenum, 1978.

____. Psi: Its Place in Nature." In Research in
     Parapsychology, 1978. Edited by William Roll.
     Metuchen, N.J.: Scarecrow Press, 1979.

Rand, Ayn. For the New Intellectual. New York: Random
     House, 1961.

____. The Virtue of Selfishness. New York: New American
     Library, 1964.

____. Introduction to Objective Epistemology. New York:
     New American Library, 1967.

Ransom, Champe. "Recent Criticisms of Parapsychology." In
     Surveys in Parapsychology: Reviews of the Literature,
     with Updated Bibliographies, pp. 424-426. Edited by
     Rhea White. Metuchen, N.J.: Scarecrow Press, 1976.

Reichbart, Richard. "Magic and Psi: Some Speculations on
     Their Relationship." Journal of the American Society
     for Psychical Research 72(1978):153-175.

Rice, Berkeley. "Messiah From Korea: Honor Thy Father
     Moon." Psychology Today, 9(January 1976).

Robbins, John. An Answer To Ayn Rand. Washington: Robbins,
     1974.

Rose, L. R. "Psi Experiments with Australian Aborigines."
     Journal of Parapsychology 15(1951):122-131.

Rossell, Robert. "Religious Movements and the Youth
     Culture." The Human Context 7(1974):621-631.

Sasaki, Y. "Psychiatric Study of the Shaman in Japan." In
    Mental Health Research in Asia and the Pacific.
    Edited by W. Caudill and T. Lin. pp. 223-241.
    Honolulu: East-West Center Press. 1969.

Scott, Gini Graham. Cult and Countercult. Westport,
    Connecticut: Greenwood Press, 1980.

Shiels, Dean. "A Cross-Cultural Study of Beliefs in Out-of-
    the-body Experience, Waking and Sleeping." Phoenix:
    New Directions in the Study of Man 4(1980):19-34.

Shweder, R. A. "Aspects of Cognition in Zinacanteco
    Shamans: Experimental Results." In Reader in
    Comparative Religion, 4th ed.   Edited by Lessa and
    Vogt, 1979.

Silva, Jose. Reflections Laredo, Texas: Institute of
    Psychorientology, 1982.

____. Mystery of the Keys. Laredo, Texas: Institute of
    Psychorientology, 1983

____. I Have a Hunch, vol. 1. Laredo, Texas: Institute of
    Psychorientology, 1983.

Silva, Jose and Philip Miele. The Silva Method. New York:
    Simon and Schuster, Pocket Books, 1977.

Silva Mind Control. Basic Lecture Series Manual. Laredo:
    Institute of Psychorientology, 1973.

____. Graduate Lecture Series Manual. Laredo: Institute of
    Psychorientology, 1973.

____. Newsletter. Vol. 15, No. 3, 1984.

Silverman, J. "Shamans and Acute Schizophrenia." American
    Anthropologist 69(1967):21-31.

Singer, Philip and Kate Ankenbrandt. "The Ethnology of the
    Paranormal." Phoenix: New Directions in the Study of
    Man 4(1980):19-34.

Staniford, Philip. "Inside Out: Anthropological
    Communication of Alternate Realities." Phoenix: New
    Directions in the Study of Man 1(1977):36-46.

Sussman, Robert W. and Linda K. "A Description of
    Divination Among the Sakalava of Madagasear." In
    Parapsychology and Anthropology. Edited by A. Angoff
    and D. Barth. New York: Parapsychology Foundation,
    Inc., 1974.

Tart, Charles; Harold E. Puthoff; and Russell Targ, eds. Mind at Large. New York: Praeger, 1979.

Tiryakian, Edward. "Toward the Sociology of Esoteric Culture." American Journal of Sociology 78(1972):491-512.

Torrey, E. Fuller. "Spiritualists and Shamans as Psychotherapists: An Account of Original Anthropological Sin." In Religious Movements in Contemporary America, pp. 330-337. Edited by Irving Zaretsky and Mark Leone. Princeton, N.J.: Princeton University Press, 1974.

Trotter, Robert and Juan A. Chaviro. "Discovering New Models for Alcohol Counseling in Minority Groups." In Modern Medicine and Medical Anthropology in the U.S.-Mexican Border Populations. Edited by B. Velimirovic, 1978.

Van de Castle, Robert L. "Psi Abilities in Primitive Groups." Proceedings of the Parapsychological Association 1(1970):97-122.

Wallace, Anthony. "Revitalization Movements." American Anthropologist 581956:264-281.

_____. Religion: An Anthropological View. N.Y.: Random House, 1966

Wallis, Roy. "A Contemporary Analysis of Problems and Processes of Change in Two Manipulationist Movements: Christian Science and Scientology." In Contemporary Metamorphosis of Religion?, pp. 407-422. Acts of the 12th International Conference on the Sociology of Religion. The Hague, 1973.

_____. "Ideology, Authority and the Development of Cultic Movements." Social Research 1(174a):299-327.

_____. "The Aetherius Society: A Case Study in the Formation of a Mystagogic Congregtation." Sociological Review 22(1974b):27-45.

_____. "Scientology: Therapeutic Cult to Religious Sect." Sociology 9(1975):89-100.

"Observations on the Children of God." Sociological Review 24(1976):807-829.

_____. The Road to Total Freedom: A Sociological Analysis of Scientology, N.Y.: Columbia Press, 1977.

Washington, Joseph. Black Sects and Cults. Garden City,
    N.Y.: Doubleday, 1972.

Winkleman, Michael. "Magic and Parapsychology." Phoenix:
    New Directions in the Study of Man 4(1980):2-6.

Wolman, Benjamin, ed. Handbook of Parapsychology. New
    York: Van Nostrand Reinhold Co., 1977.

Woodward, Kenneth. "Getting Your Mind Together." Newsweek
    Sept. 6, 1976.

Worsley, Peter. The Trumpet Shall Sound: A Study of Cargo
    Cults in Melanesia, N.Y.: Schocken, 1970.

Zaetsky, Irving and Mark Leone, eds. Religious Movements in
    Contemporary America. Princeton, N.J.: Princeton
    University Press, 1974.

SELECTED BIBLIOGHRAPHY ON SILVA MIND CONTROL

IN THE POPULAR PRESS

"Alpha, The First Step To A New Level Of Reality." Human
     Behavior, May/June 1972.

"A P.S. To Mind Control." Mademoiselle, March 1972.

"Are The Spirits Trying to Tell Me Something." The Village
     Voice, April 12, 1973.

Asher, Jules. "ESP or Your Money Back. Mind Control Sells
     'Alpha' Buys Research." APA Monitor (April 1973).

Boldt, David. "Tripping Through the Twilight Zone." The
     Washington Post Outlook Editorials. Sunday, April 30,
     1972.

"Brain Waves". The Detroit News, September 17, 1972.

Burke, Charles. "Mind Control Blows Reporter's Mind." The
     Examiner, Independence, Missouri, Thurs., Nov. 20,
     1975.

"Can Man Control His Mind?" New York Times, April 15, 1972.

"Cherokee Mind Control Course Has Started." Cherekee Nation
     News, September 20, 1974.

DeSau, George. The Silva Mind Control Courses: Effects with
     Three High School Populations. Laredo, Texas: SMCI,
     1974

DeSau, George and Paul Seawell. The Alburquerque Report.
     Laredo, Texas: SMCI, 1974.

"Faith, Hope and Clarity: Catholic Schools Are Sold on the
     'Silva Method'". New York Daily News, January 19,
     1981.

"Getting Your Head Together." Newsweek, September 6, 1976.

"Jose Silva Betting on Alpha". _Playboy_, March 1975.

"Lame-Brains". _Newsweek_, March 29, 1971.

Merrill, Sam. "Under Control." _New Times_, May 2, 1975.

Mihalasky, John. "ESP." _Mechanical Engineering_, December 1972.

"Mind Control Pays Off in Dentist's Office." _Philadelphia Enquirer_, September 26, 1972.

"Mind Over Matter." _People_, April 1972.

"Neurosurgeon's Patients Help Themselves." _Milwaukee Sentinel_, March 29, 1974.

"1,000 Hear Guru on Mind Control." _The Washington Post_, February 9, 1972.

Peterson, Karen. "Laying on of Hands." _Features and News Service_, July 31, 1974.

"Phobias, Coping With Irrational Fears." _Science Digest_, September 1974.

"Pontiac Students Probe Brain Waves." _The Detroit News_, May 5, 1973.

"Silva Mind Control: Put Your ESP To Work For You." _New London Day_, November 27, 1972.

Sullivan, Ronald. "Hospitals Introducing a Therapy Resembling 'Laying on of Hands'." _New York Times_, November 6, 1977.

"The Brain Wave Explosion: Cult and Science." _The Washington Post_, April 30, 1972.

"The Silva Mind." _Apartment Scene_, November/December 1973.

"The Story of Mind Control." _New Mexico's Teachers' News_, October 1972.

"Tuning In To Mind Control." _Family Circle_, August 1975.

"What's It All About, Alpha?" Coronet, March 1972.

"Witchcraft and Mind Control: Help or Harm For Youth?"
    Modern People, August 19, 1973.

"Your Mind." The Woman, March 1969.

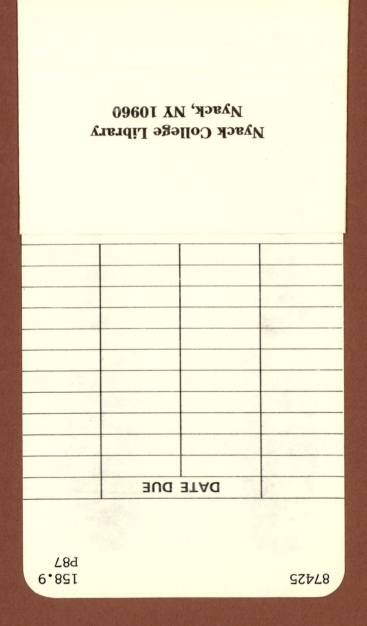